BOGEY'S BABY

Also by Howard Greenberger
THE OFF-BROADWAY EXPERIENCE

BOGEY'S BABY

Howard Greenberger

ST. MARTIN'S PRESS   NEW YORK

First published in the U.S.A. by St. Martin's Press 1978
Copyright © 1976 by Howard Greenberger
All rights reserved. For information, write:
St. Martin's Press, Inc., 175 Fifth Ave., New York, N.Y. 10010.
Manufactured in the United States of America
Library of Congress Catalog Card Number: 77-9178

Library of Congress Cataloging in Publication Data

Greenberger, Howard.
   Bogey's Baby.

   1. Bacall, Lauren, 1924-   2. Moving-picture actors
and actresses—United States—Biography.   I. Title.
PN2287.B115G7   1978   791'.092'4   [B]   77-9178
ISBN 0-312-08740-3

Contents

Acknowledgements vii

What Price Hollywood? 1

A Star is Made 16

To Have ... 29

And To Hold ... 51

And Have Not 66

The Treasure of the Canyon 75

Deadline—USA 92

We're No Angels 121

Written on the Wind 147

I'll Never Smile Again 158

Big Fish, Little Fish 179

Applause 206

Encore: As Time Goes By 213

To Selma Greenberger...
for dedication

Acknowledgements

I would like to express my appreciation to those publishers and literary agents who have allowed me to reproduce extracts from the following works in this book: Lawrence Pollinger, literary executors for D. H. Lawrence, and the estate of the late Mrs Frieda Lawrence for the quote from *Lady Chatterley's Lover*; Sherbourne Press for the references from *King Rebel* by Fred Nolan; Random House for Jack L. Warner's *My First Hundred Years in Hollywood*; and McGraw-Hill for Lewis Yablonsky's biography *George Raft*.

And thanks to Ray Hugen and Robert Reinhold for helping in the delivery of his baby!

Howard Greenberger

'*The world is supposed to be full of possibilities, but they narrow down to pretty few in most personal experience. There's a lot of good fish in the sea ... maybe ... but the vast masses seem to be mackerel or herring, and if you're not mackerel or herring yourself, you are likely to find very few good fish in the sea.*'

From *Lady Chatterley's Lover*
by D. H. Lawrence

' "Baby" went the way of all wooing nicknames
shortly after the honeymoon was over,' wrote
Sheilah Graham in a 1948 interview with the
Bogarts. 'In fact, she prefers to be called
by her real name, "Betty", and now calls Bogey
"Baby", and he loves it!'

What Price Hollywood?

Betty Bacall arrived in Hollywood during a rainstorm. Elated just at being there, the nineteen-year-old actress grabbed her suitcases and stepped off the New York train right into the frenzy of wartime Union Station. As she stood by her piled-up luggage, trying to avoid the confusion of the crowd, she clutched a copy of the March 1943 *Harper's Bazaar* with her picture on the cover that had brought her to the attention of Howard Hawks. In the hour that followed, as she waited for a representative from Warner Brothers to show up, her elation gradually turned to anxiety. Considering the rush to get her out there, she felt they could have sent somebody. But time passed and no one came to claim her.

Finally she forced herself to cope with the disappointment and telephoned Hawks. His secretary told her the director was busy on the lot and, when Betty asked about a reasonable place to stay, told her to go to a hotel in Westwood at the other end of town.

In her tiny hotel room Betty tried to relax but that seemed impossible. Adding to her troubles, she seemed to have caught a cold. Again she called the studio. This time she got the message she wanted to hear: she was to meet Hawks for lunch that afternoon at the Brown Derby on Vine Street.

Frantically, she changed and put on fresh make-up but no matter what she tried to do with her hair it was a mess. By the time she reached the restaurant, walking through the downpour, it was even

1

worse. Swathed in a raincoat now sopping wet, Betty was so unnerved she forgot to check it, and found herself being led across the elegant room to the Hawks table, appearing like a castaway washed up on a beach of a fashionable resort. Her dripping nose, that she kept dabbing with a crumpled handkerchief, made her look even more pathetic. She had to muster all her waning courage to confront the grey-haired director who was responsible for the success of many legendary actresses.

Ordering a vegetable dish, Betty began to chain-smoke as though sending up signals of help. She and Hawks were talking *at* each other. They discussed her background perfunctorily. No matter how she tried there seemed no way to engender his enthusiasm. It was obvious that Hawks was not particularly impressed.

Just three years before, believing that the only way to become an actress was to act, Betty had quit the American Academy of Dramatic Arts after the first term. The records of her brief stay at the school had notations by the teachers of her potential: 'Youthful, but unquestionably talented. Should prove worthwhile ... Not a better actress than Hepburn, but definitely a personality ... Breezy, wholesome, intelligent, colourful and temperamental ... Strikes a real note.'

One of her closest friends at the school, Marilyn Cantor, the daughter of Eddie Cantor, discovered that Betty had an overwhelming hunger for food as well as acting. After classes, Marilyn would often invite Betty to dinner at the elegant Essex House where she lived with her family. Cantor's jokes delighted Betty, but his larder was even more pleasurable. One night after Betty left, Eddie exclaimed to Marilyn, 'Don't look now, but I think the girl has a tapeworm. She doesn't want to be an actress, too, does she?'

Out among the competition, Betty found that appreciation was harder to come by but she looked upon the search for it as a challenge. Her efforts, seemingly without end, kept her trekking round to see producers, long legs stepping out, and reaching out to buttonhole celebrities with her long arms. Those neophytes without her push called her *The Windmill* in grudging admiration. When she was not hanging around with her peers at Walgreen's Drug Store, on Forty Fourth Street and Broadway, she could be seen standing in front of Sardi's. At her post she would either be selling a theatrical sheet called *Actor's Cues* for the attention it attracted or simply lurking to introduce herself to anyone of influence. If a director or a producer she did not know was on the scene, her friends were obliged to point him out so that she could go up to him and say, 'I'm Betty Bacall. I'd really be an asset to your play.' No one agreed with her estimation of herself, but for her this direct confrontation was less demeaning than trying to get past producers' secretaries.

One night she tracked down a quarry and informed him, 'I'm an actress.' Annoyed, the producer retorted, 'The disguise is perfect.'

Stars were treated to a hello and a handshake. Sometimes, if Betty was encouraged, she would fish for an invitation to be taken inside Sardi's for coffee or a coke. On the few occasions that her wish was granted, Betty was aware that she came off as a sort of country cousin visiting the élite, but that did not matter so long as she attained her objective: to be seen and noticed.

Often Betty would ask actors for career counselling. One piece of treasured advice came from Paul Lukas, who was starring in *Watch on the Rhine* on Broadway. He told her his acting secret: 'The most important thing is sincerity. Don't try to act. Live what you're doing.'

'And if you want to be an actress,' Betty could add, 'live *for* what you're doing.' Some day her friends would say, 'I'm glad she made it. She wanted it so badly.' For her, there was no other choice. Even her grandmother, disturbed by seeing Betty's exhaustion in a pursuit that seemed hopeless, asked, 'What do you really do all day, child? Why don't you get a good steady job and settle down?' But for Betty there was no other life.

Eventually she had to take a stop-gap job in order to meet the expenses of living with her mother Natalie, who had long before divorced her father, William Perske. The work experience only reinforced her resolution to pursue her avowed objective. Being a model in the garment district was a poor alternative, yet one of the few legitimate opportunities available for someone with only a face and figure to offer. Her speciality was showing Seventh Avenue copies of what might once have been inspired gowns. She preferred wearing evening dresses because she was self-conscious about the length of her legs. She felt the same way about her arms, and was more comfortable in long-sleeved models. A short fling at this repelled her so much that she quit.

Then Betty landed her first job in the theatre—as an usherette. For this she was paid eight dollars a week, graduating to eleven. The money was not important because she felt that seeing shows would help her learn about acting.

While in that job, she attracted the admiration of the critic George Jean Nathan. All she got out of it was a clipping and an introduction. Mr Nathan wrote in his 'Bests of the Year' article in *Esquire*, 'The prettiest usher, the tall slender blonde in the St James Theater, right aisle, during the Gilbert and Sullivan engagement—by rapt agreement among the critics, but the bums are too dignified to admit it.' This compliment did not do Betty much good because he neglected to mention her name. Even Betty did not know that she had been referred to anonymously until he told her.

Equally unproductive was Mr Nathan's introducing her to William Saroyan at the theatre where she was working. All the enigmatic playwright said to her was that she would be better for the movies than for the theatre. Betty assumed, of course, that he meant acting not ushering. Still, she was confused about how to begin.

'There is something in me that says I've got to win,' was how Betty explained her ability to persist despite the lack of encouragement during that trying time. 'I don't know where it comes from, but it's there and it governs everything I do. That's what carries me on.'

Auditions were scarce, and the few she got were completely negative. Particularly disheartening was the meeting she had with David O. Selznick. At first, Betty did not believe it when a press agent said that he would arrange for her to read for the producer. It sounded like all the other come-on lines she had heard and she treated it as such until the appointment was confirmed by Selznick's New York office.

The next few days Betty worked intensively at preparing a scene with an actor friend of hers. The time finally came when they were to perform for the famous film producer. Ready and on edge, they waited an hour and a half in Selznick's private office before he and the agent showed up. Immediately the producer and the publicity man became engrossed in their business, totally ignoring Betty and her friend. Another exasperating hour and Betty interrupted to remind them why she was there.

Turning to Selznick, the agent pointed in Betty's direction and said casually, 'Oh, yes, this is Betty Bacall, Mr Selznick. Isn't she cute? Doesn't she remind you of K. T. Stevens?' Selznick nodded curtly, conceded Betty's resemblance to that momentarily popular actress, and returned to his papers. Betty and her friend slipped out of the office unnoticed. If she got such treatment from the producer of the Janet Gaynor version of *A Star is Born*—who ought surely to have been aware, through that film, of the plight of struggling young actresses—what could she expect from others!

The barrage of rebuffs forced through the strong front she had tried to keep up. Her vulnerability was revealed at an audition for the producer Max Gordon that she had virtually forced him into granting. Faced with the actual try-out on stage for a road company of *My Sister Eileen*, Betty stood almost out of sight in the wings and held on to a chair for support. Asked to come forward, she began to tremble and completely threw the reading. Though, of course, she did not get the part, Betty aroused the sympathy as well as the interest of Mr Gordon, and he promised to consider her for something else, some other time.

A few months later another producer heard Betty read for the understudy to Dorothy McGuire in a cross-country tour of *Claudia*. This time Betty was in control and came across so well that she won the role. On considering how long she would be away from New York and what opportunities she might miss, Betty declined the offer.

Afterwards she regretted that decision because nothing else seemed in the offing. The only official recognition of Betty being in any way special came in 1942 when she was chosen as the first Miss Greenwich Village. Even that success lost its glow in the light of a later disclosure by the judge, Walter Thornton of the modelling agency: 'The girl I privately selected as Miss Greenwich Village was a truly beautiful redhead. But she did not live in Greenwich Village. And so my second choice was elevated to queen and crowned. Part of the prize was an opportunity to model for my agency.' And he predicted: 'Never would Betty Bacall attain a champagne and caviar income.'

Other attempts to earn extra money by modelling were dis-

5

astrous. Harry Conover turned her down four times because she looked like girls he already had on his books. And her initial foray into the stronghold of *Harper's Bazaar* was also thwarted. An editor of the magazine, Wendy Englehart, was on her way to Grand Central station when she spotted Betty carrying her modelling portfolio. Intrigued by Betty's appearance, Wendy stopped and asked her to come along for some test shots. On seeing the results, the editor Carmel Snow was appalled. She screamed, 'Who hired that girl? Never use her again. I will not have her in the magazine.' It took more than a year for Betty to be vindicated. And that period was the most frustrating she ever had to go through.

Only by persevering did Betty get into two shows and they both turned out to be flops. For the first one, Betty continually waylaid producer Roland Brown until he was browbeaten into casting her as a bar girl who did a few dance steps in *Johnny Two-by-Four*, a drama set in a 1926 Greenwich Village speakeasy. In the huge cast list Betty's name was fourth from the bottom. Her fifteen-dollar-a-week salary may not have been much, but she was in her first show on Broadway and that was enough. On March 16, 1942, the play opened at the Longacre Theater, much to the consternation of audience and critics alike. The show closed after two months, followed only by a three-week run on the Subway Circuit in the Bronx and Brooklyn. But acknowledgement came from Betty's fellow actors when they voted her the one in the cast most likely to succeed.

In the opinion of another actress in the show Betty was 'a Dead End Kid, a kid off the streets. She's heard everything, seen every-thing, but it's not for her. You'd see her sitting and staring into space, dreaming, and she's dreaming of Betty Bacall.' It was that sort of concentration on her goal that helped give Betty the drive to surmount false pride and overcome the early hurdles. Her first speaking role was snared by approaching the venerable George S. Kaufman one day as he stood outside Sardi's.

Without an introduction, she went right up to him and bluffed, 'Mr Kaufman, I'll be ready to audition for you at four. Will that be convenient for you?'

All the renowned wit could reply was, 'Huh?'

'At four, my audition. Where will you be?' Betty insisted.

'The theater, I think. Yes, I'll be there all afternoon,' was the bewildered answer.

'See you at four at your theater. Goodbye till then.' Betty ran off, leaving Kaufman completely confused.

Fortunately, Max Gordon was the producer of the play Kaufman was directing. Remembering Betty and liking her despite her disastrous *My Sister Eileen* reading, Gordon hired her for *Franklin Street* at fifty dollars a week.

One evening during the out-of-town try-out, Kaufman asked to see her in private. Betty was sure it was to give her notice. But her dread disappeared instantly when Kaufman told her he was going to switch her part. She had been playing Adele, now she was going to be Maude, and she was delighted because she had a few more lines to speak. The triumph was short-lived and so was the show. There were disappointing openings at Wilmington and Washington and the play closed, in September 1942, after three weeks on the road. Though Betty did have the satisfaction of performing for one of her idols, Eleanor Roosevelt, and the distinction of having George S. Kaufman label her 'The Little Stinker', the only tangible pay-off for all her efforts was her unemployment cheques.

After such a dismal beginning, the end of her theatrical career seemed imminent. Unemployment insurance was scarcely enough to live on even though her mother was working. Her situation became so desperate that she often had to ask the rich boyfriend of her friend Joanne Tree's room-mate to take them all out for a decent meal.

All she had to show for three years of knocking around Broadway were three playbills, one with her name hardly noticeable, and the others not even from New York theatres; a picture taken with *Hellzapoppin* star Ole Olson and Walter Thornton when she won the 'Miss Greenwich Village' title; and a publicity shot posed with Burgess Meredith at an Army Relief Benefit which was published in *Movie Life* magazine with a caption referring to her as a 'stage starlet'. There was, of course, her Actors' Equity card, but that only entitled her to being a hostess to GIs at the Stage Door Canteen on Monday nights. Betty's reaction to this void was: 'I'm going m–a–d!'

A fateful meeting changed all that. At a small nightspot, Tony's, mutual friends introduced her to Baron Nicki de Gunzburg, an executive in the *Harper's Bazaar* fashion department. His reaction to Betty was not particularly enthusiastic, but he thought he might do her a favour by presenting her to Louise Dahl-Wolfe, top photographer, and Diana Vrieland, fashion editor of the magazine.

Their reactions to her were different from anything she'd heard before in her professional life. The photographer observed, 'She has that wonderful yellow-green skin that's so good for color.' The editor added 'She's perfect all over and yet she looks like nobody else.'

Both women agreed, 'Here was someone different.' And to convince the editor who had turned Betty down so coldly before, they took new shots which were so electrifying that Mrs Snow melted.

The initial splash was big. The February 1943 issue carried nine shots of Betty. Three were shared in a two-page blouse layout with a couple of established actresses, Martha Scott and Margaret Hayes, and she was referred to as 'The young actress Betty Becell.' Her name was misspelled, but her face was noticed by Howard Hawks' wife, Nancy, known as Slim. As one of the Ten Best Dressed Women in America, she was naturally aware of models.

Immediately after the spread appeared, Betty was earning three hundred dollars a week as a model, and was given the cover of the next issue. This showed her in a bizarre, vampirish outfit, standing in front of a Red Cross blood bank looking almost ready to make a withdrawal. Nothing daunted, Slim continued to be fascinated by Betty. On his wife's insistence, Hawks called his agent Charles Feldman to find out more about Betty.

Events then proceeded with such rapidity that only later was Betty able to appraise them. 'Mr Feldman telegraphed his New York office to look me up—and over. They wired the Bazaar to ask who was the girl on the cover and where does she live. I was in Florida for the magazine. Mr Feldman's office telegraphed me at my home to suggest a screen test when convenient. My mother was confused by the secondhand message and she did nothing until another telegram arrived which was no clearer to her than the first. She wired me. I'd never heard of Mr Feldman and said to myself, "Forget it."

'When I got back to New York, the Bazaar wanted me to be their representative for *Cover Girl*, then being cast. Most of the magazines had girls representing them. When I found out I wouldn't have a line to speak, I wasn't interested. But after a lot of back-and-forth negotiations, finally I decided to sign.

'Half an hour before I was to go, came this mad phone call from Feldman's man. "Well, what about it?" he asked.

' "I'm about to sign with Columbia," I said.

' "Don't do a thing" he shouted, "till I get there."

'When he got there, we put in a call for Mr Feldman. "Well, how soon can she get here?" he asked.

'I consulted my mother and my uncle, Jacques Weinstein Bacal, a lawyer who was my manager, and we decided I'd better go out to Hollywood. It's all very well to have directors ask about you, but I knew how busy directors are and how easy it is for busy people to forget why they asked. So I thought I'd better be on hand to remind Mr Hawks that he needed me. That same afternoon they arranged for transportation for me and I was in Hollywood three days later.'

So it was that one rainy afternoon Betty Bacall came to be sitting in Hollywood's Brown Derby directly opposite the urbane Howard Hawks. Hardly looking or feeling very self-assured, she kept apologising for her limited experience, and explained that she wished he would help her learn to act. Hawks' reply gave her some encouragement. 'I hope I can teach you to non-act and to have an artful naturalness,' he said. Betty felt relieved that after their otherwise stilted conversation he had not dismissed her on the spot.

Apparently, Hawks was a fair man who felt a responsibility for her coming to Hollywood and so for no other reason, he suggested that she make a screen test. He imagined she would be best for an unsophisticated ingenue part. Betty pushed aside her insipid vegetable dish and tried to hold her cigarette more glamorously. Unaffected, Hawks decided that a combination of scenes from the film *Claudia* would be right. Having once turned down the role for the road company, she felt this was a backward step. Besides, this apple-pie part was simply too sweet and lacked the tartness Betty would have preferred, but Hawks thought it was her just dessert.

During the four weeks of preparation for the test, Betty had to fight off the attempts of make-up artists to alter her looks. She was adamant about her distinctive appearance since that was what had attracted Hawks in the first place, and refused to allow anyone to

9

tamper with her uneven teeth, oversized mouth, pointed chin, sharply arched brows and streaked hair.

'I don't get it,' Betty protested. 'When you go into a store to buy something, you buy it because you like it and can use it. You don't take a potato masher home and carve it into a spoon.'

Only Hawks' consideration saved Betty from registering total terror on first facing the camera. The entire twelve-page script had to be done in one continuous take. Getting support from the director and grabbing control of herself, Betty managed to steam-roller through the lengthy dialogue without a false move or a wrong inflection. When Hawks finally yelled, 'Cut!' there was an unbearable silence which seemed to last an age to Betty. She stared at him anxiously.

'That does it,' he said. 'See you in the dressing room in a few minutes.' And Betty was thrown into complete panic.

She wondered what was coming and sat waiting for him, tense and expecting the worst. Hawks appeared, shaking his head. 'That test is going to cause trouble,' he exclaimed.

'Trouble?' Betty quakingly asked.

'Yeah. You're going to look like an actress—which you're not. That's the trouble. Now we've got to make the test stick.'

Betty stood up. 'If the test is good, it proves just one thing. I can do what you tell me to. If you're right, so am I. And what have we got to lose?'

As soon as the film was processed, Hawks invited Betty to see the test with him. Viewing herself on the screen for the first time, she sank lower and lower in her seat and hoped that the floor of the projection room would open and swallow her up.

When the screening ended, Hawks turned to her and asked, 'What do you think?'

Apologetically, she replied, 'I think I ought to be a dishwasher.'

Hawks, however, felt that she was photogenic from every angle and that she had, in his words, a 'cohesive physiognomy'. Just like a model's, her body was flat and straight but with that went a certain grace that Hawks attributed to her 'athlete's balance.' It was obvious to him that her acting ability was limited, and at the same time showed potential. That was enough to convince Hawks that he should put Betty under personal contract. In May 1943 a seven-year agreement was drawn up, starting her at two hundred and fifty dollars a week, which was fifty dollars a week less than she was averaging as a model. The test also made Jack Warner request, and receive, a participation in Betty's contract which made her officially a Warner Brothers' player.

Signed and sealed, she was delivered into the hands of the publicity department. Her stills, they complained, had to be taken out of focus. At Hawks' behest, her name was changed from Betty to Lauren which was thought to be more memorable. Lauren was her grandmother's name, but releases reported that it had originated from an employees' 'Name the Actress' contest because that made a better publicity story. Nevertheless, she would always be Betty to those who knew her personally.

Under Hawks' own supervision, she studied acting in a style that was so carefully understated as to seem non-existent. Voice lessons and constant practice in placement made her speak in a lower register that had a provocative sultriness. Singing was also part of her grooming, and she was surprised to discover that she had some talent for it.

Developing these professional attributes, Betty was goaded on by the realisation that she had to prove herself quickly. Her contract had a six months' option and her movie career would be ended swiftly unless she came through in some special way. Exposure in a part was vital, and Betty competed with all the other contract players at the studio in testing for whatever role was available. But she always got the 'we'll call you' routine.

Some solace came from being able to bring her mother out to stay with her. After a few weeks at the meagre hotel in Westwood, Betty moved to a four-room furnished flat in a court on the wrong side of Beverly Hills, a few blocks from the fashionable Beverly Hills Hotel. Decorated with lots of chintz, maple beds with sateen spreads and nondescript pictures, her new home was hardly more than adequate. She loathed it.

Natalie, wishing to pay her own way, took a job as a secretary at the city airport. Since Betty had to be in Burbank at nine, she got up at six and made her own breakfast. In the evenings, Natalie would cook dinner and Betty would do the dishes, establishing the same routine they had when they lived in New York.

On days when she was not busy at the studio, Betty would hang around Schwab's. Like Walgreen's on Broadway, this was the soda fountain shelter for the tired, the poor, the huddled masses of actors yearning not to be at liberty. In this warm climate the crowd seemed to have a more carefree attitude compared to the cold-shouldered stage-struck on Broadway. Whenever possible, Betty preferred spending her time with the Hawks rather than with those fly-by-nights. At least, with the director, his wife and their older, established friends, Betty felt she could learn something and profit from the time spent.

Dates and nightclubbing were a rarity since there were so many pretty faces around and Betty was not interested in competing. Often she would go alone to Santa Monica with her golden cocker spaniel, Droopy, and sun herself while reading on the beach. The car she drove, a grey 1940 Plymouth, had an accordion pleat in the bumper from an accident that had occurred on Wiltshire Boulevard soon after she had passed her driving test.

Ceaseless concern over whether Hawks would use her in a movie caused Betty to lose ten pounds in the first six months before her option was picked up. That is why Hedda Hopper's remark, when they were introduced at an Elsa Maxwell party, seemed absurd. Hedda dictated, 'Whatever you do, dearie, don't play ingenue roles. You should hold out for bitch parts.' To be cast in anything at all was hard enough and Hedda should have known that Betty was in no position to exercise any power of choice.

Constantly Betty would badger Charles Feldman, who was now also her agent. 'I'd go to Charlie's office and say, "If I don't work, I'm going to go out of my head. What's Howard going to do with me?" ' she recounted. 'And Charlie would say to me, "It will be all right. Howard's got something in mind, and when it jells you'll hear about it."

'Whenever I did see Howard, he'd tell me he thought I should be in a movie with Humphrey Bogart or Cary Grant. And he'd regale me with all the Hollywood glamour, tell me about what he had said to Carole Lombard, Jean Harlow and Jean Arthur, and I'd tremble thinking I'm not going to live up to it. What will happen to me?'

One tangible prospect finally emerged. Hawks mentioned to her that a script was being prepared from Ernest Hemingway's *To Have and Have Not*. The novel had originally been sold to Howard Hughes for ten thousand dollars because Hemingway was disappointed with what Sam Wood had done to *For Whom the Bell Tolls*—Wood was the father of the K. T. Stevens whom Selznick had considered Betty's double. After a while when Hughes did not make a movie of the property, Hawks bought the story from him for eighty thousand dollars. Hemingway did not receive more than the initial payment, even though he and Hawks were friends who had gone on hunting trips in the West together.

What attracted Hawks to the property was the salty character of the hero, Steve, his relationship with his drunken friend and the suspenseful boat scenes. Ninety per cent of the original plot was altered because of censorship trouble caused by the Hays Office and by government worries about giving offence to Latin America. The locale was changed from Key West and revolutionary Cuba, as it was in the book, to Martinique and the Vichyites, causing the film to be reminiscent of *Casablanca*. The discarded story could be used for later versions of the book without having them seem like remakes.

Like most auteur directors, Hawks wanted to make the hero's loyalty to his buddy almost more important than his relationship with his girl. As soon as Betty was considered for the part, the wife in Hemingway's original began to be conceived of no longer as a spouse but as a smouldering young girlfriend. This tailoring required that the story be completely rewritten by the screenwriter Jules Furthman and his second-billing partner William Faulkner.

The star of *To Have and Have Not* was to be Humphrey Bogart, definitely not one of Betty's heart-throbs. She first saw him on screen at the age of thirteen when an aunt took Betty to see her very favourite actress Bette Davis in *Marked Women*. Betty couldn't see why her aunt should rave over Bogey—he wasn't at all handsome. She saw the picture over again, however, as she often did with Bette Davis movies, and pretended, in order to seem more sophisticated, that he perhaps had something after all. So she proclaimed to her friend Betty Kalb, 'I'm crazy about that man. Just crazy about him. I love Bette Davis, but I should play opposite him.'

Now that her passing wish might be granted, Betty was sorry she had ever mentioned it. Even though Bogey was the biggest star on the lot since his recent success in *Casablanca*, this older, sinister-looking actor was not at all the type she had had in mind as a co-star when she had dreamed about making her movie debut.

Cary Grant was much more to her taste. She expressed aversion to working with Bogey, which was based on the rough roles he played and the gross gossip about him, in her remark: 'How awful to be in a picture with that mug, that illiterate. He mustn't have a brain in his head. He won't be able to think or talk about anything.'

One afternoon Hawks decided that Betty should meet Bogey to see how they hit it off. When she and the director arrived on the set Bogey was getting ready to shoot a love scene with Michele Morgan for *Passage to Marseilles*. This film, like *To Have and Have Not*, had a war theme involving the French and was conceived to cash in on the popularity of *Casablanca*. On being introduced by Hawks during a break, Betty was polite but unimpressed, while Bogey simply tried to evaluate her as a co-star. 'I looked at her and wondered whether or not she could act,' he later admitted. 'As far as I was concerned she was merely a prop which could add a lot or could ruin the picture.'

After this brief and inconclusive meeting, Betty did not see Bogey for several months but kept hearing news which did not endear him to her. On completion of his film, Bogey went for a tour with his wife, Mayo Methot, to entertain the troops overseas. Mayo, a blonde-turned-blowzy, was also initially noticed by Betty in *Marked Women*, playing a B-girl. In the seven years since then, Betty constantly read about the drunken brawls of 'The Battling Bogarts'. From all reports, they were outdoing even themselves on this junket. Their antics included insulting a colonel who tried to prevent Bogey from battering down a door to get at Mayo during one of their usual fights, as well as playfully firing a machine-gun while they were carousing with some soldiers. The games ended with his pointing a gun at a two-star general who had him put under arrest and removed from the sector. The on-stage entertainment they had volunteered to provide seemed almost superfluous and their off-stage behaviour was no diversion from the war. Their rowdiness caused the USO to make a ruling that no husbands and wives were to go on such trips together in the future. About the notoriety they engendered, Bogey only commented, 'You should have seen the breakage bill.'

A test Betty was to make for the Hemingway film preoccupied her completely. She was trying out for one of the two female leads, Marie, described as 'a tall, hoarse, egregious, twenty-two-year-old tramp, so worldly wise that when a policeman all but slaps her jaw out of joint she hardly bats an eye'. Trying her out in a scene from the movie, Hawks now put the emphasis on her sexiness and his hunch paid off.

One morning a few days after shooting the test, Hawks called Betty into his office to tell her the news she had waited her whole lifetime to hear. 'Well, you're going to do *To Have and Have Not*.' He continued, 'Now go over to wardrobe and make-up and ...' But Betty felt so hysterical that she left quickly. Later she returned and asked him to repeat what he had told her to do.

The film was the fifty-first for her co-star. When Bogey ran into her as he was coming out of Hawks' office later, he greeted her, 'Saw your test. I think we'll have fun working together, kid.'

A Star is Made

The month before production actually began on *To Have and Have Not* was filled with tremendous activity for Betty: costume fittings, studying her part and meetings with Hawks. The producer-director was also concerned with keeping his male star happy, and so he confided to Bogey his plan for handling Betty. Hawks had discovered that she was like a child who, on being insolent, became more appealing. The grin that came over her face when she was audacious could be promoted into a unique gimmick.

Bogey did not like the idea. His personal trade-mark was insolence, not rude or disagreeable in nature, but the kind that comes from assurance and is projected by apparent laughter at the world and its quirks. He shared this cool approach only with Clark Gable, an actor he did not much admire, and he preferred not to impart that special characteristic of patronising indulgence to this unknown actress.

Hawks assured him that by giving Betty that sense of male security so that she could walk out on him in their scenes together, a provocative contest would be created that would arouse the audience. This sexual antagonism had been mildly but successfully attempted in *Across the Pacific* with Bogey and Mary Astor's casual courtship veiled in insults.

Becoming intrigued, Bogey agreed to go along with Hawks' intention. After all, Bogey's personal relationships with women

16

were always based on this type of challenge. And Hawks himself often used actresses as either siren or buddy. As a change, Betty was to be both. What made Betty run—her determination—had been discerned by the director, given an alluring interpretation and was about to be the quality she would utilise in her bid for fame.

On the first day of shooting, however, when all that Betty had ever wanted was right there in front of her, she felt weak. The sure-nerved drive to succeed she had depended on to carry her this far suddenly waned. In its place fear of failure flooded in, combined with the dread that her debilitated state would show itself, as any anxiety she ever felt always did, in twitches of the mouth and blotches on her face.

Unable to keep her head erect on making her entrance in her first scene, Betty delivered her opening line, 'Anybody got a match?' with an inclined look down under and across to Bogey. This device was a desperate measure she had just thought of to keep her head from wobbling, but the cover-up was interpreted as being intentionally seductive. Her panic became obvious when Bogey threw a box of matches in response to her request and she kept missing the catch countless times. Repeating the action only made her shakes worse.

Afraid to face the apprehension she was certain Hawks was registering, and embarrassed to look at the others on the set who must be regarding her as an amateur, she concentrated on Bogey. He was ignoring her predicament entirely. His lack of concern made her feel that flubbing could happen to any professional, and that the necessitated retakes were simply a matter of course. His off-handedness calmed her so that she could go on feeling there was a powerful force on her side. Betty was then able to do what she was supposed to: open the door, say the line, catch the matches with a smart snap, light her cigarette languorously, purr, 'Thanks', and exit.

Once the perfect take was achieved, there was a break for the next camera set-up. Still a bit dazed but appreciative of Bogey's help, Betty decided to go to his trailer and thank him. Bogey disarmed her by smiling away her expression of gratitude. She became impressed immediately that the man she had thought of as a tough guy could behave like a truly gentle man. He explained how she could have avoided tension by concentrating on her motivation for coming into the scene. There was no condescension. He told her that he had also given acting tips to Bette Davis and Ida Lupino, but they had resented it. Bette had simply ignored his advice—in the seven pictures she had made with him as only a supporting player. Ida, however, was so antagonised by his intrusive suggestions while shooting his first major starring vehicle, *High Sierra*, that she refused to make *Out of the Fog* if he were to be in it.

Being a novice, Betty valued the attention he was showing and realised that she could gain a great deal through his knowledge, power and empathy. His reaction, he confessed to his friends, was, that *Femmes*, as he referred to his leading ladies, 'give me a pain in the neck, and the reason I liked Betty was that she didn't remind me of a woman.' He demonstrated that view from the beginning by giving her such men's names as Sam, Chuck, Mike, anything butch, even Butch itself. For him, the choice of masculine nicknames for her was to show that he was secure in being 'male'. What he called her depended on where they were and the kind of mood he was in. Unflattering epithets, like 'Fish-face', were used as endearments.

Charlie was a name that added to Betty's troubles early in the movie. She had to say, analytically, 'Do you know, Charlie, I really believe you would,' meaning that she suspected he would carry out the threat he had just made. The reading that Betty gave was, 'D'ya know Charlie, I really believe you would.'

After she had done this twice omitting the first pause, Bogey cut in quickly after she said 'Charlie' with the response, 'No, I don't know Charlie.'

The point made, she corrected her interpretation. From then on, sage and disciple were the off-screen roles they essayed. Soon she began by-passing Hawks and turning to Bogey whenever she had a question. The kindness he showed in caring about her professional life made Betty go to him also for more personal problems.

'At nineteen you don't know what you're doing, so I was scared all the time,' she later admitted. 'I used to run to Bogey and he would say, "Don't worry . . . don't worry."' The wisdom of his age could settle all her doubts and gave her a sense of security. His graciousness so contrasted with his gruff exterior that it was all the more of a privilege for her to share in his privacy.

As the production progressed so did their intimacy. She would frequently visit his luxurious trailer or he would come up to her functional second-floor dressing room that consisted of a medium-sized living room, small bath and kitchen. The talk at first was serious, and then the laughter began. He provoked her sense of humour and she his. Like a couple of old vaudevillians, they would repeat ancient wheezes. They were not embarrassed by tired jokes like: *He: Didja hear what the ceiling said to the wall? She: No, what? He: Hold me up, I'm plastered.* This was followed by artificial, then real, guffaws as though they were sharing some other, more personal jest. Their conversations had the cutting edge of put-down humour that conversely kept them on their toes.

Both of them delighted in practical jokes. At the end of one day's shooting, he managed to trick her into being manacled with two pairs of handcuffs to a post in front of her dressing room. For a long time she stood like that until she got a glass of water from a page and called Bogey over to throw the contents in his face. Her spirit provoked his admiration and he bragged to friends, 'You can't hold that girl.'

This teasing carried over into the movie and the by-play of their screen characters also became a part of their real attitude toward each other. So when he saw her in the tight-fitting satin gown she wore for her *How Little We Know*, a rather louche song, and delivered Steve's line, 'You won't have to do much singing in that,' Bogey was expressing his own feelings.

Between scenes they would ride around the lot on bicycles. Lunches at the Lakeside Country Club near the studio, which used to be spent with his cronies, soon became standing *tête-à-têtes* for the increasingly inseparable pair. Their relationship started out as an unbalanced see-saw, with Bogey the both-feet-on-the-ground heavy and Betty the up-in-the-air flyweight. But the see-saw was equalising itself by her moving closer to him for safety and by his letting himself go for fun.

Though Hawks was jealous of their growing alliance, he could not complain because he was getting a better picture than he had anticipated. The plot line was not particularly strong due to the reconception of the film as a situation melodrama dominated by the personalities of Steve and Slim. Her whore-with-the-heart-of-gold character was called Slim in honour of the woman who had discovered her and had become her best friend. Steve was typical Bogey, meting out his own brand of justice to transgressors who did not play the game according to his code of ethics, and, in his own way, turning out to be the protector of the underdog.

Fortunately, unlike most movies, this was being shot in chronological order, and so Hawks was able to take advantage of the increasing closeness of the two stars by parallelling it with the unfolding of the screen romance. Originally the other woman in the story was to come between them and temporarily break them up. As the emotion they felt towards each other became more obvious in the rushes, Hawks realised that such a twist would seem impossible between these two. Constant changes were made in the script to capture the excitement of their growing relationship.

Anxious to help Betty in any way he could, Bogey even 'stood-in' off camera for her close-ups so that she could look at him and get more out of her lines than if she were addressing empty space. As proud of her as if she were his own protégée Bogey announced in a press release, 'She gives you back what you send. It's like a fast game of tennis. If you put over a good ball and someone muffs it, you can't have a good game. But if somebody drives it back hard, you drive back hard and pretty soon you have a good game. It has to work both ways. Betty sends it right back to you.'

As soon as Betty had gained confidence, due mostly to Bogey, Hawks began to evoke the 'artful naturalness' that he had mentioned at their first meeting. This technique allowed Betty to decide for herself how best to play a scene, relying on the way she would behave if the situation were actually happening to her. The improvisational freedom given her resulted in a sensuous sequence that would turn out to be a highlight of the movie.

The girl portrayed by Betty had to leave a highly charged encounter with Bogey in a sleazy hotel late at night and go to her own quarters. Betty, still feeling passionate after the scene was over, exclaimed, 'Boy, was that a dumb move.'

'What's wrong?' Hawks wondered.

'If it were up to me, I wouldn't have left,' Betty confessed. 'And if I did, I'd go back for a guy like that.'

'Then do it,' Hawks commanded, discarding the script. The cameras rolled again, recording what was honestly felt at that moment. Even the creative genius of Hemingway and Faulkner combined could not compete with the validity on film of life becoming art.

At the same time, art was also coming to life. A parallel was forming between what was happening to Betty and the lead in the mythic Hollywood tale *A Star is Born*. In that paean to filmdom, the young actress meets the older movie star who is a drunk, and, while making their first film together, they fall in love. All Betty could wish for was a far more happy ending than the one depicted in the picture.

The source of this fictional film itself was yet another manifestation of reality contributing to creativity. In the original 1932 production of the Adela Rogers St John's story *What Price Hollywood?* Constance Bennett portrayed the actress that Janet Gaynor played in the 1937 *A Star is Born*. The director of the renamed remake, William Wellman, claimed that he incorporated in the part of the young girl, Vicki Lester, the 'patient and loving' qualities of his own actress-wife.

The role of the actor in the first version was split into two characters. Neil Hamilton played the handsome star who carried the love interest. Coincidentally, Bogey made his first attempt at being an actor by rehearsing to replace the ailing Mr Hamilton during the run of *The Ruined Lady*, but he never went on because the leading lady also became ill. The second male part in *What Price Hollywood?* was a director, *á la Hawks* but a lush, who discovered the fledgling actress. Playing this character to much acclaim was Lowell Sherman, who attributed the vividness of his performance as an inebriate to observing his brother-in-law, John Barrymore.

When the second interpretation was made and the two male parts were integrated into the dipso-ego-maniacal Norman Main, a rumour was spread that the character was based on John Gilbert whose career declined while married to the ever-popular Ina Claire and later to the up-and-coming Virginia Bruce. Those in the know said that the real Main inspiration was John Bowers, an actor who drowned himself when his career waned while that of his Lester-like wife, Marguerite de la Motte, was on the rise.

The Great Profile, however, provided the greatest profile for the ageing inebriated amorist. Evidence enough was his notoriety for drinking and the headlines about the ambitious actress pursuing him into marriage. But there was more. The producer, Selznick,

21

also did several of Barrymore's films at the time. One of the writers, Gene Fowler, became the biographer of the actor. The director of *What Price Hollywood?*, George Cukor, had Barrymore play a similar part the following year in *Dinner at Eight*. The actor who played the combined lover-helper, Fredric March, trailed Barrymore in *Dr Jekyll and Mr Hyde* and gave the definitive impression of the flamboyant performer in *The Royal Family*. As actors, Barrymore and Bogart were of different schools, but as men who loved to live it up, they were of one mind.

Bogey's identification with Main was so intense that he bought a 16-mm copy of *A Star is Born* for private re-runs. Every viewing would make him weep. When queried about why this movie always moved him, Bogey replied, 'I don't know. I see this thing and fall apart. If I ever live that long and it happens to me, ...'

Now with Betty in the picture and unable to face the complications of this burgeoning romance, Bogey turned to double martinis and ceased being a one-take actor. Infuriated, Hawks threatened, 'You'd better get yourself another director.'

That was enough to make Bogey quit his dissipation. From then on he would advise everyone, 'Never drink cocktails. Whatever you drink, take it straight.' From his friend Mark Hellinger he learned to prefer Scotch and bragged, 'I never drink when I work. I get loaded now and then.'

The truth of what was going on between Betty and Bogey themselves was not only showing up on film, but was also becoming apparent to everyone on the set by the way they were attacking their parts. A few weeks into production, and their co-workers realised that Bogey was making a present to Betty of the picture and, axiomatically, assuring her future. She accepted this tribute at first with humility and then as a matter of course without admitting even to herself that it was a gesture of love. Soon she was sporting a gift of a gold identification bracelet inscribed with her name that she ascribed to 'a mysterious admirer'.

By the time her most important seduction scene came, all the great jock of the movies could do was be her solid supporter. Her lines had more meaning because they sounded like they were his, though they weren't coming out through his torn mouth this time but were being put over by her ragged voice. So often before, Bogey had carried off scenes like this with words similar to the ones she used now. Slim kisses him twice and Steve remains passive. She recommends, 'It's even better when you help.' When this remark doesn't work, she gets up from his lap and, before exiting, tells him, 'You know you don't have to act with me, Steve. You don't have to say anything and you don't have to do anything. Not a thing—oh, maybe just whistle. You know how to whistle, don't you, Steve? You just put your lips together and *blow*.'

This sexual security, which came across as a transference from him to her, had always been a part of Bogey's image. His confidence in his potency had helped him endure the years of rejection as an actor. Then when he made it, his masculinity was constantly flaunted, as in the scene in *Across the Pacific* when Sidney Greenstreet pulls out his gun and Bogey shows his, gloating, 'My gun is bigger than yours.' This was an overt expression of a philosophy basic to all gun-toting films: a man is measured by his weapon. And because Bogey's always proved the most powerful, he not only won out against his enemies, but also deserved the love of his woman. Now Bogey's gun was silenced and all he could do was follow Betty's orders in their suggestive sequence together by ending not with a bang but a pucker.

The public was tantalised by publicity releases giving rhapsodic reports of that encounter. 'From the moment she eased herself on to Bogart's lap, until the breathless second when her lips parted contact with his, the initiative was all her own. During rehearsals lip contact was delicately omitted. When the slender, negligee-clad Miss Bacall first settled on him, he uttered a loud ouch. On her next descent, he asked her if she'd prefer to park on one knee or both. During the third rehearsal, he lit a cigarette. Miss Bacall asked him if he intended to smoke through the scene. That rallied him. "What's the matter?" he challenged. "Afraid you won't get your kiss?" While the cameras were being set up, Miss Bacall admitted being not too nervous, but her hands were shaking while applying lipstick. The actual kiss burned into celluloid lasts ten and two-tenths second and Bashful Bogart went to Heroic Humphrey.'

Asked if he felt any excitement in the love scenes, Bogey responded, 'In the first place, it's business. In the second place, it's hard to feel an emotion when I see a big hairy-chested grip scratching himself.' Always he would declare, 'Mushing it up before the camera embarrasses me. I'll handle it all in the privacy of my bedroom.'

The flip that Bogey was noted for was given to Betty in scene after scene, devised not to further the quickly disappearing plot but to show the power she had absorbed from the supposed superstar of the film. In one sequence Dolores Moran, as Steve's possible other love interest, passes out. The cool one, Slim, stands by fanning ether fumes on to her. At another point in the story Bogey waits patiently while Hawks evokes from Betty an attitude reminiscent of Marlene Deitrich at her peak of confidence. In *Morocco* Josef von Sternberg had Deitrich come upon Gary Cooper holding a couple of native girls on his lap, and instead of being annoyed, she simply congratulates him. In a switch on the same theme, Slim, on seeing Steve carry the girl who fainted, quips, 'What are you trying to do? Guess her weight?'

So intentional was this moulding of Betty into a siren in total control that Deitrich, viewing the scene at a private showing with Hawks, confronted him, 'That's me, isn't it?' All Hawks could say to her was, 'Yeah', but to others he added, 'in a warmer version'.

Bogey, however, did not have to ask Deitrich's question about seeing himself in Betty's character. He knew the answer because he was instrumental in its perpetuation, just as he had consciously forged his own personality. And he was aware that whenever he got high late at night his on-screen character took over. He even gloried in the classic observation, 'The trouble with Bogart is that after eleven o'clock he thinks he's Bogart.' But now he could take mischievous delight in imagining that some day it would be said of Betty, 'The trouble with Bacall is that she always thinks she's Bogart.'

Bogey was disturbed, however, on seeing some of his characteristics in her. Between scenes one day a publicity man was trying to arrange an interview with Betty on the set. She pulled a Bogey in her refusal by using his favourite denigrating name when she yelled, 'What Kreep wants to talk to me now?'

Bogey overheard and reprimanded, 'Look, Charlie, don't get to be a character so fast.'

Not long afterwards Betty tried turning the tables on Bogey's fatherly-advice-giving. Following a take, she launched forth and gave her opinion on how the scene should have been played. Bogey came back with, 'An excellent suggestion, Miss Davis.' Enraged, she just stood glaring at him until her fury became funny even to her and she burst out laughing.

Betty was learning from a master how little becoming a star had to do with acting ability and how much depended on an actor's interior life. Bogey had found the key for himself by emphasising attitudes that were meaningful to his public. He was the unheroic hero who put self-interest before society, yet would ultimately reveal the nobility that every man wished he were capable of expressing.

The main aspect of Bogey that Betty was beginning to understand was that he was a man of integrity who had little to do with outmoded morality. Virtue had to be adapted to situations. That he confessed to being an alcoholic, a provocateur and a male chauvinist absolved him of guilt.

The public relations people were able to manipulate details about him knowing that his fans, earnestly believing in Bogey's honesty, would accept all. Even his date of birth was changed to gain the public's sympathy. Warner's let it be known that Bogey was born on Christmas Day in 1899 so that he could claim being cheated out of his birthday gifts, whereas he was actually born on January 23 of that year, rumours of 1894 to the contrary. That Christmas Day birth also gave him a Jesus association that was reinforced by his almost sacrificial screen deaths, expiring in the last frame only to be speedily resurrected for the next film. He held the record over all other actors for that type of movie martyrdom. The reason for his recurrent demises in the thirties was usually for the acquisition of thirty pieces of silver. Values being what they were in the forties, the movie-goers loved to see Bogey die carrying a cause.

The director of *High Sierra*, Raoul Walsh, explained the actor's great mortality rate, 'You can't kill Jimmy Stewart, Gary Cooper or Gregory Peck in a picture. But you can kill off Bogart. The audience doesn't resent it.'

Bogey's career began shortly after World War I when, as part of the Lost Generation, he tried to find himself by turning to the stage. As company manager for a family friend, the famed producer William Brady, he fell into performing by chance. He accepted his first role for fun, found acting to his liking and took it seriously. The twenties saw him as a white-flannelled Valentinoish

Broadway juvenile, enjoying to the hilt his part in the Jazz Age speakeasy set off-stage. In the thirties, representative of his time again, he was an unemployed actor in the Depression, forced to play chess for a living, until it was discovered in *The Petrified Forest* that he could portray the gangster-type popular in that era. Now in the mid-forties, which was his own age as well, he was the Number One hero of World War II in screenland. This recognition came much later than it did for most actors, but once more his timing was perfect. The actors who could have competed against him were away at war and though Bogey was too old for actual combat, he could simulate such action perfectly to keep up the morale of the country. Through the years, Bogey was able to express the qualities as a performer and as a person that Shakespeare had stressed in *Hamlet* as being the genius of an actor: *The abstract and brief chronicle of the time.*

According to each period of his professional life there was a wife to go with it. All three wives complemented the stages that Bogey happened to be at as an actor. All three were actresses with whom he had worked, so that he knew what he was getting and did not have to deal with the unknown. And all three engendered his love with hostility. According to this pattern, Betty seemed a likely prospect.

If Betty had noted two lines from *High Sierra* she would have been given a clue to Bogey's emotional nature. Written by his close friend John Huston, the words exposed how Bogey himself felt. In the film, Ida Lupino cries in apology for having been a shrew and Bogey forgives her by saying, 'My mother and father always used to fight. I wouldn't give you two cents for a dame without a temper.'

Bogey booted his first wife, Helen Menken, in the backside even before he started going with her. On the opening night of *Drifting*, in which she was the star and he the stage manager, the scenery drifted and collapsed. Holding Bogey responsible for the catastrophe, Menken screamed at him, and he let her have it. That kicked off the affair, and they were married on May 20, 1926. At the time she was a big hit in *Seventh Heaven*, and he was just another working actor in *The Cradle Snatchers*. For his position as a supporting player in the theatre, Helen Menken seemed ideal to be co-starring with in private life. But their battle for top billing at home resulted in a divorce after a year and a half.

Just before Menken came on the scene, Bogey had a disagreement with the woman who was later to become wife number two. He had been upstaged during his most dramatic moment in a play called *Nerves* by an actress who had the nerve to cross in front of him swinging her hips. In an angry confrontation all he got from the girl, Mary Philips, was, 'Try and stop me.' That suddenly made her an object to be won. After his divorce from Menken, the antagonists ran into each other again and settled their differences by marrying. Phillips was an on-the-way equal who provided Bogey with direction through her complete devotion to the stage. Despite several short separations and a couple of minor affairs, their marriage worked for ten years, as long as his interests—like hers—were in the theatre. The combination ended when he started to make it in films.

Round number three came immediately afterwards, in 1938, and could have delivered the knockout blow with all the violence, attempted murder and near-suicides involved. Instead, *Marked Women* woman put him on his mark. Mayo Methot's fireworks surprisingly sparked Bogey's fundamental inertia, which had plagued his career, and he rocketed to stardom.

Now up there among the highest, and worried about burning himself out, a more appropriate satellite was in order and appeared to be in orbit. The magnetism that brought Betty and Bogey together was the promise of fulfilment that the relationship held for each of them. Whatever the two had for each other was not to be given and taken directly, but to and from the third element—their love—so that growth would result.

This twenty-year-old girl realised that this forty-five-year-old man could share the burden of her life-long ambition and give it the direction she sought. For Bogey, her youthfulness was a problem, yet the accompanying enthusiasm could inspire a much-required new purpose to his frenetic life. Of course, there were plenty of other aspiring actresses around who would be more than pleased by Bogey's attentions, though he was not one to play around once committed. For Betty, there could be many men of position anxious to give some of their riches in tribute to her beauty, but she was not looking for that.

What made these two connect, so that the attraction which was not immediately there for either of them became irresistible, was the potential for growth the two sensed they would have *together*.

27

Bogey may have thought of getting someone fresh, but probably realised he could not cope with her unless—like his other wives—the woman would enhance the level of achievement of his career. Betty, in her dedication to be more than she was, could be made-to-order, but then so could many others. Betty achieved success with him, and as an actress, because she had enough daring to be provocative.

She might have had more in common with someone her own age but with two ambitious young people struggling together, conflict would have been bound to ensue. An unexpected dividend to the security in the film world that Bogey could provide, and that Betty wanted, was Bogey's heroic content that belied his calendar age and expressed the age in which they were living, not just for her but for the entire world. So Betty would actually be getting a contemporary in Bogey. And even though she was a quarter of a century younger, he admired her ageless qualities of forthrightness, stability and talent that showed she *wanted* him rather than needed him. So Bogey himself became the answer to Betty's quest—as expressed in their first movie encounter—someone to match her.

A happy ending seemed inevitable, except for Methot in her madness!

To Have ...

The circle was being completed. A turn in fortune was returning Betty to New York. Two years before, the then unknown actress had left Grand Central Station for Hollywood. Her family and four friends had brought books, magazines and candy to reinforce their wishes for her success. Dissolve to the same girl and the same place, and superimpose the date February 1, 1945. This time Betty is a movie star coming in on the Twentieth Century Limited for her first publicity jaunt and a rendezvous with her illustrious lover. Having been hurled into immediate fame by a triumph in her first movie and the international buzz of her affair with Bogey, Betty had truly arrived.

The world was her oyster and Betty was fast becoming its pearl. This local-girl-made-good could not flaunt her success. She was not allowed to act like the underprivileged youngster who vindicates years of deprivation by returning to the old slum in a chauffeur-driven limousine. Public relations dictated that she seem unchanged. So Betty wore a tailored blouse and skirt, inevitable shoulder bag with brass crest and simple high-heeled open-toed pumps to make the required understatement. Her only touch of affluence was a striped, deeply-cuffed, sheared-beaver coat. This, she let it be known, was on loan from the studio for the occasion because her own two-year-old, velvet-collared, black top coat was not warm enough. But the reception she got was certainly heated.

29

Hundreds of instant idolisers began yelling as soon as the train pulled in. Betty was escorted to the crowded platform by Jack Diamond, a Warner's publicity man. With his boss, Charlie Einfeld, he had arranged a greeting worthy of the new national heroine. The screaming, the pushing for autographs, the grabbing, all the fetishes of her new-found fans were gracefully endured by Betty and thoroughly noted by the press.

Many in the mob were called there by the zealous press agents, but most had chosen to come voluntarily in the hope that by paying homage to this recently-elevated goddess some of her luck might rub off on them. Clearing her way through this bubbling mass, with the help of men from the studio, Betty accepted the almost overwhelming adulation with good-natured coolness.

Her initial encounter with the strange world of movie fandom had prepared her. The incident happened when she was still obscure and went to Inglewood to take in a preview. One of the multitude of youngsters in front of the theatre grabbed her. Pushing his pencil under her nose, he insisted, 'Gimme y' autograph.' Betty was surprised because she had not been in a picture as yet. 'Go on,' urged the possessed boy. 'You're my favorite star. What's your name?'

Now everyone shouted her name. The popping of flashes from eight—*count 'em eight*—cameramen, more than for any previous Hollywood visitor, made the fireworks official. The usual pose of the star atop the luggage cart, her skirt lifted to show just enough of the kneecap, was followed by the expected request for more cheesecake. Her reply delighted everyone for its show of independence and awareness of the wartime idiom: 'The stuff is rationed.'

Ensconced in her suite at the Gotham Hotel, Betty refused to be photographed as a mere ornament perched on the four-foot-high mantel. This directness also garnered the respect of the newspapermen who realised that she was not one to be pushed around no matter how desperately the ten studio publicity men wanted her to be accommodating. What came across in the mass interview was that Betty had a refreshing frankness laced with enticing mystery. All this drum-beating was played against a chorus of shouts from vociferous admirers eight floors below. Above her, on the ninth floor, was Bogey, who had arrived in New York two weeks before her, presiding like a guardian angel over the miracle of celebrity he had helped wrought.

In dealing with reporters, Betty was as elusive as a general trying to conceal his manœuvres while revealing enough to create interest in his campaign.

First Reporter: Well, are you going to marry this guy?
Betty: What guy?
First Reporter: Come on. Bogart, of course.
Betty: I'd like to wait till he asks me.
Second Reporter: Hasn't he asked you?
Betty: All I know about this is what I read in the papers. I haven't seen him for three weeks.

During that hiatus, a newspaper in Cleveland had published a scoop about their relationship that had been picked up throughout the world. The attention paid their affair provided romantic respite from the war news. Besides, with victory in sight, it was time to focus on the American dream. And this story had all the elements. Movie stars, sex appeal, 'Go west, young girl, rags-to-riches, overnight success, and love conquering all including a jealous wife.' There was the well-loved hero, Bogey, older and wiser, as the soldiers would be after the war, making a new beginning by winning the pretty young girl. That was what every red-blooded man at the front, regardless of nationality, would wish for himself.

According to Bogey, this was how the news leaked: 'While I was out at Louis Bromfield's farm in Lucas, Ohio, some guy I used to know from a Cleveland paper called me long distance and asked about the rumors, which were published in London first somehow, that there was something between me and Betty. All I said to him was, "Sure I like her, but I haven't got a divorce. How can I tell you anything when I haven't even got a divorce?" That was all he needed to do a big story.'

Persisting in the attempt to break down Betty's guard the newspapers continued.

Third Reporter: You mean he hasn't said anything about marriage?
Betty: That's right. He hasn't said anything. In the last three weeks.
Fourth Reporter: You mean he has asked you before that?
Betty: Look, all kidding aside, you wouldn't want me to give away a trade secret, would you?

First Reporter: That's what I want to know. Is this strictly promotion or is it on the level?

Betty: You'll have to ask him. He started this. Let him finish it. I can't.

Fifth Reporter: Do you love him?

Betty: That's the sixty-four dollar question.

Fifth Reporter: Do you admire him?

Betty: I think he's wonderful. He's been swell to me.

First Reporter: Would you marry him if he asked you?

Betty: You're kind of pinning me down. I don't want to answer and I don't want to lie. Can't a girl have any secrets?

How different this was from a year ago when she wanted to tell the world how she felt about Bogey. All she could do then was sit in her dressing room, writing on scraps of paper: 'Betty Bogart', 'Betty Bacall Bogart', and 'Betty B. Bogart', and no one cared. Now when everyone was anxious to share her feelings, she had to withhold the truth because Bogey was still married and any statement might create complications.

When the gossip began, she would put off reporters by saying that she had a lover who was not an actor, or else she would wisecrack, 'Listen, pals, here's the lowdown. I'm secretly married to Errol Flynn.' The press, though intrusive, was sympathetic. All were on the side of 'the other woman'. Fortunately for Betty and her career, she was able to change the customary puritanical reaction to her position. The brief acquaintance the public had with Betty was enough to convince everyone that she was the ideal mate to rescue their beloved Bogey from an unhappy union.

Early in the making of the movie, Hedda Hopper came on the set to warn Betty, 'Mayo may drop a lamp on your head one day.' Betty's fearlessness in ignoring this threat may have been a part of her usual do-or-die drive. But that devil-may-care attitude made her even more admired by her co-workers, and they were all rooting for her. Everyone was aware of Mayo's constant phone calls to Bogey on the set, checking up on him. She always put in digs about Betty being young enough to be his daughter, which he repeated for the enjoyment of all. There seemed to be an unspoken agreement among those connected with the picture to protect this rising romance. Bogey, they knew, was not one to play around and he deserved better than he had got until now. So even the crew co-operated. Whenever Betty went for drinks with Bogey, and Mayo called, whoever answered would say, 'He's out with the cast.' Betty became known as 'The Cast'. Only Hawks did not succumb to the appeal of this love play. Betty would later remember that he was horrified by the 'lightning and thunder and all', and made the pronouncement that she was throwing away her career.

The memory of the beginning of their love would always haunt Bogey. Sometimes afterwards, when asked which days, if it were possible, he would like to live over, Bogey would answer without hesitation, 'When I was courting Betty. It was the happiest time of my life.'

The apparent fervour with which Bogey was pursuing Betty, and she him, was a dynamic denial of the very real possibility that Mayo could commit mayhem as she had done in the past. Dorothy Parker may have thought her description of their marriage most clever when she witticised about Mayo and Bogey, 'Their neighbors were lulled to sleep by the sounds of breaking china and crashing glass.' James Thurber may have seen a New Year's brawl at their house worthy of a cartoon he facetiously entitled, 'Jolly Times—1939.' And Mayo and Bogey themselves may have thought they were helping to perpetuate a legend of a coupling that thrived on conflicts. They even called their boat and dog 'Sluggy' after his nickname for her, and their home was 'Sluggy Hollow'. By using each other for soul-searing combat and yet being able to emerge for yet another encounter, they seemed to proclaim that they could beat the world and fate at the same time. What had they to fear when they had gone the limit on their own.

Nothing could bring Mayo and Bogey lower than the hell they were putting themselves through. Yet they thrilled to this debasement of each other. This sado-masochism as a way of life enabled them to fantasise that the game was their own creation (*life*) to try the limits of their endurance (*death*), but since they themselves set up the rules (*destiny*) and they were the only players (*mortals*), they had to be the winners (*gods*). The real reward came from a purging of guilt (*original and acquired*) that only flagellates glory (*heaven*).

This testing of the spirit was telling on Mayo. As the instigator, her looks and mind were more immediately drained by the venomous surge of her fury. Like an exhausted third stage of a rocket, this third wife was ready to be dumped. Bogey, however, was able to soar above it all because the sight of himself on the screen gave him a feedback that kept him on course. Her career had been surrendered long ago to the emptiness of not being wanted, and submerged, not by his success, but by drink. There was dignity in not trying any more and just being the troublesome wife of a star, though not for a moment did she let him think he was doing her a favour or that she was impressed by his progress.

To get through these trials, Bogey acquired an outer layer of toughness. The very stoicism he chose to bring to his life was also incorporated in the roles he played. As critic Kenneth Tynan observed, the philosophy of Bogey's screen character was, 'Accept the fact of transience, don't panic in the face of mortality, learn to live with death.' With pride and sadness Bogey attributed to his breeding the inherent strength to go on toward his goal of recognition as a great actor.

The elegance associated with the late Victorian period was typified by the luxury of the brownstone in which he was born. Located near Riverside Drive at 245 West 103rd Street, this mansion was coincidentally on the same street directly across town, as the modest tenement which was Betty's birthplace twenty-five years later.

Unlike Betty, however, Bogey would disclose, 'I can't say I loved my mother.' In order not to offend his public, he would add, 'I guess you could say I admired her.' It was for achievement in her career that Maude Humphrey DeForest Bogart merited his esteem. She was the highest paid illustrator of her time and gave Bogey his first brush with fame when her portrait of him as an infant was used in advertising Mellins Baby Food as 'The Original Maude Humphrey Baby'. As a wife and mother, though, Bogey believed her to be a failure. All the tragedies that befell his family he attributed to her complete self-centredness. Her constant putdowns, while he was growing up, provoked his publicity agent to tell Ezra Goodman in an interview for *Time* magazine, 'His relationship with his mother may be the root cause of what eats Bogart.'

Continual fights with Maude drove his once prosperous and socially prominent physician father, Belmont DeForest Bogart, to give up his practice and run away to become a ship's doctor aboard freighters. He died a morphine addict, ten thousand dollars in debt, which his son paid off. The only memento of the wealth that Belmont had lost was a ruby ring that he bequeathed Bogey. The actor was never without this grim reminder of the doom that awaited anyone who allowed himself to slip. And he also talked about the necessity for the 'F.U. Fund' that he believed everyone should keep to declare independence and be able to maintain oneself.

One sister, Frances Rose—Pat, as she was called—was always in and out of mental institutions. His other sister, Catherine Elizabeth, who was the younger, died in her early thirties—of booze. This family was strictly out of a Eugene O'Neill play and had enough Furies to drive a man to drink, which Bogey did almost out of dread of going crazy. The spectre of insanity persisted in his marriage. Mayo had been declared by a psychiatrist to be a paranoid schizophrenic but was never hospitalised.

Meeting Mayo released a rebelliousness in Bogey that he had had to struggle with since boyhood. The unhappiness of his parents made him seek other values than the traditions which unmade them. Bogey barely got through Trinity, a private Episcopal grammar school, and was thrown out of Phillips Academy at Andover, Massachusetts, for mischievousness. The Navy of World War I provided a route for his escape. After the war, his revolt against his background expressed itself through becoming an actor.

From the very start, Mayo triggered a lunacy in Bogey. Though he had seen her once in New York before he came to Hollywood, he paid no attention to her because he was married to Mary Phillips and believed in faithfulness. The very few times he did stray could be attributed to loneliness caused by being parted from his wife for professional reasons. As Peter Lorre said, 'Bogey's no ladies' man. Maybe it is a deep down decency. He has very set ideas about behavior and morals in that respect.' Maybe because he was approaching forty, Mayo brought out a need for what he thought would be a last fling.

In 1937, ten years after Bogey's marriage to Mary, she went to Broadway to do *The Postman Always Rings Twice*, leaving him to work in Hollywood. At that time, Bogey was not yet a major star, but just another character actor in Warner's 'Rogues' Gallery' of toughs. While attending the annual dinner of the Screen Actors' Guild, Bogey noticed Mayo staring down at him from the balcony.

Provoked by her brazen beauty, the intoxicated Bogey ripped a baroque decoration of a nude woman from one of the columns and with mock flourish rushed to present the figure as his personal Academy Award to her for being the most exciting actress present.

Like Bogey, but in the bit player echelon, Mayo was Broadway-imported ham for the Warner grinder. Her blatantly sexual full-faced looks were reminiscent of Mae West's, and her two-fisted conduct like Edward G. Robinson's. An actress since childhood, Mayo made her debut in her home town, Portland, Oregon, with the Baker Players and moved up to stock, finally going to Broadway in *Sapho* while still quite young. Her only triumph in the theatre came when she introduced the popular song *More Than You Know* in the Vincent Youman musical, *Great Day*. This led to her first film *Corsair*, with Chester Morris, and a stock contract at Warner's which never promoted whatever potential she may or may not have had.

Obviously Bogey saw more in her than the studio did. A few months after their meeting, Mary returned to find Mayo living in their apartment at the Garden of Allah. Bogey did not have much of an alternative as to which woman he would choose. After all, Mary preferred Broadway to Hollywood, and he was becoming known in films. Mayo was now the one who fitted into his way of life. Hadn't they just worked together in *Marked Women*? More-over, for the gangster type with which he was becoming identified, Mayo was the model moll. Mary returned to New York and won a divorce, according to a report in the Associated Press, 'by testifying that her husband had told her frequently he did not love her. Mrs Bogart also said her husband stayed away from home and refused to explain his absences.' A year before Mayo had divorced her husband Percy T. Morgan on the grounds of cruelty, claiming he would not permit her to rearrange the furniture. On August 20, 1938, a few days after Mary's decree became final, Bogey and Mayo made it legal.

During their tempestuous seven-year marriage the only thing that steered them into calm water was their mutual love of the sea. It was a fascination they had both inherited from their fathers. Hers, Jack Methot, was a sea captain by profession, while his was an ocean-going fugitive by default. As a boy, Bogey was trained by his father to regard sailing as a way to get away from all cares and to express independence from women. This was particularly necessary at their family's summer retreat at Canandaigua Lake, one of New York State's Finger Lakes. At eight, Bogey was master of the helm of his personal Great South Bay One Designer sloop. And at thirty-eight, he bought *Sluggy*, a thirty-six-foot cruiser, and was accepted as a member of the highly respected Newport Yacht Club which normally refused actors.

'We kids would pull the covers over our ears to keep out the sound of fighting', was a memory of his parents that bugged Bogey. But the barrage of his own martial marriage resounded throughout the world. Intimates realised, however, that the combativeness of the Bogarts increased the intensity of their love-making. Real trouble began when Bogey emerged from secondary roles to the first rank in Warner's roster. That made Mayo demand more attention because she was less sure of keeping him as his popularity grew and hers dwindled into nothing.

During the filming of *Casablanca*, Mayo kept interrupting shooting with phone calls, falsely accusing him of having an affair with the pretty and pristine Ingrid Bergman. With the success of the film, Mayo attempted suicide for the first time by slashing her wrists. Before this, the knife had been pointed in Bogey's direction. One night on coming home late from the baths, where he went for a little peace, she greeted him with her theme song of violence, *Embraceable You*, and stabbed him in the back. Five stitches later they were in each other's arms. A psychiatrist recommended that Mayo be put in an institution, but Bogey could not bring himself to make her go. As he explained to a friend, 'My wife is an actress. It just so happens that she's not working right now. But even when an actress isn't working, she's got to have scenes to play. And in this case, I've got to give her the cues.' This had echoes of a crucial scene in *A Star is Born*. The actress in the film explains in similar words why she has to stand by her has-been husband.

The studio publicity men became used to hushing up the more extreme manifestations of Mayo's disturbance. But a call of help from Bogey one night had them all alarmed. He had locked himself in the lavatory to escape Mayo who was pursuing him with a gun. Not wanting to involve the police, he used the bathroom phone and begged a smooth-talking publicist to come and calm the frenzied Mayo. She intended to kill Bogey because he just happened to mention that he would like to go off by himself on a little trip. That's all she had to hear and she was off and running for a gun, threatening to send Bogey where she wanted him to go with a bullet.

Until that persuasive P.R. man could get there, Bogey kept the connection to the department open. Shocked at his predicament, the studio people crowded around the phone to listen while Bogey pleaded with Mayo to relent. Her response was a roar of laughter which grew louder when his dogs, accustomed to the squabbles of their master and mistress, ignored his yelling through the bathroom window for help.

The more Bogey begged, the more hysterical Mayo became. Suddenly there was a gunshot. Their phone-in audience thought this was the end. Then they heard laughter again, but this time it was Bogey's. Only later did they learn that Mayo, out of frustration at not being sure of her target through the door, had fired into Bogey's suitcase instead. Still not satisfied, she maintained her vigil.

The sound of water confused the listeners. At first, they thought that Bogey was taking a shower. When the peace-making publicist arrived and persuaded Mayo to give up the gun, they found out that Bogey had run a bath and was relaxing in it. He felt that if he did not survive this baptism of fire, he should leave the world as clean as he came into it.

The gun, like the knife, also began to be more readily turned by Mayo from Bogey to herself. At a dinner party in their home, all she needed was to imagine she was being talked about while she was out of the room for a moment and she was incensed. Instantly she ran up to their bedroom and a gunshot was heard. Bogey rushed up, smashed down the door and found Mayo on the bed— not in a pool of blood but in tears. The gunshot had been just a ploy. So often did door-demolishing occur that there was a supply of replacements in the cellar, and a carpenter was on call to restore what they may have destroyed in their own home and in the homes of those they visited as well.

Even the studio fire department had to be used surreptitiously to put out a fire at Sluggy Hollow that Mayo had started intentionally. Usually, though, verbal attacks and physical abuse after an evening of drinking together forced Bogey out of their home. Often he would retire to a friend's house to sleep it off, but in the morning—after throwing up—he made sure he got to the studio in time. Whatever happened the night before, Bogey felt obligated to his work. Jack L. Warner, in his autobiography *My First Hundred Years in Hollywood* claimed credit for forcing this realisation on him.

One morning Warner encountered Bogey, drunk and in a dirty pair of pyjamas, riding a bicycle around the lot. Just as Bogey was about to smash into a wall, he was caught by two studio policemen. Warner confronted him in his dressing room and gave him a dressing down. 'Goddamit, Bogey, I don't care if you bust your ugly face. But there are hundreds of people depending on you in this picture, and some of them get a pay check that wouldn't handle your liquor bill for two days.'

Bogey looked remorseful. 'Forget about it, Junior, it'll never happen again', the actor promised. And, according to Warner, it never did.

The price Bogey was paying for his dissipation was marked on his face. His visage seemed to be a tragic mask to which the public responded empathetically because it reflected the human condition.

Remembering Bogey as the quiet, sensitive-looking introvert he had known in *Meet the Wife* on Broadway in the twenties, Clifton Webb could never reconcile himself to what was happening to his best friend. 'Battling Bogarts!' Webb scoffed. 'Why, any woman could walk all over him. The man's a softie.'

Others had a more critical view. They had witnessed Bogey inflict black eyes and bruises on Mayo. And she wore these wounds proudly as if they had been caused by the slings and arrows of an outrageous cupid. Mayo regarded the bad boy stories that were constantly written about him as 'Bogey Baloney', and tried to justify the notoriety by saying, 'I married a man who conducts himself like a man. A man who doesn't only offer me security, but a certain excitement.'

A favourite pastime was a public display of boxing with the burly actor Broderick Crawford. These matches were staged in any night club that would still allow them entry. Not only would Mayo play referee, but also, if some outsider tried to get into the act, she would knock him out. Often she would encourage Bogey to bop a fan who came over to the table, or else—egged on by him—she would do the punching herself. Their own personal fights could simply be started by his coming home from the studio and mentioning how tired he was. Then she would begin a tirade

on what a sissy the big manly star was for being so delicate. Sometimes just a word from an outsider would be all that was needed
to get her in a fighting mood. One of the friends, as a tease, would
mention MacArthur. Immediately she would begin attacking
Bogey for not liking the general and for being a cowardly 4-F
shirker, and she would wind up by throwing her glass at him. Laughing it off, Bogey would brag that he did not mind because he knew
when to duck, and besides his wife was a bad shot.

Any hint of dissatisfaction with his sparring partner was strictly
not for publication. He tried to encourage Mayo's career by giving
her the spotlight in a personal appearance they made at Broadway's
Strand Theatre in December 1940, just before he began to hit it
big. On screen was the Bette Davis movie, *The Letter*, and the real
stars of the stage show were Ozzie Nelson and Harriet Hilliard.
Bogey was thrown in as a promotional filler and Mayo came along
for the ride, desperately trying to give her almost non-existent
popularity a boost.

The act the studio devised for them had all the embarrassment
of actors showing their inadequacy as entertainers just to satisfy
the lust of fans for the flesh of film personalities. Naturally, Mayo
sang her standard, *More Than You Know*, just to remind the
audience of her one moment of glory. Then after a cavalcade of
flashes from a dozen pictures in which Bogey was shot, he came
on live, tumbling down a flight of steps, pretending to be wounded.
After a few jokes, he actually sang, which prompted one critic to
write, 'In the latter role, he is far more terrifying than in his bad-
man parts.'

On leaving the theatre, after a performance one night, they
became separated by a waiting mob of his fans. Bogey rushed into
a cab, thinking Mayo was behind him, and quickly drove away.
Stranded, Mayo let out with her customary curses and someone
in the crowd exclaimed in amazement, 'She's tougher than he is.'

'The trouble with the world,' Bogey would often philosophise,
'is that it is three drinks behind and it should begin to catch up.'
Perhaps the Bogarts were countless drinks ahead. Fortunately, he
began to develop an internal barometer as his career progressed.
He knew when he was running dry and would supply himself with
just the right amount of replenishment required to keep a glow-
on all the time while still being able to function. Because Mayo

did not feel any responsibility to anyone or anything, she exercised no such self-control.

A trophy they proudly displayed on the wall over the focal point of their home, the bar, was a receipted bill for breakage from the Hotel Algonquin in New York. As with many of their stories, they told variations on how they got that prized possession, depending on what would make themselves more pertinently colourful at the moment. Sometimes they would say that it was a memento of the beginning of their private war, their honeymoon. On other occasions the bill would be attributed to a tipsy mix-up later in their marriage. She threw him out of their suite at the hotel, and when he returned to find her gone he took another room to play it safe. Then she came back and, not seeing him there, booked herself elsewhere. The next day they finally came together in the original room and the clash that resulted gave them this souvenir. The bill was a proud proclamation that they could afford to do whatever they wanted regardless of the cost, even to themselves.

If Mayo really intended to kill Bogey, she would have. She had plenty of opportunity to do so, but she was not ready to ring down the final curtain on their farce. Instead, she forced him into joining her grotesque clown act. At first, he did not mind running in circles under threats of violence because he always scoffed at the values of others, and this ridiculous demonstration of living by his own standards gained the attention of the crowd.

The pain she inflicted on her partner, in addition, made him a man of action. Unexpectedly, he was rapidly moving away from her, and they could not play off each other any longer. So the crazy carnival would have to close. Out of desperation she would go to greater extremes to reach him the further he advanced. Finally she brought about the very isolation which she dreaded. Inadequacy promoted jealousy, and that forced a schism between them. Like most people who feel victimised, Mayo helped create the competition she had imagined. Ultimately, she drove Bogey into Betty's open arms.

Bogey flaunted his affair with Betty like a man who had already paid the penalty for a crime he had yet to commit. He felt free of guilt and wanted the world to know it. Although his friends were about his own age, they soon also became *her* friends. She did not seem to mind the lack of people of her own generation if that meant being with Bogey. His was the life to be supplemented. She had no alternative.

'Probably my first major adjustment under the Bogey regime was "Learning-to-Love-a-Boat",' Betty declared, realising that his enthusiasm had to be hers. The first time she took the wheel of his pet sailboat she ran it down at its mooring. Everyone at Newport Beach Club watched and laughed. Then in her maiden attempt to pilot the cruiser *Sluggy*, nerves made her put the engine in reverse and toss a line overboard that got snarled in the propeller.

Within a few weeks, she learned not only to master the cruiser, but also to manœuvre the sailboat so well that in one of the club sailing races, she came fourth. Altogether, there were only four competitors, but at least she made a worthy showing. To finish at all, Betty had had to plead with oglers on other boats, 'Please get out of the way. Can't you see I'm racing?' Soon she could announce, 'Bogey claims I am a good helmsman. I could handle the wheel or sails—except in a race or a gale.'

Betty helped with the chores to disguise her repugnance at being aboard. So active was she in covering up her real hatred of boats that she was considered a good sport. The kitchen, though, was her real nemesis. She had no aptitude for cooking other than making coffee and a simple breakfast. Because of her height, she was able to hoist supplies aboard easily, so the weekend sailors called her 'Ladder Legs'. This pleased Bogey because, ever since school when he was called 'Hump', he believed, 'You can't trust a person who doesn't have a nickname.' A similar wariness was expressed about teetotallers.

The openness with which Betty and Bogey behaved resulted in a particularly embarrassing predicament from which they were extricated by the quick thinking of friends. One evening they pulled into the yacht club and did not appear on deck until the next morning. The conservative members put two together and were scandalised.

Before action could be taken to bring about the dismissal of Bogey, a married couple he knew came out of the cabin wearing pyjamas and making a big show of stretching and yawning. Since the pair were recognised as respectable and it was assumed they were chaperones, the incident was dismissed. Betty and Bogey, however, were just as surprised as anyone to see their friends aboard but were quite relieved. They found out later that the couple came to pay an unexpected visit, grasped the situation, slipped below unnoticed, and changed their clothes. Betty was discovering that the impudence and sexiness she had developed as an actress had to be used cautiously off-screen.

Talk spread about what had happened. A few weeks later, while Betty was lying alone in the bunk below, Bogey having gone on an errand, Mayo stormed aboard. Hearing the jealous wife shout their names, Betty lunged into the head and locked the door. This time it was her turn to avoid the wrath of Mayo by hiding in the bathroom. Betty could hear the angry woman searching and swearing in her frustration. Then there was a long silence broken by an occasional clatter. Obviously Mayo was determined to wait and Betty was just as resolute in avoiding the confrontation. This could hardly have the refinement of a Bette Davis–Mary Astor movie. Dialogue might be impossible because Mayo would rather use a weapon than her tongue. Whatever Mayo's intention was, Betty was not anxious to find out.

Half an hour later, though it seemed longer than that to the trapped Betty, Bogey arrived. After an argument with Mayo, he forced his wife to leave. Betty leaped out of her confinement to hug her rescuer. To be sure, cowering in the john was very unbecoming to a star, and most unlike the carefree position Betty had always assumed previously. But then she had never been so close to the menace of Mayo before, and never would be again.

So much of their romance revolved around the boat that it was not surprising when Bogey used the occasion of a yacht club dinner to make public for the first time his intention to marry Betty. Rising, he asked everyone in the dining room to lift their glasses, 'to toast my fiancée, Betty Bacall, the future Mrs Bogart'. This was news to Betty. The guests made no fuss, and the press totally ignored this announcement.

No formal proposal was ever made to Betty. Bogey never even said, 'I love you,' but only talked about what they would do when they were married.

Much later, however, a movie magazine carried an article by Natalie Bacall in which she described Bogey asking for Betty's hand. It was too lovey-dovey ever to ring real. 'Love for them is ridiculous as well as sublime,' she wrote. 'A weird, whimsical sense of humour miraculously shared.... There's that wonderful humility each feels before each other. "Mom, could there be a guy like that? How could any girl be good enough for him?" And Bogey coming to me one evening to ask if he could marry Betty. Earnest, awkward, "She loves me, Nat. Imagine the luck of that! That magnificent little kid ..."'

There was an understanding that as soon as they had finished shooting their film, he would have his confrontation with Mayo. If they could have supplied the script for a movie made of that scene, the action might have gone like this: Bogey and Mayo, to get away from it all, board the boat for a sober talk about their situation. After a minor hassle, they come to terms and agree to a divorce. Even though it might be early in the morning, Bogey leaves immediately and calls Betty to pick him up on the road. As the lovers intertwine, their happiness reaches a crescendo; the old relationship has ended amicably allowing the new one to proceed smoothly. Cut! Only that wasn't the way it was to be.

Second thoughts made it necessary for Bogey to rehearse his real-life part more than once. Unexpected remorse about leaving Mayo to slow disintegration began bothering Bogey. Also, he had qualms about a permanent commitment to a girl young enough to be his daughter. And he feared the death threat that Mayo held over all three of them. So even though he kept moving out of his home, misgivings forced him to return. This indecisiveness lasted only a few weeks, but to the people concerned it seemed an eternity.

No longer in control, Betty was crying all the time, and all she could say was, 'What else can I do?' Her future was up to Bogey. A factor she did not take into account was the movie they had completed. True, she had put everything into it and had received some immediate happiness from it. What she could not anticipate was that the success of her introductory film would result in her ultimate fulfilment.

A sneak preview of *To Have and Have Not* was held at a small theatre in Huntington, far enough away from the regular Hollywood crowd so that the audience was composed of more ordinary human beings. Jack L. Warner, along with Hawks and an entourage of tired studio executives, drove down to see what they thought would be just another picture to ride on the crest of *Casa-*

blanca. Though most of the experts had seen either part of the film or all of it, none of them would commit themselves until they got the response of non-professionals.

Seeing herself on the screen in a theatre for the first time and wondering about the public's reaction was painful for Betty, but Bogey was immune. There was a smattering of applause when the credits came on and the audience realised they were going to see a Humphrey Bogart movie for free, but then he had made so many mediocre pictures that they could not be sure of what they were getting. The crowd remained quiet and seemed not too impressed until the door to Bogey's hotel room opened and Slim slammed a home run. The theatre resounded to wolf calls and whistles, and everyone clapped with delight at her two songs. The love scenes played to the accompaniment of sighs. And to cap the amazing response, the applause at the end was overwhelming.

A stunned Jack Warner rushed over to Hawks in the lobby and exclaimed, 'Ye gods . . .!'

Betty's reality immediately became more exciting than her most extravagant fantasy. She was suddenly the centre of everyone's attention and admiration. But until she heard from Hawks soon afterwards about his great plans for her future, Betty was afraid this might be just Hollywood hoopla that would pass quickly. The release of the picture was going to be held up a couple of months so that both she and the film could get the build-up they deserved. And as a reward for merit, she would be rushed into another movie—with Bogey, of course—to exploit the winning team. This was predicated on his getting off the suspension he had been on for the past few months for refusing to do a movie he did not like.

Hawks himself would direct them again, despite his original intention to put her in the hands of another director. Part of his reason for originally wanting to change her supervision was that he wanted to vary her experience. But, even more, he also wished to avoid the contest with Bogey for authority over her. The hit she had made altered the professional triangle, just as, in the future, it would straighten out the romantic one.

The screenplay for the next movie, *The Big Sleep*, based on a Raymond Chandler novel, was written in collaboration with Faulkner, in only eight days. And if Betty believed that her life at that time was in a state of confusion, it was no more of a jumble than the plot.

Hawks revealed, 'I don't know what the title refers to, probably death. It just sounds good.' Others thought it was about the effects of drugs which was one of the problems of the plot because it was not mentioned directly. 'I never could figure the story out,' he admitted. 'I read it and was delighted by it. All we were trying to do was make every scene entertain. We didn't know about the story. They asked me who killed such and such a man. I didn't know. They sent a wire to the author and he didn't know. They sent a wire to the scenario writer and he didn't know. The main idea was to try to make every scene fun to look at.' The reason they had to telegraph Faulkner instead of calling him for a story conference was that Jack Warner agreed to the author's insistence on working at home without realising that to the writer home meant Mississippi.

A while later, Betty met Faulkner downing a martini alone in a bar. When she questioned him about his drinking habits, he replied, 'After one martini, I feel bigger, wiser, and taller. After two, it goes to the superlative. After three martinis—well there just ain't no holding me.'

This time the philosophy of the making of the film was to influence what the leads did off-screen, instead of the other way round as in the previous opus. Betty and Bogey quit trying to solve the troubles that were almost poisoning their love, and made an effort to enjoy whatever happiness they could rescue.

While again working with Betty nearly every day, Bogey realised that any permanent reconciliation with Mayo was impossible. With the attitude of taking things as they come, they once more dated regularly, a routine Bogey had resisted when they were between pictures. Now they had old haunts to go back to, and Emil Coleman's orchestra would always—as before—strike up their song, *That Old Black Magic*, when they entered the Mocombo. This time around their affair had the quality of 'bittersweet chocolate', a description that Betty had once given of her own personality.

For the time being, Betty suspended her annoyance at Bogey's frequent flights back to his wife. She even reconciled herself to his giving Mayo a diamond and ruby ring for Christmas while she still wore her old chrysoberyl. A little patience would be well rewarded, Betty knew, because she had a good idea what lay ahead for her.

The accolades began pouring in. Even before the picture was released, every newspaper and magazine wise man in the field of entertainment heralded the birth of a new star in the west. Then when the film hit the screen, there was an explosion of adulation in words and pictures heard and seen around the world. High-powered publicity ignited the initial fireworks, but the devastating bombardment of the public became self-generating and ever-expanding once her rumoured talent and romance were confirmed. Covers and feature stories telling of the meteoric rise of this Bronx youngster vied for attention on the news stands. Not only was Betty fresh fodder for movie magazines, but she was also immediately dignified by the attention of the more serious media.

Unprecedented for a newcomer, she achieved both the front cover and four pages in *Life*, three pages in *Look*, a page in *American Magazine* and in *Liberty*, two pages in *Collier's*, special stories in *Time* and *Newsweek*, a front cover in the *Sunday News* and *Mirror Magazine* sections, three pages in *Sunday P.M.*, a front-page feature in the *Sunday New York Times* drama section, and innumerable news items elsewhere. Story after story was put out about her by every Hollywood reporter. For the first time Walter Winchell devoted a full column to a new personality and called it, 'The Bacall of the Wild'.

The personal reviews, which were the most unanimously ecstatic since the heyday of Garbo, to whom Betty was being favourably compared, reached their zenith in a rave by Bosley Crowther. In the *Sunday Times*, he wrote, 'Marlene in her salad (and salacious) days, a haunting resemblance to Katy in her style, a wisp of Veronica Lake (arrogant hank of hair), and in her lurid moments— Mae West.' The column was titled, 'A Big Hello, Welcome to Two New Screen Personalities'. The other newcomer being so graciously received was Clifton Webb in his *Laura* debut. By coincidence, not only was he one of Bogey's best friends, but also Betty had been an usher when Webb was starring on-stage in *Blithe Spirit*.

'The Look' was seen everywhere. That label was credited to Bogey who had used it to sum up the insinuating glance she threw at him in her first scene. Sidney Skolsky published the scoop that 'she sleeps only in the jacket of her pajamas and she curls up in bed. When she's asleep in bed, she has that Look.' Betty let it be known in turn that Bogey should be referred to as 'The Hangover'.

Another distinctive feature that became a subject for talk was her low-pitched voice. Hawks described it as 'exciting to men, but it's the women who love it'. Stories abounded of 'how she shouted her way to the top' by going out to the mountains and screaming everything from Shakespeare to restaurant menus. While doing this, *Time* reported, two policemen almost took her away. Skolsky had another version of the source of this phenomenon. 'She always had a deep voice and, because of it, she was called a tomboy as a kid.' And he wound up his column with such particulars as, 'Hips, 35", waist $23\frac{1}{2}$", bust 34", but she's flat-chested.' As for her singing voice, which was considered extremely suggestive, Betty constantly had to protest that her own was used in the film and that it was not dubbed in by the young Andy Williams or some adolescent boy.

One of the many awards she acquired was from the National Academy of Vocal Arts which recognised her as having the Sexiest Voice in its list of the ten most outstanding women's voices in the world. Another title came from the United Press and the Associated Press who picked her as 'Most Interesting Actress of the Year'. Fashion magazines chose her 'Model of the Year'. Letters came from troops overseas naming her as winner in their popularity polls. One pigboat outfit in Japanese waters broke the silence of the silent service by voting her, 'The girl we would most like to sink to the bottom with.' From the personnel of the 15th Hospital Centre in England came the name, 'Miss Pulse-Rate of 1945'.

Soon she was guesting on the radio shows she had grown up listening to. Her first broadcast was with Bob Hope and Bing Crosby, and they both had to hold her around the waist as she spoke her lines so that she did not collapse from mike fright.

The demand for her was so great that she finally complained to Bogey about her weary load.

'Oh, for God's sake, Charlie,' he replied, 'shut up!' Betty stared, but Bogey continued, 'Listen, Kreep, you wanted to be an actress, didn't you??'

That made Betty smile. Understanding his annoyance, she answered seriously, 'Yes, I did. I always did.'

Although Betty made a quick jump from twenty-fourth to sixth place in popularity among all Warner's players within only a few months, she was not due for a pay rise for another half year, and even that increase would not be commensurate with her box office value. Before the completion of *The Big Sleep*, Hawks turned down $75,000 from another studio for a loan-out.

This time Hawks admired a particular aptitude of Betty's. 'Not only does she soak up everything you tell her, but also she absorbs things by just walking through a room.'

Bogey put his own realisation of that trait in another way. 'She's like a chameleon. She takes on the color of things around her.' This ability showed up in filming *The Big Sleep*. During a scene in a gambling joint Betty was supposed to say in a Park Avenue accent, 'Spin the wheel. Want another play?' Just before this line, she had been watching Bogey do his rough stuff. When her turn came, she unconsciously dropped into his manner and came out with, 'Spin dat wheel. Wanna 'nother play?' Everyone on the set broke up at her out-Bogeying Bogey.

This talent for mimicry was evident, according to Betty's mother, from the time her daughter was fourteen months old. Even at that age, Betty was able to duplicate any expression that crossed Natalie's face so perfectly that the proud mother concluded, 'The die is cast,' and foresaw that she would be an actress.

That early prediction was confirmed as soon as Betty learned to talk, and it was discovered that she could also imitate other people's voices. Natalie's husky speech and Granny's heavy Rumanian accents were ideal targets. Both older women thought it was 'scary' the way the little girl could sound like them. Sometimes Betty would do a Granny bit by calling, 'Nat-a-lie', from another room, and her mother would respond by rushing to the old woman at the other end of the apartment.

This bit of mischief reinforced Granny's belief, which she often repeated to Natalie, 'She has a great gift, your little one.' Granny furthered the interest that Bettylein—as she called the child—was developing in things dramatic by reading from her own favourite author, Shakespeare. Just before Betty got her first taste of film glory, Granny died, cutting a secret bond that had always been between them.

This absorption with the character of others resulted in an incident, when she was three, that her mother described as 'devilish'. At that time, there were already indications that she was becoming a strong-willed blonde beauty. Her family would always tell her that from the time other girls started becoming aware of the world around them, all Betty's thoughts were directed inward. On that bizarre afternoon, they turned outward with near-tragic impact. As a special treat Betty was being allowed to take a nap in her parents' room, and her mother was to join her. When Natalie saw Betty had curled up in one of the two beds and was lying quietly, she relaxed in the other and fell asleep. All of a sudden Natalie was awakened by an alarming scream. What she saw was a nightmare come to life. There was Betty atop her husband's chest of drawers and the little girl's face was covered with blood. Holding up her father's straight razor which she had run across her cheeks, giving herself a gash, Betty cried, 'I was just being Daddy and look....!'

As a reminder of that frustrated attempt to seek love and attention through assuming the identity of someone else, Betty got a lifetime scar on her right cheek. Yet there was some compensation. Betty's self-inflicted wound was in the same place as Carole Lombard's scar. If anyone asked Betty to choose the star she would most like to emulate, she would reply, 'I wish I could be Carole Lombard's kind of actress,' knowing that at least they shared a facial defect.

Another hurt that Betty had in common with Lombard, as well as her other idol Bette Davis, was an emotional one. All of them suffered from early desertion by their fathers and were dependent on domineering mothers for guidance.

Like Lombard, too, Betty had been directed by Hawks, who was famous for *Scarface*. The Lombard–Hawks combination was responsible for *Twentieth Century*, which co-starred John Barrymore, one of the prototypes for *A Star is Born*. Their film together was memorable for the wild mating of an actress with her Svengalilike lover aboard the very train that had brought Betty back to New York. The rowdy reel relationship was similar to Betty and Bogey's real romance in that both climaxed on their arrival in Gotham.

•

And To Hold . . .

To be a celebrity, Betty was discovering during her gruelling week's stay in New York, meant to carefully expose all past and present actions, as well as future hopes, in such a way that people could find out exactly who she wanted them to think she was.

For the achievement of the desired impression, Betty was scheduled for sixty-two interviews, both mass and individual, and endless bookings for photos. Special fashion shots were in demand because of her modelling experience and her affinity for casual clothes. To replenish her personal wardrobe, she slipped off to Loehmann's, a designer discount outlet in Brooklyn she used to frequent in the early days.

Every interviewer was looking for an exclusive angle, especially one that had a connection with Bogey. An eager columnist came up with an imaginative observation that Betty was anxious to confirm. Asked if she did not have a lisp à la Bogey, Betty sucked her lips sweetly to reinforce the possibility of this mutual defect. She wished it were true, yet she was forced to admit, 'Not that I know of.' Quickly she relented with, 'Well, maybe I have a lisp . . . a little one.'

All her beliefs had significance for those anxious to expose the factors that go into making a success. 'To get to the top,' Betty opined, 'you've got to concentrate all your thoughts on your career. I don't happen to think it's worth it. Life is too short as

51

it is without making it more so by spending your time reaching for the stars. I prefer to concentrate on being happy.'

To another columnist, she revealed, 'Perhaps things wouldn't have come so swiftly if I hadn't pushed. I like to think I helped.'

Still another view was printed that said, 'I guess it's a good thing I'm a fatalist and take things as they come. Otherwise I might not have gone to Hollywood. I might still be trying for that hit play.'

In an obvious attempt to cement her relations with the newspaper crowd, Betty told of an initial ambition she never pursued 'I started out with the idea of becoming a newspaper reporter. I suppose I am the kind of girl who likes excitement, and I guess I also liked the idea of my name in the papers. That is the reason I am so happy now. To tell you the truth, I get a thrill every time I see myself mentioned, and good notices puff me all up. After all, screen players don't get real applause.'

Wishing to emphasise her individuality, although she was compared to every star in creation, Betty spoke with humility, 'I don't want to be another Bette Davis. We're not the same type, and I'm not "another" anybody. But I want to be as good as Bette if I can.'

A story was told of how Bette Davis gave Betty her first mention in the newspapers when she was still in her early teens. Betty and her inseparable friend, another Betty with the last name of Kalb, revered the Bette of the movies. The star-struck youngsters mooned about her constantly.

When Davis came to New York, a friend of a relative of Natalie's who knew her was able to arrange a meeting between their heroine and the two Bettys. As dawn broke on the great day, the anxious girls reached the Gotham Hotel to wait for the star's arrival. Hours later they saw Davis swoop through the lobby with her young blonde daughter. More than a few minutes were needed for the girls to regain their composure. Pulling their newly acquired matching skunk coats around themselves and wobbling only slightly on their heels, they made it to the room.

Once inside, Betty Kalb withdrew to the far end and froze in awe while the more energetically nervous Betty paced about until Davis patted the pillows beside her on the couch as an invitation for the girls to sit there. That seemed to relieve the tension somewhat, and after a while the three of them had an easy conversation about New York, Hollywood, movies, acting and all the revelations the novices wanted to hear from their superior.

After what seemed too short a time, publicity men entered and the girls made a reluctant exit. Turning excitedly to Betty Kalb, Betty saw only a pile of skunk skins in the hall. Her friend was lying underneath in a faint. The alert publicity men got the item in the columns the next day, giving both Bettys the initial entry in their scrapbooks.

Now it was Betty Bacall's turn to be the visiting celebrity at the Gotham. The presence of her cocker spaniel was a warm touch everyone noted, especially since this was the first time an animal was allowed in the hotel. This was retribution, she explained. When Betty was a teenager, she and another friend Marcella Markham had tried to crash a party there. As with all Betty's stories, when stars are mentioned, those involved always worked for Warner's. The guest of honour at this event was Priscilla Lane. Asked for invitations, the girls became flustered and were shown to the door. But this time it was Betty's party.

Between the hundred phone calls a day she was receiving during her stay, Betty was still able to express her opinion about anything and everything to interviewers. Gladys Hall was told, 'Bogey and I go out together. We're good friends, as I told you. Not to go out with him would be idiotic. Sheer insanity. Phoney. Listen to this, pal. The gossip stuff doesn't bother me. If you let it get you, you'd end up in an insane asylum. There are more bewildering stories going around. One I heard the other day is that Bogey isn't well. He's fine. Feels good. I've been a fan since I could read words of one syllable, and so have read all the stuff and things for nearly fifteen years. Some of it has been so silly. Some of it hasn't. So what? Besides, I don't think it will do me any harm. Way I figure it, on Shirley Temple it wouldn't be becoming. But on me, considering the type I turn out to be on the screen, it's okay.'

Expressing her feelings about marriage, Betty revealed to another columnist, 'I used to think I wanted to give my life to acting. Die in grease paint and all that. But now I'm not so sure. There's something sort of empty about it, you know. Look at all these movie stars. Happy? Uh-uh. When they get what they want, they don't want what they get. After all, women were meant to be wives.'

As for the other half of the duo, Bogey refused to share the spot-light and so let Betty have her solo. His pungent views on corre-sponding subjects, however, were always widely quoted to the delight of some and the irritation of others, as was his intention.

His feelings about women were, 'They've got us. We should never have set them free. They should still be in chains to the home, where they belong.'

About women in the profession particularly, Bogey growled, 'I once said ninety percent of movie actresses are dumb dames. I figured every one of them would automatically include herself in the ten percent escape clause I'd left them, but they jumped all over me. So I have since amended the statement. *Ninety-five* percent of all movie actresses are dumb dames.'

Concerning love, he crowed, 'A critic once referred to my face as a triumph of plastic surgery. Good looks have nothing to do with a happy marriage. Women love through their ears. An intelli-gent man can charm the pants off them, while a good-looking, callow youth can bore the hell out of them.'

The May–December romance everybody was writing about, he justified with, 'Career girls don't want to go through the struggle of marrying a young man who's searching for a job. That's what Betty told me. . . . She liked the idea of moving into an established home. Most girls today aren't the covered-wagon type. They prefer older husbands.'

Their published horoscopes gave the public an insight into how the stars were ruled by the stars. Bogey was pure Aquarius, ideal-istic and disillusioned. Having Jupiter with Scorpio in mid-heaven meant that he was slated for prominence that he simply took for granted. Venus in Sagittarius would account for his multiplicity of marriages. Betty, born September 16, 1924, showed that she was 'a siren—à la Garbo, also born Virgo—the planet of personality is in the sign which rules the throat and is restricted by Saturn, so she can't help talking that way. Smooth and smart, and when the stars are on her side, she speeds up; when they're not, she slows down to a walk.' Her future it was predicted was 'very promising' and she had 'an old soul'.

The probing of the press into Betty's persona included a hand-writing analysis by Muriel Stafford printed in the *New York Mirror Sunday Magazine*, that stated, 'There is a seething cauldron of im-

54

patient emotion—including temper—in the lightning strokes of this gifted handwriting. But the left slant of the lettering indicates self-control despite occasional flairs of temper. She knows what she is doing all the time. She is constructive, intuitive, ambitious and stubbornly self-willed. The consistent up-slant of the T-bars for ambition. The deepening strength of both T-bars and underscore for determination. Large, swiftly written disjointed backhands with truly distinctive letter formations are rare and significant. They know others are drawn to them and are able to make the most of their charm and ability. Women like this do not always choose a career. They almost inevitably marry well. They cannot be flattered or swayed. Her capitals are simply made, meaning she judges herself totally accurately.' An added observation was, 'She will stay a long time.'

Newsweek, referring to the analysis that gave the impression Betty was ruled by her head and not her heart, printed her admission, 'It's true up to a point. If my heart got interested in something, don't you believe I'd let go. Not easy.' Betty agreed to the supposition that she was self-possessed and persevering, and to the *Newsweek* conclusion that she was 'not the Rita Hayworth type', and would be around for a while. 'Sure, if you don't use your head where will you be five years from now?' Betty added. 'Stars don't last unless they've got brains, too.' About her trip, she commented, 'Do you call *this* a vacation? No sir, this is work and I don't mean maybe. But a girl has got to think of her future.' Betty ended the interview on a note of modesty, 'I'm good, but really I'm not that good.'

Life magazine's cover story by Francis Sill Wickware held that Betty 'displayed the curious mixture of extreme aggressiveness, narcissism and exhibitionism which characterises stagefolk. . . . Her toughness is protective, acquired during early Broadway years. Friends said, "People were never nice to her." Betty learned to expect little from promises and never to expect something for nothing. . . . Tough most of the time, coy never, Bacall on celluloid has much in common with Amber St Clare, and the instantaneous success of these two ladies no doubt is of deep sociological significance.'

Life also described the gusto with which the press celebrated the Betty–Bogey romance as 'rarely equalled since the Simpson–

Windsor nuptials'. To be the principal in any love story, especially one that was being compared throughout the world with the legendary amours of all time, was a new role for Betty. Until now the only love scenes she had played were acting exercises. These began in her quarters at boarding school, doing parts of *Romeo and Juliet* with her room-mate.

After Betty's parents were divorced, and Natalie was forced to return to work as a secretary in a firm of food brokers, her mother's family came through with the child support William Perske refused to pay and she was sent to the stylish Highland Manor in Tarrytown, New York. Betty was 'crazy' about it from the minute she arrived. 'Above all,' Natalie recalled, 'she loved her room-mate, Gloria Hofpaüir, who was almost as addicted to make-believe as Betty was.' As for her demeanour, one teacher remembered, 'She was certainly a lovely little girl. Wherever there was Betty there was pandemonium.' When she left the school at twelve, her souvenir yearbook predicted, 'She would break men's hearts.' That was predicated on the naïve notion that her obvious good looks meant success in love. Usually the effect was just the opposite because, as one friend maintained, she 'blitzkrieged' her suitors like an anxious actress overdoing her part to capture an audience that was withdrawing even further because of the pressure being exerted.

An early emotional setback that indicated what her pattern with men would be occurred the summer after graduation from Julia Richmond High School at the age of fifteen, two years ahead of the other girls. Betty tried to barge through the barrier that often separates beauty from brains. Every previous summer she had been going to a camp in Maine, where she had become a swimming instructor by forcing herself to overcome her fear of water. This particular year she was hired to be dramatic counsellor at a camp in Connecticut. It was the first money she was to make from her interest in the theatre.

On the train ride to the country, she met Marcella Markham who turned out to be one of those 'special' friends of whom Betty was intensely possessive for a long time. The same relationship had existed with Gloria Hofpaüir at boarding school who was replaced by Betty Kalb in high school. Just like them, Marcella was fascinated by the theatre and resembled Betty in lithe loveliness.

The focus for all the applause.
Syndication International

MOVIE LIFE OF LAUREN BACALL

1 LAUREN BACALL—seven months old, here—was born in New York City on September 16, 1924. A baby-sitter let house-to-house photographer snap this.

2 FOUR years old, she was busy with swings. Her name then was Betty Joan Perske, later became Bacal. Hollywood added extra "l."

3. BETTY-LAUREN was five-and-one-half years old when snapped on Long Island (N.Y.) with a few cronies. She wore out both slide and dress that day.

4. NOW NINE, Lauren was at Highland Manor, a private girls' school in New York. She spilled a chocolate malted on the coat, tried vainly to get it off with toilet water.

5. LAUREN WAS 10, above, when she posed for her first professional picture—which went into the files of John Robert Powers, to little avail.

6. STUDENT, still, at Highland Manor, the 11-year-old Lauren strikes a glamour pose for a classmate photographer.

7. GRADUATION, at 12 from Highland Manor school. Pictured with Helen Bakewell, classmate and friend.

8. SENIOR, at Camp Cannlhaw in Connecticut, whose duties included looking after the junior campers. Senior Bacall was 13.

9. SHE MODELED children's clothes (above) when she was 14 and a junior at the Julia Richman High School in New York. Next year, she graduated 459th in class of 884. Then, American Academy Dramatic Arts.

76

Betty's early life—part of a *Movie Life* profile.

Fan portrait. *Ronald Grant collection*

MOVIE LIFE OF LAUREN BACALL *Continued*

19. IDEAL VISIT—a call on MOVIE LIFE magazine while visiting New York. Lauren was *going up!*

20. SERVICEMEN fans had a look at The Look in Washington, liked what they saw and kept her after school writing *Lauren Bacall.*

21. PIANIST and appreciative audience. It was *Vice President Harry Truman* when this photograph was made by a cameraman who has since been knighted by the studio. Occasion was a Press-Club entertainment for servicemen.

22. STILL WRITING her name for soldiers and sailors in the many canteens and camps she visited. "Make it, 'To my dear pal Smiley!' willya?"

23. LUNCHEON for columnist Drew Pearson drew stars Bogart and Bacall, as Jack L. Warner, studio vice-president, played luncheon-reception host.

24. HELEN TURPIN, head of the hair-dressing department at Warner Bros. and a customer who usually wears hair simply—with pin-curls brushed well.

25. DROOPY, the dog, eavesdropped on chat with Bogey. New dressing room

26. RARE SHOT of girl in shorts was taken at Lakeside Golf Club, where Bogey

27. KISS, à la Bogart, while prophetic, was actually called for in script of *The Big Sleep*, a Bogart-starrer. Bogey helped coach her in her first two films, says, concerning

Fan fare. More of the *Movie Life* profile.

28. TRAIN of events had resulted in Bogart-Bacall engagement (1945), leave-taking for Ohio wedding ceremony.

29. PAUSE in Chicago (for a patriotic celebration), enroute to novelist Louis Bromfield's Ohio farm for their wedding.

30. WEDDING, May 22, 1945, of Humphrey Bogart and Lauren Bacall, at Malabar Farm, home of Louis Bromfield (extreme left), near Mansfield, Ohio. This was Bogart's fourth marriage, her first. He was 45; she 21.

31. LA RUE, where the newlyweds were a focal point for every photographer in town. They'd set up housekeeping in Beverly Hills, were both working, planned some sailing.

32. SAILING is Bogey's second love, an enthusiasm that's shared by this fair deck hand. Boat, a 55-foot yawl named Santana, is a race-veteran.

33. TARS at work luffing the anchor, or thereabouts. An accomplished sailor, Humphrey found a willing pupil in Lauren.

34. LESSON proceeds with study of sails in a healthful classroom. Love me, love my

35. INSIDE DOPE from Big Bill Tilden during tennis matches at the Los Angeles Tennis Club. Mrs. Bogart had added a coronet braid to usually plain

36. FIRST RADIO appearance and opposite Bogey in To Have and Have Not, on Lux program. Smiling

37. HARVEY (left), a boxer, and friends he was visiting on set of their new movie, *The Dark Passage*.
38. Fame and a congratulatory hug from Baby as Bogey made cement-record of prints at Grauman's.

MILESTONES IN THE
MOVIE LIFE OF LAUREN BACALL

39. PARTY and rarely-seen evening clothes. Note sandals.

40. WHISTLE, Bogey's gift, a gag from first movie, was to summon Humphrey. It did!

1. TO HAVE AND HAVE NOT, 1944. Her first and with Walter Brennan and Bogart

2. CONFIDENTIAL AGENT, 1945. It was opposite Charles Boyer.

3. THE BIG SLEEP, 1946. Whodunit with Bogey as detective *Christopher Marlowe*.

4. THE DARK PASSAGE, 1947. Another whodunit—with Humphrey.

Even more of the life of a film star. *Movie Life*

10. $15 A WEEK was pay as walk-on extra in Max Gordon play, *Johnny 2x4*, on Broadway. She's at right, chin on hand.

11. COVER PICTURE on *Harper's Bazaar* interested director Howard Hawks and resulted in her Hollywood career. It was the work of Louise Dahl-Wolfe.

12. IN HOLLYWOOD she underwent intensive training, then was put into lead in *To Have and Have Not*. MOVIE LIFE gave a page to this shot, her first publicity.

13. RELAXED, momentarily, she was dead serious about acting, making good. Hawks had lowered her voice, taught her "naturalness" notable in her first film.

14. THE MAN and The Look—Humphrey Bogart and Lauren—going back to work on *To Have and Have Not*, and arm in arm, after lunching together.

15. TRIO, Walter Brennan, Lauren and composer-actor Hoagy Carmichael, discussed counterpoint, arpeggios and *Stardust*, on the set.

16. CHESS game between takes is an old Bogart custom; this was *To Have and Have Not* set. Blonde kibitzer was surprise chess move.

17. OOMPHY love-making, such as above from *To Have and Have Not*, accounted for much of her smash personal success in the film. Studio promptly made Lauren a star.

18. TRIUMPHAL visit to New York following stardom after first movie, and the customary photographic-hoopla amidst a mob of avid fans. 77

Bogey's Baby. *Keystone Press*

As soon as the girls reached the camp, they surveyed the competition and agreed that they themselves were the prettiest around. They then drew up a list of available males to conquer for the season. Out of the limited possibilities, Betty chose Sam—a handsome young leftist—as the object of her affection, even though he was a little red in political colouring. Unfortunately, he had his eye on someone else, Georgine, who had a passable face that became immediately ravishing when she discussed Marxian dialectics.

One night well into the season, after having been frustrated by Sam's resistance to her onslaught, Betty caught the ingrate with the visually unworthy Georgine. Confronting him afterwards, she wondered, 'What do you want to go out with her for when you could have me?'

The reply was polite but pointed. 'You're gorgeous, but she can talk. She knows politics and the world situation.'

Still insistent on winning him, Betty screamed, 'I can talk. I can talk. Ask me anything. Go on, ask me.'

Betty never got to play it with Sam even once.

Undaunted by her failure in private encounters, she hoped to devastate them all once the *bonne chance* printed in her high school yearbook, *Spotlight*, came true:

> 'Popular ways that win.
> May your dreams of becoming an actress
> Overflow the brim.'

A more astute oracle would have realised that those dreams were already in full flood and that she was having enough trouble just keeping her head above water. Betty would do anything to gain attention and would constantly play around in class. The teachers noticed and put such notes on her records as, 'Full of the devil, but an industrious student,' 'A nice girl, but talks too much,' 'Tardy too often.' When her tomfoolery and truancy were not enough to make it obvious that she thought rules were for others, she resorted to malingering and hanging out at the off-limits-during-school-hours pharmacy named for another dreamer, Don-Q. Because she was smart enough to justify anything she did, Betty got away with more than most girls and was graduated 459th in a class of 884. Yet long after Betty left school she would hear about the impression she made on her first teacher who recalled that Betty kept saying, 'I am going to Hollywood.' An administrative assistant later spoke about her, 'I've been here seventeen years. When you graduate eight hundred girls twice a year, you remember the very good ones and the very bad ones. I remember Betty very well.' Betty had succeeded in leaving vivid recollections behind her.

Despite all her carryings on about the theatre and behaviour worthy of the most temperamental star, Betty did not bother with high school dramatics but saved her talent for part-time classes at the New York School of Theatre.

To be known by her classmates as, 'The only girl who could wear those awful gym bloomers and still look like a dream,' was not enough for Betty. Besides, she had some doubts about acceptance and was 'stupidly sensitive and hurt easily. I'd see two girls, heads together, whispering, and be sure it was about me, and brood over it.'

To prove her superiority and earn extra money after school, in her spare time, with her mother's enthusiastic approval, she would make the rounds of the modelling agencies. At first, when a photographer told her that she had 'legs like a colt', she broke into tears, thinking he meant she was like a horse. Later she could laugh at herself when she looked at her pictures in playsuit ads, and agree that her legs did look 'nine feet long'.

Because she was 'not the least bit *femme*', as she remembered, she once got 'pebble legs' from a fall while riding a bicycle too vigorously. For all this outside activity, her studies did not suffer. Often she and her friend of the time, Betty Kalb, would do their homework together while listening to and commenting on their favourite radio programmes, *Screen Guild* and *Lux Presents Hollywood*. All the while, both Bettys would be dreaming of the future when they would gain universal approval.

Until that happened, the attainment of even a modest one-to-one response from a man eluded Betty Bacall. Just after the *Harper's* cover came out and before the Hawks talk began, Betty went to St Augustine, Florida, with Mrs Louise Dahl-Wolf for some location shots. Although recognition was at hand, Betty did not relax, and applied the same pressure on an unsuspecting prospect that had made males shy away from her before.

Betty met a young Navy lieutenant assigned to the Information

Office whom she liked and had no inhibitions about chasing. He was attracted to her, but held back because he was engaged. That did not stop Betty, just as Sam's prior commitment at camp had not deterred her. Not that she intended to steal him away from his fiancée. What she needed was someone to escort her around so that she could have fun during her stay. He was the one she chose for that function, and like it or not he was going to fulfil her needs. So Betty barraged the lieutenant with persistent phone calls and finally got her date.

That headstrong drive was described in the Yiddish word her mother would use, 'chutzpah'. Some viewers of Betty in action admired this quality in her and thought it showed strength of character. Others were repulsed and even refused to interpret her impatient, outspoken and nervy qualities as overstatement due to insecurity. Whatever the cause, having 'chutzpah' was basic to her nature.

A clash of wills with her father had showed that determination even at the age of three. William Perske took Betty to a restaurant, and when she demanded ice cream for dessert, he refused to order it. Betty exercised all her tiny wiles and cajoled him into surrendering. When the desired dish was set before her, she looked at him and laughed, 'I get anything I want, Daddy.'

Now a big girl, Betty was getting everything she had ever wanted: fame and, even more, a famous consort to add his name to hers. Her feelings about her triumphal return to New York were revealed to Ezra Goodman. 'How wonderful, how simply scrumptiously wonderful, I thought, to be a movie star, a real honest to gone movie star, to be beautiful and chosen and one of God's very special creatures. It was just thrilling to be alive and in the presence of those wonderful people.'

Nuances of behaviour, likes and dislikes, everything Betty believed in, all were explored by reporters to get at her essence. The most outstanding characteristics she disclosed were a sense of humour, a natural manner, unpretentiousness and a hatred of phoniness, all of which she shared with Bogey.

Personal trivia were also exposed, such as liking to chew gum and eat artichokes, and preferring not to wear make-up or nail polish. The fact that she smoked heavily and played piano occasionally were made a matter of importance. Stories were syndicated that were supposed to show she was 'real'. Much was made of her being a good sport because she came to an interview one rainy day wearing men's galoshes. Also considered worth reporting was an incident that occurred when she first started going with Bogey. He took her to a posh restaurant that catered to celebrities. Even Clark Gable was there. Unimpressed, Betty only paid attention to Bogey until she spotted a man he did not know, and screamed out, 'There's Sam Friedlander!'

'Who,' Bogey asked, 'is Sam Friedlander?'

'Why, I once modelled hats for him,' Betty smiled.

An ironical item was printed that told of the famous Broadway producer Gilbert Miller calling to have Betty appear in a new play of his. 'A very short while ago,' Betty replied, 'that would have been very simple. Mr Miller could have stepped to his reception room and crooked his finger. I was sitting there on and off for two years.'

The darling of the day had so many commitments that she had to neglect her darling of the night. And 'the Great Loner', sharing his suite at the Gotham with his friends, Louis Bromfield and Bromfield's secretary and business manager George Hawkins, could not stand being without her. During a particularly lengthy press session, Bogey phoned to inform her of his annoyance at being deserted. Immediately Betty cut the conference short and rushed to his room. When she entered, he burst into tears for the first time since she knew him, and exclaimed, 'I didn't think you'd come.'

Always the practical joker, Bogey decided to upset an interview Betty was having with a reporter from the liberal newspaper *P.M.* Bogey made an entrance wearing his usual trenchcoat, but hobbling on a cane. When the reporter opened with, 'What do you think of the New York school system?' Bogey let him have it. 'What kind of stupid question is that to ask, you silly son of a bitch?'

With the help of George Hawkins, he proceeded to get the reporter drunk. On stumbling out, the man from *P.M.* gurgled, 'If you want anything, all you have to do is whistle.' Like everyone, he misquoted her line from the film. This condensed version of what was actually said was to become a classic wrong-liner like Bogey's 'Play it again, Sam,' which he never spoke in *Casablanca*. The next day the story appeared in the paper with an editor's note, 'We sent our reporter to find out about Bogart and Bacall and he came back with a confused version of the happenings. The moral of this story is: "Love Conquers All." '

Bogey's petulance made Betty find more time for him. Together, though their movements were constricted by crowds, they went to all the shows in which her old friends had parts and visited them backstage. This gesture was in recognition of a promise she made to Betty Kalb one day when they were attending a benefit at Madison Square Garden. The girls caught sight of Helen Hayes and Tallulah Bankhead in loges at opposite ends of the arena, making a show of themselves by waving enthusiastic greetings across to each other. Here were two great ladies of the theatre, the kind that the two Bettys longed to be, behaving in a way that the young hopefuls could imagine themselves doing some day. Both girls vowed that they would wave like crazy should they encounter each other under similar circumstances when, not if, they made it. So far only the waving of one got any notice.

'It was something. Very romantic, the whole thing,' was how Betty described to Goodman the excitement they provoked and the mob scenes they collected wherever they went. Sneaking out of the hotel, avoiding the crowd waiting for a glimpse of them, they would head for Bogey's favourite spot in the city, the '21' Club. Their special nook became known as 'The Cradle'. At the bar one night, Bogey made headlines and gave Betty the nickname that would forever be attached to her. Leaning across a drunk seated between himself and Earl Wilson, Bogey grabbed Betty's hand and told the columnist, 'When I get a divorce, I'm going to marry Baby.'

This was the break the media were waiting for, although they had ignored it when he first made the announcement at the yacht club. Undoubtedly Betty's emergence into the celebrity limelight since then made this an earth-shaking revelation. Betty and Bogey's every move in New York was followed by hordes of fans and reporters. With 'fatherly concern', as one magazine described his actions—since this was a touchy time with him and Mayo—Bogey would make sure that no pictures were taken of them 'à deux'. However, they were snapped when they attended a party for the Navy, and Bogey went to the Navy Public Relations Office himself to make sure it would not be published. That is why he was particularly annoyed when Warner's sent him a telegram reprimanding him for his conduct while in New York. His wire in reply was typical of his attitude toward their inconsistent policies. 'Do you want me to come to coast to handle Errol Flynn's publicity? Regards. Bogart.'

Before leaving New York, they had lunch with Moss Hart. Wishing to pay her a compliment, the playwright took up a Cassandra ploy. 'You'd better retire now, Betty. You'll never top the reviews you got for your first picture. You can get out with glory now.' Of course, Hart meant what he said in good-natured jest, but it came off as an ominous prophecy which she would never forget.

After creating enough publicity in seven days to last most actresses a lifetime, Betty and her press agents headed back to Hollywood. They stopped off in Washington DC for an appearance at a National Press Club entertainment for servicemen. Dressed in a suit, Betty draped herself atop an upright piano and showed enough leg to grab attention while Vice President Harry Truman played an old-fashioned waltz. The photograph that was taken of the old timer and the newcomer provided an appropriate exploitational topping to one of the most successful publicity tours in the history of motion pictures.

Coming back to the studio was a letdown. Perhaps what Hart had said about getting out while she was ahead was true, but she could not face it. And she could not take the disappointment expressed by the studio about her performance in *The Big Sleep*. Bogey came across stronger than she did. He seemed more concerned with compensating his fans, who saw him in the rather submissive role before, than with cushioning Betty. The other actresses, Martha Vickers as a dope addict and Dorothy Malone as a nymphomaniac, were more outstanding too because their parts, though not as long, were more interesting than Betty's straightforward role.

To add to her chagrin, Hawks was bowing out of her life. She gave her view of this setback, 'Howard Hawks was so furious with the fact that Bogey and I had fallen in love, and that he had lost control of me that he sold my contract to Jack Warner.'

So except for Bogey, there was no one who had a personal interest in her career. Even her mother had left her, remarrying to become Mrs Goldberg. As though all these blows were not enough, Warner's decided to hold up the release of *The Big Sleep*, not for a build-up as before, but so that she might be able to redeem herself in another film and not lose the public's interest as quickly as she had gained it.

The new movie planned for Betty was *Confidential Agent*. This time her leading man would be another screen lover, Charles Boyer. Also cast were Katina Paxinou and Wanda Hendrix whom the studio may have thought would give Betty strong support, but instead made her fight for every inch of film. The director was Herman Shumlin who had made only one picture before, *Watch on the Rhine*, and he did that from his own stage production. Playing the part of a high-class English girl called for acting skills which Betty had not yet exercised. She would be expected to be totally professional and would not get the special attention she knew she still required.

An edgy atmosphere pervaded the shooting. Shumlin turned out to be something of a martinet and kept the set closed. When Betty tried to kid around as she had done before to relax her nerves, Shumlin warned, 'There will be no making fun of the lines.' That made her even more tense, especially since she knew that her screen future would depend on the outcome of this picture. The overnight success could be a one-night stand!

Until now Betty had looked to Bogey for encouragement and enjoyment. At this crucial time, what she wanted was his protection. Bogey could provide the security she needed because he knew the ropes and was venerable. Their relationship now seemed vital to her survival in Hollywood.

Bogey still probed the problem of her youthfulness and feared the fickleness that usually accompanies it. 'I don't know how the hell I got mixed up with a nineteen-year-old girl,' he would wail to friends in private.

Peter Lorre somewhat allayed Bogey's concern about the disparity in their ages by advising him, 'It's better to have five good years than none at all.'

Losing patience with Bogey, Betty facetiously remarked, 'I suppose eighty is the proper time for getting married because then you can be sure it will last.'

Finally, this strong silent hero of the movies decided to stop procrastinating and start taking the action which might give him some happiness. An out-of-court settlement was reached with Mayo. Details of the agreement were kept secret, but it became known that he gave her a great deal of money as well as his investment in two Safeway stores. Bogey complained that Mayo had stripped him and announced, 'I paid a high price for my freedom.' But at last Bogey was rid of the 'More Than You Know' wife and could marry the 'How Little We Know' girl.

On May 10, 1945, Mayo was awarded a divorce in Las Vagas on the grounds of mental cruelty. Bogey broke the news to Betty that night while they were dining. Then he told her that he was going to Chicago for an 'I Am an American Day' celebration, and asked her to meet him there so that they could go to Louis Bromfield's farm to get married and 'kill two birds with one stone'.

After Bogey delivered his patriotic speech at the rally in Soldier's Field, he took Betty and her mother and headed for Mansfield, Ohio. Passing through this small town on the way to the Bromfield estate, Malabar, in Pleasant Valley, they saw reporters in the main square waiting to cover the wedding the next day.

At six in the morning of May 21, Betty and Bogey, with Natalie as well, were back in town for the marriage licence. Natalie had to come along because Betty was not quite twenty-one so the permission of one parent was necessary. Her mother gladly gave her consent. Her father, whom she had not heard from in ten years, made a statement to the press from his home in Charleston, South Carolina: 'In my opinion, Lauren is far too young to marry a man more than twice her age. But she's a girl with a mind of her own, and chances are that she will marry Bogart. If the wedding happens, it sure won't be with my approval. My daughter's studio advised me to keep my trap closed, but I just felt like opening it.'

Bromfield's home had been chosen for the wedding because the author had been Bogey's friend for twenty years. Bogey had once said, 'I couldn't marry unless Louis were the best man. By the third time, he'll be good!' Bromfield had influenced the actor's choice of roles by telling him long ago, 'The man in struggle, not the man arrived, holds the interest of an audience, single-handed and alone, if possible.' Perhaps Bromfield could have a further influence over Bogey's life. The author's stable ways might rub off on Bogey and encourage him, with this fourth marriage, to begin a more domestic phase in his off-screen character.

Dozens of people from all over the area came to catch a glimpse of the celebrated couple, but Betty wanted the wedding to be very private and very simple.

Before the ceremony, she ran into Bogey as she was coming down the stairs in her wedding outfit. She wore a rose-beige suit cinched in at the waist by a leather belt and topped with a brown scarf and white orchids. 'Aren't you going to say, "Hello"?' she asked.

'I did say hello,' he replied. Betty smiled softly and leaned against him for a moment. The encounter set the mood, exerting a soft, gentle and emotional spell over the wedding.

Gathered in the great central hall of the house, where the rites were to be performed, were Betty's mother, Bromfield, his wife, his mother, his three daughters, the butler and his wife, the cook and Lieutenant Robert McElhiney of Boston, one of the servicemen the Bromfields put up in their home for rehabilitation. Municipal Judge H. H. Shettler stood before a huge recessed window banked with ferns and snapdragons that overlooked the landscape. Bromfield's boxer dog, Prince, came in unexpectedly and lay on the tiger-skin rug at the judge's feet. Hope, Bromfield's seventeen-year-old daughter, was at the piano and began playing the Warsaw Concerto, which had a certain sentimental association for the couple. The Lohengrin wedding march began, and Betty was escorted down the hall by George Hawkins who gave her away to a subdued and serious Bogey, very close to tears. Immediately prior to taking the vows, Bogey downed a martini and whispered, 'Oh, Baby,' to the bride.

The special service written by the judge to Betty's specifications contained a little of everything except the word 'obey', for which she substituted 'cherish'. Bogey cried during the brief three-minute ceremony. 'The words got to him,' Betty explained later. Bromfield was so nervous that he handed Bogey the gold link rings with the chains all meshed together. The groom had to force Betty's ring on her finger. She smiled and whispered, 'It's all right.' He whispered back, 'It goes on all the way.'

At the end of the service, they just stood still until the judge told them, 'It's all right—you can kiss her now.' When Bogey did as the judge directed, Betty screamed, 'Oh, goody,' and a whole joyful round of kissing began.

Giving her mother a hug, Betty murmured, 'It's wonderful—and it's over! I'm Mrs Bogart—Mrs Humphrey Bogart . . .!'

And Have Not

'We were down on the boat at Balboa when the picture opened and the notices began coming in,' Bogey recalled, describing their response to the critics' attack on Betty's performance in *Confidential Agent*. 'I watched Betty's reactions, not knowing at first how to help her. She was badly hurt, there was no doubt about that. Then I decided that the only way to handle the thing was to kid her, and pretty soon we got to the point where she was kidding about it, too. She has a sense of humour, you see. She has a sense of values, too, and she has guts.'

The sudden and complete reversal of her ascendancy happened only a few months after their wedding. Until that unexpected shock, Betty had believed she had proven herself if not an actress then certainly a star. And according to Bogey, 'We were happily married and she decided the time had come to be a homemaker for me. I didn't want to influence her one way or another. I didn't feel I had the right.'

In the middle of Betty's quandary, Warner's offered her a new deal at a substantial increase in salary. Aware of her difficulty in making the choice, Bogey acknowledged, 'My heart went out to her, but I kept my mouth shut. Then when this blast hit her everything was changed. She couldn't quit. It would look as if she were running away. There was nothing else to do but take the rap and then go on to prove that her first success was no fluke, that she could really act if she got the right opportunity.'

His defence for her disastrous second outing was that she had been miscast, and the studio bosses should have realised their mistake in putting her in this inferior film right after seeing the rushes. He believed that their eagerness to cash in on her current popularity had caused the disaster.

Creating special vehicles to enhance a newcomer was not Warner's way. Having become a major studio by introducing sound, the outfit looked for a newsworthy gimmick from then on that had topical value at the box-office. If a formula succeeded, they would repeat it until a self-feeding cycle was formed. And so great batches of musical, newspaper, gangster, historical and war films were churned out until each vogue was done to exhaustion. Instead of grooming stars like most studios did, Warner's maintained a stock company of actors who were usually regarded as types because they were required to do the same kind of role repeatedly. Since so many of Warner's films had the common touch, some of the contract players who were most bold reached the public and became favourites. Even then, the studio refused to grant them the special treatment that was given established stars hired from the theatre. Only by going on strike did the actors who emerged from the stable finally force Warner's to concede that eminence of stars and not the immediacy of themes was to be promoted for profit.

Still clumsy about the unique handling required to build a star, Warner's had repeated the mistakes of the still-withheld *The Big Sleep*. The wrong role and flashy supporting cast were enough to wipe out any star quality Betty could have shown in either film.

Soon after the devastating reviews, Betty became known as 'The Million Dollar Bubble' that had burst. It made it seem as if the studio had foolishly spent exactly that much money on her promotion but they had, in fact, only laid out comparatively little. A quarter of a million had gone into the publicising of Ann Sheridan as 'The Oomph Girl', but no real expenditure had been needed for Betty because of her sensational screen personality and her romance with Bogey. Now that those factors were no longer working, Betty was regarded as a deficit.

Once Betty got a perspective, she was able to give this account of her relationship with the studio: 'I was always insecure about my career because Jack Warner convinced me very early that I was no good, worthless, rotten to the core. He was very good at that.

I knew they would have no respect for me as an actress, a talent, a potential, and I was right. I was a commodity, a piece of meat.'

Bogey confirmed that Betty still had lots of fight in her by announcing 'Now she's out to show them. She won't quit until she does that, and I'm backing her up all the way.'

But another knock was forthcoming. The Hollywood Women's Press Club was considering naming Betty as the most unco-opera-tive actress of the year, even though she had given interviews galore and had only turned down relatively few because of prior com-mitments. Her competition for the booby prize, Greer Garson, was entrenched enough not to mind.

To take the edge off this twist of the knife, Bogey had a scheme he divulged. 'I began phoning my newspaper friends asking them to vote for Betty. I put on a regular campaign to boost her into the cellar. I told my newspaper friends that we really ought to have an award of some kind in our family. Betty was very much annoyed, of course, to get a slap in the face, and that is why I did it. I was afraid she really might get that title and if she did it would go hard with her unless I could find some way of kidding her about it.' Due to Bogey's efforts the race was closely fought, but Garson got it.

Some time later Betty disclosed her real feelings about the press: 'Most people in business get their reputations by being honest, ac-curate and fair. Hollywood columnists are the only people I know who can be successful by being dishonest, inaccurate and unfair.'

Until Betty permitted herself to make this admission, she had attempted to elicit sympathy for her diminished status by conced-ing that her comeuppance was deserved. To Louella Parsons she confessed, 'I'm not an experienced actress. I need plenty of help in every scene I play before the cameras. I have to be told what to do with my hands and feet and which way to turn my head. The studio failed to take this into consideration when they gave me Herman Shumlin, a stage director, to handle me. In the future I am going to say the first thing on the set, "Boys, I need a helping hand. Please help see me through."'

This show of penitence appealed to the high priestess and Parsons proclaimed, 'Well, if the girl does that, you'll see her go farther and farther in her career—and I predict it.'

Humbling herself like that was completely unlike the attitude that Betty had assumed only a year before when she told *Life* magazine, 'Back in New York I memorized three-act plays with no trouble at all. Here I learn two or three lines at a time. On stage you have to move around and you can make a fool of yourself, but in front of a camera you know just where you have to stand, and if you make a mistake they can keep taking the shot over again all day. That's why I don't think there's such a thing as movie acting.'

Based on his observations of Betty's capacity for quickly acquiring sea legs and making herself handy around her first big house, Bogey asserted, 'I think that ability of hers to learn and to conform to the rules in all kinds of activities shows in her acting. She's a good actress, not the greatest, not the most inspired maybe, but she's got the stuff in her. There are very few really great actresses on the screen. There are great personalities and I think Betty is one of them. She has a simple, direct way of delivering her lines which gives a distinct individuality. Furthermore, we work well together. We have fun on the set and we both get a kick out of going over our lines and studying our parts at night. I think *The Big Sleep* will show some of Betty's real qualities as an actress. I'm not going to stick my neck out with any prediction. Let's all wait and see.'

Warner's were not going to take any chances. To insure their investment, they decided to throw into *The Big Sleep* the sexiness the public wanted from Betty. Out of desperation, Hawks was called back to help her.

'About eight months after we finished the movie,' Hawks recollected, 'they asked me to make another scene between B and B. They said they didn't have enough scenes together. It was during the racing season at Santa Anita and I had some horses out there and so I made them talk about riding a horse. I was thinking about racing and I thought, "Well, I'll do a scene about a little love argument about racing." The plot didn't matter at all. I saw some of it recently and it had me thoroughly confused.'

The new sequence, between her as the vivacious Vivian and him as the mellow Marlowe, barely made it past the watchful eyes of the Hays Office because of its raciness.

Vivian: What do you usually do when you're not working?
Marlowe: Play the horses—fool around.
Vivian: Women, too?

Marlowe: I'm generally working on something most of the time.

Vivian: Could that be stretched to include me?

Marlowe: I like you. I've told you that before.

Vivian: I liked hearing you say it. But you didn't do much about it.

Marlowe: Neither did you.

Vivian: You spoke of horses. I like to play them myself. But I like to see them work out a little first—see if they're front runners, or come up from behind. Find out what their hole card is. What makes them run.

Marlowe: Have you found out mine?

Vivian: I think so. You don't like to be rated. You like to get out in front—open a big lead—take a little breather in the back stretch—then come home free.

Marlowe: You don't like to be rated yourself.

Vivian: I haven't met anyone yet that could do it. Any suggestions?

Marlowe: I can't tell till I've seen you over a distance of ground. You've got a touch of class, but I don't know yet if you can go a route.

Vivian: A lot depends on who's in the saddle. (As he looks at her in silence) Go on, Marlowe. I like the way you work. In case you don't know it, you're doing all right.

Marlowe: There's something I can't figure.

Vivian: My hole card? (As he nods) I'll give you a little hint. It isn't sugar. Everybody tries that and it doesn't work.

Marlowe: Then what are you trying it on me for? Who told you to sugar me off on this case?

The titillation of the couple sharing a private dirty joke—with Betty doing all the provoking—did not help her performance. Adding an extraneous sequence with Betty singing also failed to arouse excitement. Nor was there any improvement made by inserting Bogey's standard comment that he had used on Mary Astor in both their movies together and to Betty in their previous one, 'You're good—very, very good.' Even the heavy advertising campaign, using the extravagant claim, 'The Film They Were Born For', did not convince the public that Betty had fulfilled her initial promise. Her track record showed she was a loser.

With marriage to Bogey, Betty had her heart's desire, but not what she had set her heart on since the age of six: to be a star. From the time her father left home she had constantly reiterated, 'I am going to Hollywood.' The fixation was so strong that soon her family took this aspiration for granted. Four uncles, who were helping in the child's support, one night treated Natalie and Betty to dinner at a restaurant near their home in Brooklyn. As a souvenir of the occasion, Betty asked them all to sign the menu. Natalie knew that her inscription would delight her daughter. She wrote, 'To a future Hollywood star,' capsulating Betty's wish into the dedication.

That encouragement was vital, but the inspiration originated from being a child of the Depression when people lived for tomorrow instead of today, and looked for any salvation from everyday dreariness. Betty's every action was guided by her desire to join the adored on the great white sheet.

As an only child and all that her mother had in the world, Betty was expected to excel. Natalie would see to that. Her mother was a first-generation offspring of Rumanian-Jewish stock that came to America bent on producing 'a somebody'. And Betty Joan, as she was named, was the chosen one of her people. 'You ought to be in pictures,' the most overworked line of the generation, was an appropriate motto for a girl of her looks to live by. What else could give such commensurate rewards for being beautiful?

No sacrifice, and there were many, was considered too great by Natalie to compensate for Betty being deprived of a father. That man who was a stranger to her, William Perske, of Russian-Jewish parentage, was a medical supplies salesman. This was all Betty ever cared to divulge about him. She had not seen him since he had gone down South when she was eight, and that was the way she preferred it to be. As soon as Natalie was free of her husband, she dropped the Mrs Perske and reassumed her maiden name. This time, she translated the Weinstein—'wineglass' in English—to its Rumanian equivalent, Bacal. Using the name professionally later, Betty added another 'l' because people were constantly rhyming Bacal with crackle and that annoyed her.

As her mother saw her, she was a 'reasonable' little girl who 'never' had to be spanked. Betty would describe herself more modestly: 'I guess I was a nice child in a repulsive sort of way.'

71

From the age of twelve, until they moved to Greenwich Village after she left school, Betty lived with her mother in the Louis Morris apartments on the Grand Concourse, a wide avenue of modernistic buildings in The Bronx. The neighbourhood resounded to the din of violins as good Jewish boys sawed away submissively and to the pounding of feet on the floors of dance schools as good Jewish girls hoofed heartily. While the youths secretly yearned to be movie heroes carrying fiddle cases with tommy-guns and the girls imagined themselves tapping their way to the top, the more serious parents did not go along with those mundane objectives. They dreamed of making a contribution to the alien culture by training their progeny to be prodigies à la Heifitz and Pavlova. The local residents worked for self-betterment, and 'self' meant '*der kinder*'.

Betty's donation to this burgeoning of talents was made at Ruth St Denis's ballet school. She had attended this Manhattan-based shrine of modern dance since she was three years old, and continued there for thirteen years until the realisation was finally made that she had the 'wrong' feet for the art. Drama lessons, however, began when she was ten and continued until she was a professional. At the age of fifteen, while still studying, she set herself a 'Ten Year Goal' to be a star. If she did not make it by the time she was twenty-five, she would give up, she decided.

The desire to be a star was different from wanting to be an actress. A star was universally loved not necessarily for showing ability at characterisation but for being the essence of a single facet of the audience's personality. In any situation, the onlookers could anticipate the star's reactions and behaviour and participate in the action. In the movies a star had to function as an acter-out of emotions who moves, and moves for, an immobilised spectator who dreams of being not only the character portrayed but also the star.

Basically, the American standard for a star was a heart of gold that would shine through either one of two portrayals of the schizophrenic national character: puritan or whore. Betty's whore-star was born out of artificial insemination. A real brazenness had been impregnated by a faked sexuality. Combining the actual force with the deceptive superimposition demanded all her powers of creativity. The distraction of acting a role with more complicated qualities made her give a false delivery. Even her natural drive

72

seemed to dissolve in the confusion. She appeared to have passed her climax in her second and third try, and, with nothing to sustain her, as they saw it, the critics rewrote the story that until now seemed to be her destiny. No longer did it seem she would outshine her husband as in *A Star is Born*. This alteration to a *Sunset Boulevard* has-been image became the subject of widespread speculation for gossips. Self-proclaimed analysts theorised that Betty, bereft of her father, had sought sublimation through becoming a star, and that having found the total father image in her husband, she had lost her power as a performer for the public and her impetus to overcome being just Bogey's Baby.

'Nobody was ever born great,' Bogey had been quoted as saying in a *Billboard* interview the very year that Betty came into the world. 'They become great through concentrated effort. The failure of many with talent proves that talent without effort is wasted.'

His view twenty years later was: 'Hostile critics can help.' To make his point, he referred to a review that he used to carry with him all the while until the paper crumbled. The clipping was of his first critical notice when he played the juvenile lead in *Swiftly*, a play that closed very quickly. 'The aforementioned sprig', wrote Alexander Woollcott, 'was what might mercifully be described as inadequate.'

But in his review of *Nerves* Woollcott was forced to admit: 'Mr Bogart is really capital. He is a young actor whose appearance here two seasons ago in a terrible play called *Swiftly* was recorded by your correspondent in words so disparaging that it is surprising to find him still acting. Those words are hereby eaten.'

Bogey attributed his progress to following the advice of a fellow actor, Holbrook Blinn, who told him, 'Just keep working. If people see that you're busy, they'll think that you're good.'

Rising from adversity was Bogey's phoenix-like pattern that, until their meeting, Betty's spunk had resembled very closely. His unhappiness with his parents made him independent. His shortness caused him to become tough. His split lip gave him a lisp that he used so distincitively it became his trade-mark. His discontent turned him to acting. His unemployment during the Depression forced him to change his image to get *The Petrified Forest*. His second-string status at Warner's gave him the George Raft rejects—*High Sierra* and *The Maltese Falcon*—that gained him stardom. His age kept him out of service during the war and increased his popularity at a time when male stars were at a premium. His miscasting opposite an unlikely co-star in a movie version of a flop play that no one believed in (Dennis Morgan, Ronald Reagan and Ann Sheridan were originally supposed to be in *Casablanca*) proved him a romantic idol. His torment in his domestic life with Mayo impelled him to Betty. Just as in the catharsis of Greek tragedy, Bogey grew by extracting good from evil.

The crisis that was besetting Betty did have an easy way out that meant she would not have to exercise the powers of propulsion that had put her ahead previously. She was, after all, Mrs Humphrey Bogart and thus was kept in the spotlight. Her view of living in reflected glory was told in an interview with Roy Newsquist for *McCall's*: 'I slid down the ladder so fast that it was all I could do to catch myself midway. I hadn't the training I needed to protect myself.

'As a compensation, though, I was Bogey's wife. And was thought of as Bogey's wife by my friends and my friends were producers and directors and writers. I was Bogey's wife first and an actress second and as a result I gradually had fewer and fewer opportunities to find a place for myself. I had terrible frustrations about my work. I chose always to have my marriage come first. If I had the choice to make over again, I'd do it the same way. But I felt moments of frustration and anger because people didn't think of me the way I thought they should ... as an actress.'

Bogey made the observation, 'Betty sky-rocketed from an anxious nobody to a scared somebody.'

The Treasure of the Canyon

Raves came from Bogey for Betty's performance as his wife. 'I didn't know what happiness was until I met Betty,' was his feeling. 'Class,' he would say, 'that's what she has—real class.' And even though he was usually reluctant to discuss personal sexual matters, he was not above divulging, 'She's great in the sack!'

Their honeymoon began at Louis Bromfield's farm, and ended at sea aboard *Sluggy* one week and four days later when they had to go back to work. As Bogey carried her across the threshold of their small suite at the Garden of Allah, the hotel that had been the scene of his clandestine affair with Mayo while married to Mary, he quipped, 'You weigh a ton.'

That dig set the tenor for what was to come. Any weak spot was a target. Some of their friends thought that the Bogarts' darts were aimed to give themselves a self-effacing sophistication, like Nick and Nora in *The Thin Man*. Others believed that their constant needling was symptomatic of a serious struggle for supremacy, and bet on Betty to win because she had youth on her side, despite the fact that she decried being considered young. The kidding never erupted into public outbursts because Bogey disliked making a scene with Betty, even though she could hold her own like his other wives. He was also embarrassed by any show of affection in front of people and would push her away when he felt she was getting mushy with a 'G'wan now.'

Their publicised nicknames were also jocularly used in their

75

jockeying for position. 'Baby' now applied to him and was interpreted by the press as a change of status at home. Columnists made
so much of this switch for so long that Betty complained to her
mother, 'Why do they harp on this Baby business? It makes our
marriage sound cute. It's not cute, it's good.' According to Natalie,
Bogey, irked by the Baby talk, would use only men's names when
he wanted to address Betty affectionately. Later, in reminiscing
about this loss of her famous identifying tag, Betty spoke wistfully
to Ezra Goodman, 'He used to call me "Baby" all the time. He
doesn't any more. When he is angry, he calls me, "Betty" or "Miss
Bacall". I've always loved "Baby". I think it's...I don't know.
I don't really look like a Baby.'

Bogey soon considered himself an authority on how to make
a marriage successful and advised, 'You've got to work at it.' Then
he expounded, 'Occupy the same room and sleep in the same bed.
If you've had a quarrel—and show me a married couple who
hasn't—I defy you to wake up in the same bed and NOT speak to
each other!'

Betty made no pretence that they had an idyllic union. They
argued frequently, but they made up quickly. 'The disagreement
usually starts when he begins to think he's Bogart and says, "Listen
to me." I can always tell. He gets lost in the characterization.' She
took these difficulties in her stride, probably remembering an
observation she made in 1943: 'Wives are expendable, but good
husbands are hard to find.'

Anxious for a home, Betty was excited when a friend told her
about a house that was being vacated because the owners were
moving to South America. They decided to take this nine-room
residence in Coldwater Canyon. Since it came completely
furnished, even to dishes and sheets, Betty and Bogey could set
up housekeeping immediately. One of the most unusual features
of this rather uninspired place was a blue tile bathroom that had
a Roman bath they kept drained for fear that some soused guest
might get doused.

The first alteration made in the modern Chinese decor was to
remove the bamboo bar from the games room. Pictures of the two
of them soon lined the living room. A touch of kitsch hung from
a wall bracket—a driftwood, raffia and shell doll that she adored.
Bogey had bought this toy for her one night at the Beachcomber

restaurant. For sentiment, on the mantel were the bride and groom figures from their wedding cake that she had mounted on an old newel base and encased in a glass dome.

Bogey liked living on top of a hill, but this house was built on three levels and was steep even for him. Every morning Betty had to pick up the servants by car at the bus stop because they could not make the climb to this remote high place. Three of the staff of four were Bogey veterans. A recent addition was an elegant English-bred Jamaican butler, Fred Clark, who slept in. The cook, Mrs May Smith, the part-time gardener, Aurellio Salazar, and the secretary, Mrs Kathleen Sloan, had been with Bogey for such a long time that Betty was prompted to remark, 'Wives come and go, but they stay.'

In the middle of the next night after moving in, there was a knock on the door of their bedroom and their butler called anxiously, 'Milord, Milady, please come out. Something has happened!'

Rushing to follow Fred to the lower floor, they were horrified to see the living room floating in a foot of water. The deficient cliffside construction had created stress on the pipes causing one to burst. The entire evening was spent bailing and sweeping water out of doors and windows. When they thought they were through, they observed to their consternation that the parquet floors of the room had swollen, curving convexly until there was a huge bulge in the centre.

The next flood was of wedding gifts. Those closest to them encouraged their persistent smoking, her mother with a silver cigarette box and his sister with a silver ashtray. Mark Hellinger presented them with drinking glasses for every occasion, though Bogey was trying to cut down on his liquor. Jack Warner, in a magnanimous mood, let her keep the black convertible she had driven in *The Big Sleep*, and Bogey, not to be outdone, decided to redo the interior of his own car in the same red leather. Jack Kreinlander of '21' sent them gold whistles which, they told reporters, were used to call each other from one floor to another. He attached his to his key chain, and she put hers on the slave bracelet she had been so sensitive about before the marriage. Now she disclosed that the other side of the plaque which bore her name was inscribed, 'From the Whistler'.

Betty's present to him was a gold key with a locket top that contained her picture and was engraved with their wedding date so he would not forget their anniversary. For some time he did not reciprocate, but he finally gave her a chrysoberyl pin to match her ring. 'Just because it says I must is no reason I'm going to do it,' Bogey would protest as an excuse for delaying gift-giving.

Her reaction was, 'I know that although Bogey will pass up occasions, a few weeks later he'll bring me a present for no apparent reason. I don't expect it. I am always thrilled by it. When he does give me a gift, it's usually with a crack meant to take the sentiment out of it.' On presenting her with a gold cigarette case that had a ruby-set snap, he grunted, 'I'm tired of seeing tobacco in your bag.' A matching lighter came with, 'Now you can light your own cigarettes.' But Betty felt that underneath it all Bogey was really a romantic, saying, as she once did, 'Bogey is the kind of guy who sends roses.'

At their first Christmas—on time this time—he presented her with something she had always wanted, a mink coat. It came from Bergdorf Goodman in New York and had her initials B.B.B. embroidered on the right panel with a miniature mink appliquéd beneath. Immediately, she took childish glee in throwing the coat on to the floor and walking on it barefoot. This innocent play was the antithesis of the show of defiance Mayo once made with a mink he had given her. Climaxing one of their usual brawls at Chasen's the enraged wife had thrown the mink 'right into his kisser', as Pat O'Brien described it. Betty, however, prized her mink. One night she was ready ten minutes early for a dinner at the John Hustons', and this was unusual for her. Bogey looked for her all over the house and eventually found her in the kitchen, polishing the silver while wearing her coat. She could not wait to put it on.

'Betty thinks a day has twenty-six hours,' he exclaimed in exasperation. This bothered him, especially since he was always prompt and if he were delayed even a few minutes, he would call to apologise. Because her estimation of time was an issue, he gave her a gold and ruby cuckoo-clock lapel watch with two tiny dangling chains; when one was pulled the doors flew open to expose the bird.

Except for a St Christopher medal, the gold gifts that she bought him to wear on his key chain—a monocle, a ball and chain, and a toothpick—were chosen, she acknowledged, 'just to bedevil our friends when we dine out'. His buddies would go along with the game by offering to buy Betty's charms from him but would receive an exaggerated refusal. When asked why he did not give her gag gifts in return, she replied, 'Bogey has a sweeter nature than I have.'

Two serious presents from her that Bogey especially valued were a Huson sextant and a skilfully executed model of his recent acquisition that he loved above any other material thing, the yawl *Santana*.

A few months after settling down, he sold *Sluggy* and allowed himself to buy the fifty-five-foot sailboat that he had longed to own. The name *Santana*, like Errol Flynn's yacht *Sirocco*, meant Devil Wind. The boat had come in first in the Bermuda race, and was placed second in the San Pedro-to-Bermuda run, which Bogey had planned to enter that July fourth until a picture commitment interfered. Dick Powell and June Allyson were the former owners. The Powells had bought the *Santana* from George Brent, another member of the Warner Brothers family. This made Bogey joke about expecting to find a few of Ann Sheridan's bobby pins aboard. Brent had converted the cabin into two rooms, but when Bogey saw the construction blueprints he restored it into the original large single room.

All of Betty and Bogey's spare time was devoted to the *Santana*. They would constantly be polishing the teakwood deck, and when people came aboard they were obliged to wear soft-soled shoes to avoid scratching the high shine. Fans would harass them by sneaking aboard to carve graffiti. Bogey admitted that the *Santana* was his pet luxury which he accessorised with every possible piece of equipment made for boats. 'Dough spent on a boat isn't really extravagant money,' he explained. 'We get our recreation there, and it's a lot cheaper than spending our spare time in a night club.'

In speaking of Bogey's love for the *Santana*, one friend asserted, 'Here Bogey could escape all that he detested about Hollywood— the parties, the phonies, the compromises. Bogey knew that Hollywood had misused his talent in too many shoddy films, but his boat was another world, a clean world.'

Not always interested in escape, Bogey would take a stand on public issues that others in Hollywood thought dangerous. 'I spoke up when I was a long way from having arrived, too,' he remembered. 'I'll confess I practically scared myself to death when I did so.'

Betty agreed with his liberal attitudes. Together they took action when Congress tried to exploit the movie colony during the 1947 Red Scare. The House Committee on Un-American Activities, in which Richard Nixon was first noticed, attained the propaganda they sought by confronting a group of creative people who refused to testify whether they were, or had ever been, members of the Communist Party.

When the 'Hollywood Ten' were jailed and exiled from the industry, nearly everyone in filmdom feared any connection with these outcasts. But Betty and Bogey, despite warnings from Warner's, fought against this infringement of rights by leading a Hollywood contingent of twenty-five celebrities, among whom were Sterling Hayden, Danny Kaye, Evelyn Keyes, John Huston, Richard Conte, Jane Wyatt and Paul Henreid, in a protest flight to Washington.

'We went in there green and they beat our brains out,' Bogey conceded. To make him even more red-faced from embarrassment, the Communist newspaper, *The Daily Worker*, published a front-page story implying that he was the vanguard of the party. Though Bogey apologised for blundering in his attempt to make the House Committee on Un-American Activities cease their un-American activities, no one really minded because he lived up to his reputation as a troublemaker.

True to his nature, just to be contrary and prove that he had not capitulated completely to married life, he issued a statement that made a case for misogamy: 'I should have remained a bachelor. I never learn. You think it's going to be all right. That you've learned all the tricks. You've learned that you must put away that bath towel and not leave bristles in the basin after you've shaved. And then the next time it's something different. You have a cupboard for drinks and you want the glasses arranged so you can get at them, and you find your wife likes them fixed in neat pyramids and you go wrong again.'

Also, he spoke up for misogyny: 'Women are troublemakers, not sensible, unsatisfiable, dull, not delicate, and expect too much of men. Only Betty is the exception. But then, as she says, I can't go through life marrying every five minutes. I've got to like it.'

It took some time for Betty to make the perfect rebuttal, but finally she declared, "I think, when he married me, Bogey thought I would be, like his other wives, a companion for his semi-bachelor existence.' As for her reaction to her marriage, she professed, 'I don't know what my life was like before I met Bogey. ... We have fun with a capital "F".'

After sixteen months of doing little more than being a married woman, Betty found her own outlet, a new home at 2707 Benedict Canyon. One day she heard on the radio that Hedy Lamarr and John Loder were selling their house. 'You should have heard Betty describe the place when she saw it,' Bogey later teased about her to a columnist. 'She came home after rushing there with the real estate man and said, "Bogey, I've found a dream place—one that even you'll like. You go through a door and turn to the right into a dreamy kitchen where there's a little coffee grinder." How do you like that for a description of a house—a door, a kitchen and a coffee grinder!'

'What I meant when I told Bogey even he would like this house,' Betty elucidated, 'was that before we found it his idea of pleasant living revolved around a ship's cabin or a drawing room on a train. Once he saw this place he completely agreed.'

'It was a revelation to find that she had such an astounding drive,' he said with pride. 'When she wants something she gets it. Like our house ... she did sell our other house and she did buy this one the very same day. What's more we made quite a profit out of the old house we had.'

To reconcile the hundred-thousand-dollar, eight-room house overlooking the valley with her image of unpretentiousness, she felt obliged to announce, 'I said when I first went to Hollywood that I intended to live my life my way. I still intend to. I said I didn't want a big house, lots of servants, lots of clothes, the chi-chi. I still don't. If I had ten million dollars, I wouldn't live in a forty-room house. Or a thirty-room house. Or a twenty-room house. I like cozy places. Get lost in big ones. And I always have a favorite room with a favorite chair to sit in. Or spread in. I can't help sprawling.

'It's just as well I feel this way for I firmly believe that now that this war is over, fame, position and money aren't going to matter. All that's going to matter is what you've got here,' she pointed to her head. 'And here,' she touched her heart.

As soon as they moved in, Mark Hellinger paid them a visit. When Bogey showed him the room Hedy Lamarr had prepared as a nursery, the gangster-style producer remarked, 'You'd better put in a pool table.'

At Bogey's insistence the bedroom was frilly and had a five-and-a-half-foot by six-and-a-half-foot bed. One particularly masculine red plaid room had a small table with a placard Betty had ordered to be printed. It read: BOGART'S MAD ROOM ... BEWARE!!! DO NOT ENTER UNLESS HE KNOWS YOU! Another warning was posted: DANGER—BOGART AT WORK! DO NOT DISCUSS: POLITICS—RELIGION—WOMEN—MEN—PICTURES—THEATRE—OR ANYTHING ELSE!!! There were twelve pictures of Betty in the room, and she explained, 'He can't get away from me if he tried.'

Parties were not a regular part of their routine since Bogey was considered a provocateur and was not welcome in too many Hollywood homes. 'I've never gone along with the social structure of this town,' Bogey commented, 'and as a result I don't have many friends who are actors.'

The usual large functions did not appeal to Betty either. She confessed, 'There is or has been a shyness in me—probably because of the forward thrust of my vocal chords. I don't walk into a crowded room feeling wildly confident. I'm always nervous when I go into a large gathering. In fact, I rush to the bar and get my first drink, so that I can cope with it. As a girl, I don't suppose I was as noisy as I am now, but I'm fairly reserved. I stay very much within myself, though no one believes it except close friends. I got used to the uninhibited horseplay that goes on between Bogey and me: lots of fooling around, very quick retorts. This always leads people to believe I'm in command of the situation and that I can handle myself no matter what happens.'

Whenever they did go to a party they would separate, but she felt protected because she knew that Bogey was hovering not too far away if she needed help. 'Occasionally, when he has too much to drink,' she revealed, 'I have to step in and make myself known. I am not above making a fuss if necessary. Bogey hates that and he has no heart for the chase anyway. So the problem of other women doesn't exist.'

His boozing, though not quite kicked, was almost being nudged out of his life. Most of the time, Scotch before and Drambuie after dinner were all that he allowed himself. Betty attributed this semi-sobriety to an increased sense of security. She never tried to keep up with his drinking and would pay no attention when he did get drunk so that he could never have the satisfaction of getting a rise out of her.

To the persistent probing about how to tame a roustabout like Bogey, Betty gave her formula: 'Let him run wild. He'll always come home then. It's a mistake to annoy a husband with matters of household and, likewise, a wife should never ask her husband how he feels in the morning. He knows how he feels. Why bring it up? I reach for the lipstick in the morning, practically before Bogey's eyes are open.'

Her advice about marital problems was widely published. 'What's wrong with Hollywood marriages? I think it's the wives' fault,' she averred. 'I always said before I married that when I did, I wanted it to last and would do everything to make it last. I still say the same thing. I'd give up acting if that were necessary. Bogey hates being alone, so if we can't work approximately at the same time and enjoy ourselves together, I'd rather forget a career.'

Aware that Betty was a natural-born psychologist, Bogey described her technique: 'When I get into one of my tirades at the end of the day, she smiles and says genially, "And how did things go at the studio today?" Or, "Oh, you don't care that much." Our sense of humor saves many situations. She never asks me where I've been, what I did; instead, she sits back comfortably and lets me get out of the mess myself. I never get the "Look-what-you've-brought-on-me" routine. She's a backseat driver in every way.'

Bogey expressed the view: 'We enjoy our home and we enjoy our boat. If we spend our time in those two places, keep away from night clubs and Hollywood parties—and the misunderstandings that seem to sprout there—we'll stay out of trouble.'

Betty countered with, 'Humphrey does nothing around the house, but nothing. He is not a house man. He wants everything to be just so, but he doesn't build barbecues or stone walls and he has no recipe for spaghetti. Furthermore, he will not turn a spade of earth. He is not a farmer and has no interest in tilling the soil.'

The kitchen was not Betty's province. She had learned that she had no penchant at all for cooking the moment she tried to prepare more than breakfast in the galley aboard the boat. One night when they were in dock, Bogey expressed a desire for some asparagus for dinner. Quickly she got to a phone, called a friend and was told, 'Put a pot of water on the stove. When it comes to a boil, dump in the asparagus. Let it boil for twenty minutes. There's nothing to it.' Betty followed the instructions, but as soon as the water came to a boil she turned off the jet and ended up with un-cooked asparagus. On another occasion, her attempt to pour off the fat from some pork chops she was frying almost caused a fire and resulted in a badly burned finger. Bogey moaned, 'This is the first time I've had a real home. If only my wife could cook.'

Conscious of her limitations in running the house, she would 'confer' with the help rather than give orders. All she could con-tribute to housekeeping was neatness. At their first dinner party, confronted by the formal setting—all the silver and linens bore the intertwined B & B crest she designed—Betty was nervous until Bogey suggested that she take hints from Fred the butler on how to proceed.

One day Bogey overheard her bawling out the grocer on the phone. Shocked, he asked what it was about. 'He said he'd close our account because we weren't buying enough with him,' she answered.

'How much did we spend last month?' Bogey inquired.

She replied, 'I only charged a head of lettuce.' Bogey made her write a letter of apology.

Buying antiques was much more her style, especially if they were bargains. With the help of a decorator, she furnished the place in early American, Dutch and French provincial. She developed a passion for Delft and pewter. When she tried to tell Bogey that investing in antiques made sense because not only are they beautiful but they also increase in value, he retorted, 'They also fall apart. Now take that clock on the living room mantel. It's the only one in this country. It's rare, it's old, it's significant. It also doesn't keep time. We are very lucky people.'

So involved was she in the house and the boat that Betty told friends, 'If I never make another picture, I won't really care. I have everything a girl could want anyhow. Everything is so different when you're married. Bogey and I can sit together for hours without exchanging a word yet there's no feeling of strain. There's only a wonderful companionship and a sense of completeness.'

Word got around town that Bogey had 'mellowed' and he resented the expression. He always thought of himself as a cultured gentleman who enjoyed reading and could quote Shakespeare. If he liked 'outsiders'-and behaved like one on occasion, it did not mean that, despite his surface roughness, he had lost his innate dignity.

Betty saw him as he saw himself. Once she said to a columnist, 'I married an old-fashioned eighteenth century man. He is a prude. This surprises you. These are not the terms in which you think of him. Bogey, because he is not a secure man, is a very deceptive man.'

Mary Astor observed some time later, 'I think the remarkable Lauren Bacall knew who he was, let him be who he was and, in return, he was at last able to give something no other woman could grab from him: his total commitment.'

While Betty trusted implicitly in things working out, Bogey was a worrier although everything was running smoothly. 'His eyes are always sad even when he's happiest,' Betty commented. 'At first when they looked that way, I thought it was because of something I had done. It worried me. Now I know.' He had a passion for reducing problems to their lowest common denominator. This was apparent from his habit of choosing the same food to eat, and from his limited wardrobe. He had four suits, including the flannel he had bought for the wedding. Betty began choosing his accessories. But he would always wind up changing into the same tasselled moccasins and sportcoat or towelling jump-suit after work.

'I'm inclined to be impatient and it isn't easy for me to hide my feelings,' Betty stated. 'Like those times when we've planned a quiet evening at home and someone drops in unexpectedly. I say, "If a person behaves like a dope, why should I put up with it?" He answers, "We've got to realise that everyone isn't as lucky as we are—maybe they're lonely." So I'm learning to be more patient.'

Her ability to persist until she got what she wanted was now applied to her home and it gave her the beautiful rear lawn that she thought would complete the look of the place. Despite everyone's protests that she could not have one in the back because the lot was on a hill, she insisted and it did not slide as was predicted by all, even the expert gardener.

Tending to the chicken coop became an adventure for the city-bred Betty. 'We have one hundred and forty-eight chickens,' she said. 'We started out to have about fourteen for fun and atmosphere. They grew on us. I got crazy about them and bought fifty more and the poultryman gave me an additional fifty because I was such a good customer. So where once we had the chickens, now the chickens have us.' She maintained that only the eggs were eaten.

To complete their blissful picture of domesticity, they acquired a boxer dog from Louis Bromfield. Her golden cocker spaniel, Droopy and offspring Puddles, had been left with her mother when Betty married since Natalie had become so attached to them. Betty and Bogey's new dog was named Harvey because, as Bogey put it, 'He's the invisible hound. He's never around when you want him.' Soon the dog was joined by a mate named Baby. Their pup was called George after their friend who gave her away at their wedding, George Hawkins.

Harvey roamed around the vacant lot near their home and would pick up ticks from the shrubs. Betty always de-loused him immediately, even in the middle of a dinner party. 'I have protested repeatedly,' Bogey said. 'But the domestic meaning of the word protest is to whisper an objection while a steamship whistle is blowing.'

Bogey was called a 'hero' in the newspapers when they reported an incident involving the dogs that happened one night at their home. A commotion on the back porch made him run to see what was going on. He found a rattler had bitten Harvey. Stomping on the snake, Bogey killed it and rushed to the vet with the dog. On his return, a wildcat was disturbing the female boxer and he quickly routed the attacker with a few rifle shots.

Though they were only ten minutes from Beverly Hills there was plenty of wildlife in the environment and it disturbed Betty tremendously. To avoid the wilder human life on Sunset Strip, they had quiet dinners at home, but once a week they would go to her mother's, the Hellingers' or La Rue's restaurant.

Although Bogey had influenced her to soften her almost too casual style of dressing so that it became more feminine, she hardly ever decked herself out. Once when they were going out with the Hellingers for dinner, he told her, 'The trouble with you is that you cheat your public. You're a glamorous actress. They expect drooling sex when they see you in person. Once in a while, at least, you ought to give them that hot, burning screen personality.'

That challenge prompted her on this occasion to put on her most daring gown, mink, jewels and even a black cocque feather skull cap. Playing the bored sophisticate to the hilt, Betty kept in character while Bogey and the Hellingers spent all evening trying to break her up. After a couple of hours, she finally relaxed into her natural self.

When asked about some specific attributes of Betty's, Bogey answered, 'Slinky? I suppose you could call her slinky all right, but *only* on the screen. Heck, what do you think I'm married to, a snake? Her smokey voice? I reckon it's smokey all right. Sometimes when she answers the phone at home people think it's me.

'For a while she was imitating me more than she should have. A female Bogey around the house was a trifle disconcerting. For a few weird weeks her voice got lower than mine.' She even began to eat the same bacon and eggs lunch he always had. But at dessert time she would switch back to her old likings, always winding up with something gooey, like lemon meringue pie. Bogey's comment was: 'She's the only girl I know who can eat all that sweet stuff without putting on weight.' His simple tastes for dinner annoyed her. He liked only broiled steaks, chops or roasts, also seafood. If he enjoyed zucchini one night that did not mean he would want it again.

A source of contention, also, was the use of foul language. 'A four letter word I find most expressive is *shit*,' she confessed. 'That is his least favorite. But he'll use words I sometimes can't bear. I don't like dirty words.'

Betty could have been reproached—by those ever-watchful critics, film and otherwise—for her at-liberty status if it were not for her at-home activity. The only professional intrusion on her playing housewife was to provide a gag tag with Bogey to the Dennis Morgan–Jack Carson comedy, *Two Guys from Milwaukee*. She was her off-screen self as the dream girl a prince wants to meet on coming to America. When he sits next to her aboard a plane in the last sequence, Bogey interrupts to ask for his seat back. It seemed that this way Warner's was avoiding the problem of how to handle Betty in her next film.

To add to the confusion of her career, a new actress, Lizabeth Scott, was moving ahead rapidly by almost parodying Betty's gestures, voice, hair-do, clothes, even to wearing a checked suit and black beret. Many years earlier, back in New York, both actresses had competed once before. Two struggling actors bet each other that he could come up with the prettiest date. One showed up with Betty and the other with Lizabeth. It was considered a draw. Without any compunction, Bogey helped compound the comparison by accepting a loan-out to Columbia to co-star with Scott in *Dead Reckoning*, a take-off on *The Maltese Falcon* and *The Big Sleep*. So while the original star was languishing for the time being the counterfeit star was flourishing.

The only thing memorable about *Dead Reckoning* was an attitude Bogey expressed as the character in the film and later adopted as his own chauvinistic viewpoint: women should be small enough to put in a man's pocket and only pulled out when they are wanted.

Betty, however, had the satisfaction of reading Bogey the bad reviews for both the film and Scott. Then *The Two Mrs Carrolls*, which he had made two years before, was released and the fourth Mrs Bogart took delight in the panning. But a couple of mistakes did not matter to *his* reputation. He had been one of the top ten box-office favourites since 1942, earning himself nearly half a million dollars and besting everyone at Warner's, including Bette Davis.

Feeling obliged to rescue Betty's career, he decided to make a movie with her again, *Dark Passage*. The idea of the film would make it seem natural for Betty to walk off with the honours. Throughout the first half of the movie, the subjective camera technique showed what was happening through his eyes. And when he was seen at last, his face was completely bandaged for a long time. Even with this advantage, she had a hard time holding her own because in the cast was one of the great scene-stealers of all time, Agnes Moorehead, acting what she did best, a psychopath. By playing a good-natured normal girl, Betty had nothing. The electricity Betty and Bogey had once generated by seeming intimate together on the screen had only low-voltage power here except for one candlelight dinner scene with *Too Marvellous for Words* being played in the background.

As an actress Betty was still in trouble, but a catastrophe hit Bogey during the shooting of the film. As a result of hormone shots his hair suddenly began to turn white and to come out in alarming patches. Although some hair grew back, he was still so bald that from then on he had to wear a toupee. This could have affected the future of most other actors, but it only helped him decide to end his 'Image Period'. Rather than play Don Juan, he decided from now on to seek roles to challenge his acting abilities.

Tired of being Pygmalion as well, Bogey publicly resolved to stop trying to vivify Betty's stoniness. Even though publicity shots showed them happily visiting landmarks in San Francisco—where *Dark Passage* was shot—he wanted everyone to know that 'as far as movie-making was concerned, Betty was now completely on her own'.

That put her nowhere because, until she was cast opposite him again in a low-keyed role among high-powered actors in *Key Largo*, she did not act again for many months. The lull was spiced by tagging along with Bogey to Mexico for the making of *The Treasure of Sierra Madre*. Otherwise, this would have been the first separation since their marriage.

While the rugged filming was being done in the hills, she and John Huston's wife, Evelyn Keyes, waited in the hotel of the nearby town of San Jose. For nearly two months, the actresses were playing the role of patient wives by spending their days taking baths at the spa, sunning themselves or shopping until their men returned from work at night. The completion of the picture coincided with the Bogarts' second anniverary, and they took a five-day second honeymoon touring through the hinterlands of Mexico.

From the beginning the artistic intentions of *Treasure* inspired only antagonism at the studio. For some reason they had bought the B. Traven novel on which the film was based and had simply sat on the property for ten years. Huston exhumed it, but the greed theme was too much of a morality tale for Warner's taste. And when they saw the grubbiness of the characters in the rushes, and the mounting production costs, they wanted to call the whole thing off. For a change, they even resented Bogey dying at the end. But the insistence of John Huston and the power of the producer, Henry Blanke, prevailed and a masterpiece was created. Though Walter Huston won the Academy Award, justly, for his supporting role, and Bogey lost out in the Best Actor category, his performance as Fred C. Dobbs was considered the finest of his career.

Louise Brooks, known as 'The Lost Star of the Silent Films', was inspired to write about Bogey in this film. 'He lies in dirt, about to drag himself to the waterhole. He has endured all for gold—and now must he give it up? Wide open, the tragic eyes are raised to heaven in a terrible beseeching look. Despised and most abject of men. In the agony of that beautiful face I see the face of St Bogart.'

Bogey's talent may have raised him to sainthood to the discriminating, but his drawing power rendered him a god in the commercial world of Hollywood. As tribute, Warner's negotiated a new contract that paid him five million dollars for doing one picture a year for fifteen years. Allowed to make outside films, Bogey formed his own company with a Columbia release for four pictures. Called 'Santana', the production outfit was a partnership with his business manager, Morgan Magee, and Robert Lord, a former MGM producer who came in as a replacement when Mark Hellinger died during the negotiations.

On completing one of the biggest deals ever made in Hollywood, Jack Warner moaned, 'What am I doing, signing an old actor who's going bald?'

Bogey's retort about the contract was: 'What are you trying to pull off here? I've checked this thing three different times. The way it works out, at the end of fifteen years, I'll be seventy-five cents short.' He paused and added soberly, 'They think I'll be dead by then but you wait and see.'

Further glory came from *Key Largo*. The picture itself was unimportant. Its main significance was that the film dramatised how far Bogey had come as a star in twelve years. The plot was a variation on *The Petrified Forest* theme. This time Bogey played the lead, a Leslie Howard idealist, who slowly moves to take action against Edward G. Robinson personifying 'Bogey-man' evil. When *Forest* was brought to the screen, Warner's wanted their big-man-on-the-lot Robinson to do the Duke Mantee role that Bogey created on the stage. But Howard had promised Bogey that when the film was made, he would not do it unless Bogey was part of the deal. Howard telegraphed Warner's from London to that effect. After putting Bogey through thirty screen tests, Warner's eventually capitulated.

Afterwards, in film after film, Robinson wiped out Bogey with his bullets. Then in *Largo* it became Bogey's turn to get Robinson. With his beautiful but ineffectively-cast wife by his side and his best friend, John Huston, directing—to make his triumph complete—he cut down Robinson for the first time in their last picture together. Even more killing for Robinson as an actor was Bogey finally getting top billing over him.

Approaching fifty, Bogey no longer flaunted his sexual powers, but boasted about his acquisitions instead. 'I have the best boat in the world, the best home, the best wife, the best servants and the best dogs.'

Betty could not help but comment, 'You notice who got third billing?'

Deadline—USA

'All of a sudden when our son was a year old, Bogey realised he was a man with responsibilities,' Betty observed in 1954. 'I know he is aware of the responsibilities because lately he has the strange notion he is in the twilight of his existence, both as an actor and as a human being. He is always talking about having something to leave me and the kids. He feels he must amass a lot of money. In some ways I suspect that this feeling is due to the difference in our ages.'

Old age and the prospect of death, an awareness of which was intensified by the great span of years between him and Betty, gave impetus to Bogey's desire to provide future security for his family. Although he saw himself as being in the 'twilight of his existence', his star had never shown brighter. In his private life he had challenged time by having his first child when other men his age were grandfathers. In his public life he was in great demand and was able to, work continuously, often in roles with wider range than before—and this at an age when most actors would be forced into retirement. In his fifties, he was attaining his most memorable achievements as an actor and his finest ones as a man. From facing the future squarely, he extracted from what he saw as the ultimate evil, the greatest good.

But, being over half-a-century old and set in his ways, it was hard for him to make adjustments, particularly in the case of his son. Often, before Betty became pregnant, Bogey had said he was 'too old for that kid stuff'. His version of how Betty told him the news was quite different from hers, but both stories show that the prospect of fatherhood was upsetting for him because, as his wife realised, 'it was another brick in the house of conformity'.

Betty's telling of the tale is a sentimental one. A wife is waiting in front of the house for her husband to come home from work. She has news for him. The doctor says she is pregnant. He puts his arms around her and they go inside. Later, for some minor cause, they have a major row, their biggest ever. Perhaps he felt that the oneness they shared would be jeopardised by having a child. Maybe he realised his resentment at this moment when they were so close.

Bogey's version of the same event keeps him in character as a character.

'The day came when my spouse walked in the door with the words, "Well, the doctor says you'll never forgive me, but I'm going to have a baby."'

In response, he makes the prescribed noises of elation. 'Frankly, I think I did them pretty well,' he later cracked, 'considering it was my first "take".' But then he remembers what Betty had stated. 'Why am I never going to forgive you?' he asks. 'To me a baby is a baby.'

'Summer is coming, isn't it?' He nods as she continues, 'Well, I'm not going to be able to do much sailing, you know.'

'Oh,' is all he can respond to this sudden awareness that there would be a change in the focus of their relationship from now on.

The impact of impending fatherhood really hit when he decided to spend some time aboard the *Santana* after finishing the first production for his own company, *Knock on Any Door*. Betty stayed at home since now, being pregnant, she was made ill by the rhythm of the boat. The *Santana* was fifty-five miles out when Bogey started to miss her. Characteristically not wanting to show that he longed for her, he decided to make a joke of it—albeit a romantic and very expensive one. He decided to put a call through to her by way of London. The twelve-thousand-mile round-trip phone call just to hear Betty's voice seemed to him great fun, but he could not convince the operator at Claridges in London to make the connection. A call from California via London back to California, he was told, was just too ridiculous. So he had to be prosaic and divulge his loneliness via a direct call home.

For the first time since becoming a major star, Bogey was going to play the part of a parent on-screen in his own next production, *Tokyo Joe*. To show that he had actually chosen his off-screen role as a father, he rationalised: 'I can't say that I truly ever wanted a child before I married Betty. For one thing, in the past, my life never seemed settled enough to wish it on a minor. I was in the theatre in New York, or going on tour around the countryside. And in Hollywood, I was either trying to consolidate my foothold in pictures or was preoccupied by something else.

'But Betty wanted a child very much. And, as she talked about it, I did, too.

'For one reason—which may seem a little grisly, but true nonetheless—I wanted to leave a part of me with her when I died. There is quite a difference in our ages, you know, and I am realistic enough to be aware that I shall probably leave this sphere before she does. I wanted a child, therefore, to stay with her, to remind her of me.

'And for another reason. I simply wanted a child. Period. I didn't care whether it was a boy or a girl, though Betty did: she hoped desperately for a boy. She beat her brains out with the problem of what to name *him* and chose *her* name quite casually.'

As a double reminder, the baby was called Stephen Humphrey Bogart (Bogey's own name) and there was also a reference to *Steve*, the character Bogey had played in *To Have and Have Not*. Bogey gave as his reason for the choice: 'We wanted our son to be part of our happiness at having met.'

The new life that was on its way gave Betty an excuse to revitalise their home by redecorating. In the middle of Bogey's sleep one night, Betty woke him to say they had to redo the butler's pantry. That room was the wrong colour for a home that was to have a baby in it, she declared. And so began the endless middle-of-the-night home improvement sessions. This all seemed a lark until the bills started coming in. But Bogey continued to comply with her wishes, not wanting to upset her. After the house was almost completely redecorated, he was startled to see her reading books, not about the care and feeding of an infant, but about the latest in gadgets for the home. Alarmed, he called his business manager Morgan

Maree and told him that she was studying 'how to equip our home like the house of the day after tomorrow', and asked him to take over the supervision of Betty's purchases.

From then on, Betty had to clear everything through the manager. 'Maree was really tough,' she said. 'A couple of times he held out for as long as a month before giving in.' Bogey's and Maree's final token of surrender was to give Betty a model of the refinished house with all the changes made by her. Bogey, however, still complained to Mike Romanoff, 'When other wives are pregnant, they're supposed to demand pickles, ice-cream or strawberries out of season. Mine just wants money and thirty-room houses.'

'The most discussed baby-to-be in Hollywood' was how the press referred to the forthcoming event. But rumours of Betty being pregnant had always been rampant. Once, extremely annoyed, she had told a journalist, 'Listen, you columnists have been having me with a child since I was married fourteen months ago. This must be the longest maternity in the history of the world. I belong in a carnival.'

Another time, when they came home late one night, Fred the butler congratulated them on being expectant parents. He had heard a false report on Jimmy Fiddler's Hollywood gossip radio programme.

Now that Betty was truly pregnant, Bogey tried to put off nagging reporters by stating, 'I think most people think too much about having a baby. What's so remarkable about it? People have them every day. Why, right now it seems like half the people Betty and I know are having babies. Why the fuss? I tell Betty that the American Indian had the right idea. When her baby came, the squaw stepped a few feet off the trail, had her baby, and pretty soon got back on the trail. The quicker she got back, the shorter the distance she had to cover to catch up to her old man. Especially if he were riding the family horse.'

This sardonic attitude was an apparent façade to cover the panic he was registering inside at becoming a parent. He had to find out what it would be like as a father and so tried to take an interest in his friends' children. Perhaps he tried too hard—the children didn't really take to him, and their rebuffs multiplied his terror.

Some respite from his growing concern came from a comic stag baby party his friends held for him at Romanoff's. The highlight was a mock baby delivery that had John Huston using fire tongs to wrest an imaginary baby from a pseudo-pregnant and prone Bogey. Later the actor was touched to receive all the baby gifts his friends presented to him and he tried to describe his feelings about becoming a father in a speech, but the booze made him blubber.

Three days into *Tokyo Joe*, on January 6, 1949, just before the lunch-break, he got a call from Dr Krohn informing him that Betty was in the obstetrician's office and was having birth pains. The prospective father had to rush off to take her to the hospital. Half an hour later, a pale and nervous Bogey was registering an inwardly anxious yet outwardly composed Betty at Cedars of Lebanon Hospital. For a while he tried to keep her company in the labour room, but unable to take the agony, he went to sit out the wait in the 'Fathers' Room'. Soon he was joined by a newspaper pal, Jack Rosenstein. At Betty's orders, since the delivery was not immediately imminent, the doctor took Bogey out to dinner. 'Now you take care of Bogey,' she had told the doctor. 'Don't let him get too worried.' After their return, about midnight the nurse announced that Bogey was the father of a six-pound six-ounce boy. Instantly, Bogey brought out the flask he had in his pocket from which he and his friend had been taking nips to sustain themselves. To celebrate, he poured drinks for all the fathers-to-be in the waiting room. After rushing down the hall to view 'The Boy', as he would refer to him, he saw Betty being wheeled into her room. Holding her hand, tenderly caressing her, though she was unconscious, he stayed with her until the nurse asked him to leave.

The next day it was Bogey who received a big bunch of red roses with a card that read, 'Dear Dad, It was a tough fight, but we made it. Stephen Humphrey Bogart.' Betty's turnabout gave him the laugh he so badly needed.

Five days later, in a blizzard unusual for Los Angeles, Betty and Stephen were delivered home in an ambulance that had difficulty driving up the hill because of the snow. An avalanche of gifts from fans soon followed. The only ones that were refused were machine-guns, because Bogey said, he 'did not want his son to follow in his Dad's footsteps'. He hoped Stephen would become 'something respectable, like a doctor or a lawyer', in accordance with the post-war goals of conformity. Among the presents Mr and Mrs Bogart prized were a pair of bunting boxing gloves from Sterling Hayden and godfather Louis Bromfield's silver cup on which was engraved 'To S. H. B. from L. B. From One Capricorn to Another and God Help the World'.

A memento Bogey wanted he never got, although he claimed on occasion that he had. It was a cancelled cheque for twenty dollars, the stake in a bet with Harry Truman. The President had predicted that the baby would be a boy. When Bogey sent Truman the winnings, he attached a note asking, 'Please cash it, PLEASE!' But the President never deposited it.

Getting used to being a father, Bogey expressed his appreciation by saying, 'Betty gave me a son when I had given up hope of a son.' On the same theme he added later, 'She is my swan song. She is everything I ever wanted and now, Stephen, my son, completes the picture.' Asked about how he rated as a parent, Bogey replied, 'I don't know what constitutes being a good father. I *think* I'm a good one, but only time, of course, can tell. At this stage in a child's life, the father is packed away, put aside and sat upon. The physical aspects—feeding, burping, changing, training—are matters before the Bogart committee which is, as of now, a committee of one—Betty. I dare not make a statement for fear of incriminating myself. So, I won't take over for a while yet. When I do, I'll handle the boy as I would any human being in my orbit. That is, I'll let him be himself. I won't push him into anything or try to influence him.'

Betty added, 'He's crazy about our son but the only time he ever pinned diapers on him—except in some dire emergency—was for the benefit of studio publicity photographers. So then what happens? People get the idea he has the cribside manner. Well, don't let the picture fool you. When it come to diapers, that's why wives and nurses were born.'

In Erskine Johnson's column she was quoted as saying, 'Stephen's reaction to Bogey's singing lullabies is just to curl up into a ball and stick the ends of his diapers in his ears.'

A change from the parental pace soon came when he finished *Tokyo Joe*. Together, the Bogarts went on a nationwide tour to promote *Knock on Any Door*, which turned out to be as prosaic as any of the movies he had protested against but had made when he was a contract player at Warner's. A prolonged stay in New York gave Betty a chance to go on a shopping spree, which was important to her since she had recently been voted one of the ten best-dressed women in the country—joining the ranks of her discoverer, Slim.

One night after seeing Bobby Clark in *As the Boys Go* on Broadway, they were stormed by their fans just as they were getting into a taxi with Louis Bromfield, who was palmed off as Fred Allen. Everyone was shouting, 'Give us a look at Baby.' A beaming Bogey turned on the ceiling light of the cab and held a burning cigarette lighter over Betty's head to give her the full spotlight.

The need to be in the real spotlight as a performer still bothered Betty. 'Despite all the hammering, Miss Bacall has somehow managed to stay among the living,' she let it be known. 'Professionally, that is. I'm alive, and a little older, and perhaps even a little smarter, too. Smarter because I know that all of us, in pictures or out of them, are always climbing stairs.

'Climbing and resting, and climbing again, and perhaps even stumbling once or twice when you miss a step or two. But climbing—moving upward. Coming of age, professionally. That's the important thing. When you know that you can stand on your own feet—I have nothing against Bogey's Number Tens; I think they're elegant—you've come a long way up those stairs.'

On making her first picture in two years, *Young Man with a Horn*, Betty achieved the only acting satisfaction she had felt since her initial film. One day on the set the crew broke into spontaneous applause after a scene she did with Kirk Douglas. She felt that the approval of the glamour-weary men meant that Bacall had *come of age*—'I wasn't just the girl Humphrey Bogart had married and helped along; I was an actress and I had put that scene over. I've still got to prove—to myself, primarily—that as an actress Lauren Bacall can go it on her own.'

Bogey gave her his vote of confidence by stating, 'I'm happy Betty now feels she finally has a place in the scheme of things. Becoming certain of herself as a wife and a mother accounts for this. She has the drive of a steamroller, yet she is genuinely modest about her own qualifications.'

On the first day of shooting *Young Man with a Horn*, Bogey had sent her a bouquet of roses as he always did when she started a picture. This was followed by a peculiar present from her co-star Kirk Douglas. He showed up in her dressing room with a caviar and jam sandwich in remembrance of a vow she had made six years before when they were both unknowns.

While making the rounds of Broadway producers' offices, they would often run into each other at Walgreen's and share a 'dry' sandwich together. Betty had sworn that if she ever became a star, she would eat caviar and jam. Now that the strange concoction she wished for was given to her, she had to force herself to consume it.

In those early days Betty called Kirk 'Big Shot' because of her great admiration for his acting ability. They had both studied at the American Academy. He had to work as a soda jerk and part-time waiter to pay his way through school. Years later, while he was still doing bit parts on Broadway, Betty and Bogey were on a train to New York and happened to meet Hal Wallis. The producer told them that the purpose of his trip was to search out new talent. Immediately Betty suggested that he look up Kirk Douglas. Hal Wallis did and brought him to Hollywood. When Kirk arrived, Bogey helped him to find an agent and gave him advice on his career. Now a real 'big shot' as a result of *The Champion*, Kirk was returning the favours by encouraging Betty so that she felt more secure about their scenes together and by making sure she got the best camera angles.

A most incisive comment was made to Betty by the director of the film, Michael Curtiz, who had done *Casablanca*. She had a habit of flaring her nostrils when she was tense just before starting a scene. 'Like a runner getting himself set for the sound of the starting gun,' she described it. Mike came over one day and stared at her for a while, then, in his mangled English, asked, 'Listen why do you make faces, faces all the time?'

'I'm sorry, Mike,' she laughed, 'but I'm not making faces. It's just something I do unconsciously.'

'Well then,' the director exploded, 'don't be so unconscious—be conscious!'

Being conscientious as well did not help Betty. The film turned out to be a run-of-the-mill production and ground down the hope that her frank portrayal of a lesbian would at last bring recognition as an actress. This was all the more disappointing since this was one of the few parts she had ever been eager to do. Over the past four years she had been suspended by Warner's six times for refusing roles. Turning down *The Girl from Jones Beach* because she was reluctant to appear on screen in a bathing suit, she protested, 'I've got to stop being sultry and sexy some time. It just isn't a solid career. It's a good thing I have a husband. Suspensions can get awfully rough on the pocketbook.' Once both Bogey and Betty walked out together rather than co-star in *Stallion Road*.

One more picture, Betty's seventh, and she terminated her contract with Warner's by buying herself out a year and a half ahead of time. Not until later did she realise that, because of studio cutbacks due to television, they would have let her go just for the asking. Her final film as a Warner star, *Bright Leaf* with Gary Cooper and Patricia Neal, had her playing a turn-of-the-century madam with as listless a quality as the picture itself had. Yet despite the lack of critical and public enthusiasm, Betty was always able to garner a 'She-was-never-better' compliment from the columnists. This had all the sincerity of Louella Parsons' standard line for Marion Davies: 'Marion was never lovelier.' Though Betty was constantly disappointed and disappointing to the vast majority, she had a following which kept hoping for even a flicker of that first flame which had ignited their interest. Now she had no studio to protect her or to protest against. All she had was a powerful husband who could express the force and strength of a whole studio executive body by himself.

'Naturally, he's right there to advise me, like any good husband, when I need his advice,' she divulged. 'But when it comes to pictures, he agrees with me in my thinking. What I want is a chance really to say something in pictures—to find out what I can really do. I'm frank enough to admit that I have a special and definite field: I'm no Duse, and I don't want to run the gamut of emotions. Nor do I feel that I'll ever make an Academy Award.

'Like Bogey, I believe that motion pictures were founded on colorful, exciting personalities, rather than on superb acting. I believe that most movie fans would rather see Bing Crosby being Bing, Gable being himself, and Danny Kaye and Gloria Swanson just being Kaye and Swanson, instead of some weighty problem play in which these personalities—or others like them—are anything but their well-loved selves.' She had the same to say about Bogey, justifying his lack of creativity in his latest film, *Sirocco*.

'Personally, I don't think it matters very much if you're off the screen even five years—if you're a personality movie-goers really want to see. Maybe I'm wrong, but I'm willing to find out. I can't act with sincerity in a picture I don't think is right for the kind of screen personality that I believe Lauren Bacall should be. In pictures, people either like me or hate me; there's no middle ground—and I'm happy it's that way.

'I have a ten-year plan and I have supreme faith in the future. When the right part comes along—a role with humour and one with a definite personality, I'll know it. And I'll grab it.'

For the next three years, there was no golden role to reach out for. Though she kept moving in Bogey's élite circles, her own merry-go-round was at a complete standstill.

This hiatus was startling. Bogey's reaction that he expressed to columnist Gladys Hill was, 'If she didn't work I'd have more time with her, sure, but as long as she wishes to go on with her career, it's the better part of valor. For, three years from now, you know, or even in thirty years I might hear, "I could have been Ethel Barrymore if it hadn't been for you." And she might have me there, who knows? What is more, I wouldn't know what to do with a wife who didn't work. All my wives have been career girls. A wife who sat around at those chicken à la king luncheons playing Bridge or Canasta would be a stranger in the Bogart ménage in Beverly Hills, California.

'Besides, work is a good discipline. Keeps your brain alive, your muscles flexed and your face before the public where, let's face it, an actor likes his face to be.'

During this barren period only Betty's voice was heard professionally. With Bogey, she played in a syndicated radio series produced by Santana, called *Bold Venture*. He was Slade Shannon and she was his 'ward' Sailor Duval, a pair of uninhibited characters who owned a boat and a small hotel. Every weekly action episode was spiced with their typically zesty by-play. The five thousand dollars per show salary his company paid them, they said, was being kept for Stephen's future.

More than ever before, Betty made her home her world. The influx of antique pewter mugs, plates and plaques never ceased. Bogey would yell, 'Hey, how much more of that stuff can one house hold, anyway?' But that did not stop Betty from trying to find out.

The garden also became her passion. The enviable results inspired a columnist to remark to Bogey, 'Isn't it wonderful how lucky Mrs Bogart is with her flowers?'

'Yes,' Bogey countered, 'isn't it wonderful? The harder she works, the luckier she gets.'

Although interest in Betty as an actress was virtually nil, she still maintained a fascination for newspaper and magazine readers by constantly reminding them of her strength in standing up to Bogey and of her equality with him off-screen. Through such confessionals she fulfilled the essential ambition that Mike Romanoff ascribed to her: being a celebrity. At the same time, the restaurateur believed that all Bogey wanted was to go through this phase of his life with as much contentment as possible. The wife-who-could-hold-her-own-against-the-toughest-man-in-the-world was an ideal subject for human interest columns. Her tale was not one concerning a rough babe or a tear-stained slavery. Here was a contemporary woman, a perfect match for her mate who had become that by not competing nor complying, but complementing. And as a paragon of pairing she had a grip on the imagination of people throughout the world. This was the marriage that everyone had said wouldn't survive more than a few months. And now it had become the universal object of admiration as the ideal, if not idyllic, twosome. Betty's conditioning of Bogey to her image of the life she wanted—while accepting the best of his nature and working through the shortcomings—gave her stature in the public's estimation.

As a preface to one interview, she set up the premise, 'To my mind men are much more mysterious than women. I don't honestly think that any two husbands can be managed in exactly the same way.

'Still,' she continued, 'during all our years of bliss and battles, I've chalked up a pretty good batting average, keeping Bogart from turning into Bogart more often than behoves his blood pressure. And mine.'

So that the world would know the measure of her achievement, she issued statements like, 'He's a complex guy and hard to live with, but I'm not dazzled any more. I think I can handle him.'

Her motto was, 'Scratch a "bogey-man" and you'll find a human being.'

Curiosity about Bogey's drinking habits never relented—even though Betty often stated that he had cut down 'one third' on his alcohol intake. Seemingly desirous of helping hordes of desperate wives in what appeared to be a widespread problem, she would reveal her method in coping with her husband's liking for drink: 'I'd wait until he was sober, then go about telling him what an ass he made of himself. He didn't like to hear these things and gradually he let up on his drinking.'

Bogey, however, had a reputation to maintain as an ornery cuss in his cups. To the incessant inquiry, 'Do you drink any more?' his standard response was, 'Not any more. The same amount.'

His New York capers in particular gained him further notoriety. The Bogarts' trips to the city became more frequent because he was promoting pictures made by his own company. This gave him a chance to combine business with pleasure, but at the expense of his privacy.

A Broadway columnist described a lunch with the Bogarts which he thought was typical:

He: How do you feel, Baby?
She: I'm fine. What do you want? Soup?
He: Scotch Mist.
She: I'm definitely a soup girl.
He: I don't even want to think about something to eat for two more drinks.

In a *Time* interview, he explained his attitude toward carousing: 'I have politeness and manners. I was brought up that way. But in this goldfish-bowl life, it is sometimes hard to use them. A night-club is a good place not to have manners.'

Whenever and wherever possible, he put that belief into action, especially at El Morocco. Once, when on entering that elegant club with Betty, he refused to check his hat and the manager Roy Dill-man insisted he obey the rules. This resulted in an unsuccessful attempt by Bogey to put out his cigarette in Dillman's face. On being ushered out of the club, he was taunted by Betty's sarcasm: 'They can't do that to you, Bogey.'

Vindicating himself to the press, he announced, 'I wised up some people about the notion that they can push celebrities around. I'd say it compares with the Dreyfus case. I struck a blow for freedom, not to mention the pursuit of happiness.'

Six months later, he was back at the same stand with a pal. Each of them was carrying a gigantic stuffed panda weighing twenty-two pounds. At his previous stop, the Stork Club, Bogey had suddenly decided that two stuffed pandas would be the ideal present for his ten-month-old son and had sent one of the waiters out to look for the toys, even though it was well after midnight on a Sunday. The mission was surprisingly successful and cost Bogey a total of fifty dollars. Several versions exist of what happened next at El Morocco—even the number of toys keeps changing. The fanciest one had Bogey protecting his honour as well as his pandas. A model, Robin Roberts, was leaving as he came in. When she saw him with his stuffed animal, she made a play for him to get the toy and though he protested, 'I'm a happily married man,' she tried to run off with the panda and he had to tackle her to retrieve it.

In the simplest telling of the tale, Bogey offered Robin the panda as a gift, then tore it away with a push that bruised her chest.

Violence formed a part of still another rendition of the incident. This interpretation began with Bogey and his friend depositing the pandas as soon as they entered because they had spotted a friend and had gone off to join him for a drink. Within a few minutes they were back, only to find the pandas gone. Two young ladies, one of them Robin Roberts, were carrying the toys off. Quickly, Bogey made a flying leap at Robin's friend, causing dishes to fly. A plate hit Robin on the hip. The clatter that resulted was heard on teletypes around the world.

Right away, Sheilah Graham called Betty in New York to ask, 'What will you do?'

'I will do nothing,' Betty answered, 'He's too big to hit and too old to spank, so I'm treating his hangover and putting him to bed.'

To another columnist, Betty commented, 'That's the way those guys get when they're pushing fifty. This burns me up.'

Facetiously, she declared to a persistent reporter, 'This [censored] husband of mine has to go out and get loaded. I'll have to take him to a dark corner and burn his ears. But after all, he was only out with a panda.' To make sure she came across as an understanding wife, she added, 'You can quote me on this: My husband is wonderful.'

Cornered by reporters, Bogey protested, 'I'm a lovable character, about as tough as Shirley Temple.' To the question, 'Were you drunk at the time?' he came up with the classic retort, 'Isn't everyone at three o'clock in the morning?'

An action for twenty-five thousand dollars was instituted by Robin Roberts who claimed hip injuries. The judge dismissed the case, summing up with: 'Bogart was only using force to protect his property.'

Prodded about the panda, Betty exclaimed, 'That animal is the exclusive property of Stephen and Bogey. I want no part of it.'

Years later the incident was still remembered and talked about. A columnist referred to the fracas while interviewing Betty who responded, 'Funny thing is that when he took the thing home, Steve wouldn't look at it. And didn't for three years. After, when he was four, he used to ride it when he watched cowboy films on television.'

The Stork Club was also to make news by barring Bogey. One night as Bogey was entering the bistro, Sherman Billingsley, the owner and the host of the television interview show emanating from there, asked him to appear on the programme. Bogey had to refuse to go before the cameras impromptu because he was not wearing his toupee. This antagonised Billingsley who became abusive. Finally, Bogey exploded with, 'You ham, you stink up the entire show.' And that got him axed from the club.

One of the first things Bogey taught Stephen was to respond to the question, 'Do you like Sherman Billingsley?' with an emphatic, 'No!'

Betty's characteristically caustic reaction was, 'If you had any ambition, Bogey, you'd get barred from Madison Square Garden this trip. That would give us the doubles championship and we could turn pro. I'm telling you, there's money in it.'

Betty herself took on the role of 'bouncer' once while Bogey was away from home. Late on September 4, 1950, a certain aspiring actor broke into the house. On seeing Betty, he made lewd advances. She fended him off by talking calmly to him. While she outmanœuvred him verbally, her secretary phoned the police from another room and they quickly came to cart the intruder off to jail. Once again Betty had proved herself an expert in manipulation through words, a talent she attributed to years of countering Bogey's barbs.

One of his favourite ways to get a rise out of her was to say, 'I had to marry you. You chased me until I had my back to the wall. I did what any gentleman would do.' If anyone overheard his remark, she would explain in an especially subdued tone, which she always used when desiring to appear in control, 'This, of course, is not true. I think he married me because I was younger than he and he felt he would get a new lease on life. It would have been a big mistake on my part to act older in an attempt to keep up with him. It was much wiser and better for him to adjust in the direction of youth.'

Part of Betty's emphasis on youthfulness expressed itself in her attempt to be positive about everything. She made certain that there was nothing indefinite or vague about herself. Her sureness sometimes made the words she was saying sound as though they had come from a text printed in upper case. If a person or a condition did not measure up to her standards, she made her opinion known quite emphatically. She was as absolute about minding her own business as in demanding that others mind theirs. Live and let live was her attitude.

All these ideas coincided with Bogey's, but she endowed them with a certain freshness because of her greater dynamism. She was becoming more and more a female counterpart of him through years of absorbing his concepts of individuality. And, symbiotically, he thrived on the reinvigoration of his ideals.

Her views reflected Bogey's outlook. He spoke for both of them when he said, 'You have to be yourself. I reserve the right to go where I please when I please, cultivate people I like, and ignore those I dislike. I am called a character, I know. There's too much of this sticking on labels, like calling people "tolerant" or "liberal" or "independent". Those were good words originally, but they are misused.' Such opinions were accorded respect because Hollywood's original Dead End adult now had screen success and an admirable life with Betty.

Free-thinking, for them, meant free-doing. If tagging a person was poison to him, he did something about it. When his black butler played a small part in *Mr Peabody and the Mermaid*, he was

106

driven to the studio by either Betty or Bogey on their days off just as they were chauffeured by him when he was not working in the film. 'But what did I hear about myself, all of a sudden?' Bogey complained. 'I heard I'm on a crusade. I'm being "tolerant". Well, I wasn't being anything of the sort. I wouldn't patronize any human being by being "tolerant" with him or her. What I did for Fred, I did for a friend.'

Not simply content with being someone who tried to be true to himself, Bogey proclaimed that he could forgive anything but a lie. Often he would voice the warning to Betty that if he ever found out she was having an affair behind his back, he would never have anything to do with her any more. He believed that it was not enough to have character, you had to act it out at all times.

Many years later, Elizabeth Taylor on the David Frost television show acknowledged Bogey's influence in making her be more of her own person. She recounted, 'At a party, Bogey took me aside and said, "Love," and you know he was very virile, "you're an absolute crumpet. You follow Michael Wilding around like a puppy. You just kind of listen to his conversation and sort of either say yes or no, or agree or disagree in monosyllables. Get out on your own. Go out in the room, talk to other people and make some kind of statement—a statement of your own, that's your very own. If you're disagreed with, then disagree back if you believe in it." I started doing that. He told me, "Get you finger out, baby."'

Directness was usually Betty's way, but when she anticipated a negative response from Bogey she would be oblique in order to wangle what she wanted from him. He was not unaware of her wiles. 'She infiltrates my ideas. She drops a word here and there,' he said, 'and six months later nurtures it with a few more words. A year later her first words have given root and I'm sitting under a giant oak tree—and I never ever saw the acorn.'

Without using the 'acorn' method, she drove him 'nuts' for years with pleas for a trip to Europe. 'All you do is sit around on your fat behind,' she admonished while he grinned. 'You never want to do anything or go any place.'

'European trips are like appendicitis,' he laughed; 'a wife should have taken care of it before marriage.'

A few days aboard the *Santana* was Bogey's idea of getting away. He spent short spells between pictures lounging around the house, reading and sleeping, but always lunching at Romanoff's. At his special booth, the second from the left of the entrance, he would hold court with his entourage, eating and drinking, exchanging the latest news, dreaming up practical jokes or playing chess. The trips he took always involved business. Although he worked an average of thirty weeks out of the year in front of the cameras, much of the remaining time was occupied with arranging production details, properties, investments, promotion, residuals and rights.

The satisfaction of being a combination actor and business man was described by Bogey to Art Buchwald: 'When a picture of mine is released, there are five hundred prints made and they're sent out all over the world . . . there are five hundred of me, and I'm working all the time, bringing in money.'

From 1949 to 1951, his company's first six films were moderately successful. But the only reason they made money was his drawing power as a star and not his canniness as a producer. Often he was quoted as saying, 'People who write plays with a message give me a pain.' And he would follow this with the bromide, 'If they have a message, let them use Western Union.' Most of the movies he was making looked as though they were scribbled on inter-office memo pads. He even refused to play Captain Ahab in John Huston's *Moby Dick* because he thought it was like doing Shakespeare or reading poetry. 'My audience,' he declared, 'are those beer-guzzling guys who fall asleep in front of their television sets.'

His only daring was in using unknown casts and crews. Once he had to explain his choice of relatively inexperienced director Nicholas Ray for a couple of films and said, 'I don't believe in the theory that only directors who have been in the business for years are any good. I like the idea of giving the young guys a chance. We should do more of that out here.'

At the start of his own film career, Bogey had told Ed Sullivan, 'After I finish acting, I want to stay in pictures. I'd like to be a director. I keep my eyes open on a set and hang around the camera to find out what it's all about. I watch those directors.' Now, as part of the upper echelon of the industry, he let it be known that in all his vast experience, he had only found a handful of directors that he really believed were true creative artists.

A similar change of heart was expressed about the entire motion picture profession. In the beginning, he had felt, 'There is nothing I resent so much as the digs that are taken at the movies. It is a comparatively young industry and the progress has been sensational. The movies have been swell to me and they've been swell to a lot of people. If I were to forget that, I'd be a dope.' But, several years later, his original enthusiasm was past remembering, submerged in the bitterness garnered from experience, and he told a *Time* reporter, 'I don't give a damn about the industry. If they go broke, I don't give a damn. I don't hurt the industry. The industry hurts itself—as if General Motors deliberately put out a bad car.'

Bogey's change of attitude toward Hollywood was dramatised by the difference between how, in earlier, more halcyon days, he had regarded having his footprints recorded in the cement in the forecourt of Grauman's Chinese Theater and how, when later Betty's turn for distinction came, he saw it then. It had been right after *The Big Sleep* when he had allowed a big fuss to be made over pressing into concrete the 'lucky shoes' he wore in that film and in *Casablanca*. Beside his footprints, he had written, 'To Sid. May you never die till I kill you.' Years later when Betty was asked to step into that hall of fame, Bogey no longer took the distinction seriously. For a lark, he talked her out of accepting the honour by convincing her that the prestige had gone out of the invitation and that the ritual was too undignified. But Betty would always regret losing the chance to cement her fame.

Acting was, for Bogey, like a mistress he took for granted once the conquest was over. To stir any of the former passion would require tremendous effort and he was becoming too comfortable to be bothered. So he spent his time making provocative statements and playing mischievous games. Anything more creative seemed not to be worth the strain.

Then, with Bogey in his fifties, there came an opportunity that made him want to exert himself. Taking up the challenge, Bogey was able to prove he was still a man of his time by expressing the disillusioned realism of the 1950s in a performance that was to give him the greatest triumph of his career just when he desperately needed a hit.

At the start of the decade an old association came to a close. After twenty years, Bogey parted from Warner's by mutual agreement because the studio was not doing that well with his recent films and he was not too happy with the properties they gave him. In George Raft's biography, written by Lewis Yablonsky, Raft says, 'Bogart was in a mellow mood after he left Jack Warner and reminisced with a tinge of fondness, "I kind of miss the arguments I had with Warner. I used to love those feuds. It's like you've fought with your wife and gotten a divorce. You kind of miss the fighting." '

Also in 1951, Bogey lost another former sparring partner when Mayo Methot died of cancer at the age of forty-seven. She left a fifty-thousand-dollar estate and fourteen hundred dollars in cash.

Although he would hardly admit it to himself, Bogey was in low spirits. So he found a new height to scale. As soon as John Huston and James Agee decided to adapt the 1935 C. S. Forester novel *The African Queen* into a movie script, they both agreed that Bogey had to play Charlie Allnut, the gin-guzzling pilot of a decaying riverboat. Author-critic Agee's opinion of the actor was, 'He has charm and doesn't waste energy pretending to act. He has a sinister-rueful countenance which acts for him. He has an exciting personality and lets it do the work.'

As for the female lead role of the prim spinster, Rose Sayer, Bogey took credit for suggesting Katharine Hepburn, whom he knew through his close friend Spencer Tracy. The actress was just completing her widely-acclaimed appearance in *As You Like It* when she was offered the part. Even though she was told that the film would be shot in Africa and they would be living in primitive conditions for a few months, she was not put off, but accepted.

'Interesting girl,' Bogey told columnist Gladys Hall, about Hepburn, soon after that meeting, 'very stimulating girl. And—like Betty—as different as possible from what I may describe as the "formula" female. First time John Huston and I interviewed Katie neither of us had shaved. Obviously suspecting the worst, the great Katharine plied us with black coffee saying hopefully, but firmly, "Now, if you boys will just straighten up." We've now planned that in Africa, we'll show up with glasses of dark brown iced tea in hand so that Katharine can put us on the wagon. Funny thing, there's a dash of the reformer in every fabulous female.'

No matter how close Bogey thought he was to Huston, the director had his own ideas of their relationship, as he described in his biography, *King Rebel* by William F. Nolan: 'I hate stars.

They're not actors. I've been around actors all my life and I like them, and yet I never had an actor as a friend. Except Dad. And Dad never thought of himself as an actor. But the best actor I ever worked with was Dad. All I had to tell Dad about his part of the old man in *Treasure* was talk fast . . . a man talking fast is an honest man.'

Just as three years before when he went to Mexico to make that film, Bogey wanted Betty to be with him on location for the new one. 'I don't see the purpose of getting married if you prefer being separated,' he explained to Hedda Hopper. 'If you want to be single, don't get married. Being separated is one thing, but being apart for a period of months can wreck a marriage.' Undoubtedly, that lesson had been learned during his marriage to Mary Philips when she had gone off to Broadway leaving him alone. He hadn't been able to bear it and had turned to Mayo. So vehement was he about the necessity of being with his wife all the time that the columnist asked Betty about the possibility of their pairing in a picture again. Betty replied, 'I wouldn't object if it were a good story, but I'd rather not appear in a film with Bogey. I'd like to prove to myself and others that I can go it alone.'

While Betty was tremendously excited about going abroad for the first time, Bogey was less than enthusiastic. She did all the packing, and the shopping, and the racing around; he just sat back and let it happen. Her projected image of what would occur in Paris was that Bogey would sit in the Ritz Bar all day but, if he did that she predicted, 'All he'll see of me then will be a swift gust of wind trailing after me.'

Now that she was realising another one of her ambitions, Betty was contemplating her next project. 'When we're back in Beverly Hills after our safari, we're going to have to look for a new house nearer town,' she revealed to a columnist, 'so that Stephen will have some friends of his own size and age to play with. Bogey doesn't even want to think about that, yet. But although a hilltop in Benedict Canyon was fine for the two of us, Stephen needs companionship of the youngsters he'll go to school with, and if we have another child, as we hope to, we'll need the additional space even more. As it stands now, we've got plenty of hillside, but very little house for a family.

'Before we were married, I was always an apartment girl. It took

111

me a year to find just the house I wanted and now we've got to look for another one. As a frustrated interior decorator, it's taken me a couple of houses to find out just what I like, but Bogey would much rather not hear about it. Once he's settled, he hates to pull up stakes. He can't see the shortcomings of our tiny kitchen. He's used to it, so he likes it. Once we're moved and settled again, he'll be amenable to that. Meanwhile, he'll let me do the worrying about it.

'It all goes back to the basic impulse to want your own way. Most everybody wants his own way. There are very few self-sacrificing people in the world. And those I've met bore me. He doesn't.'

Before leaving, they whizzed through the recording of thirty-eight of their *Bold Venture* radio shows in three weeks to guarantee more 'sheckels' for Stephen as Bogey described it. Their plan for the way back was to have their son flown over to meet them in London for a stay, then they would all take the *Ile de France* to New York.

A few minutes after they took off from Los Angeles International Airport to catch the *Liberté* for Europe, their son's nurse, Alyce Louise Harley, suddenly collapsed at the departure gate while holding the two-year-old in her arms. Betty's mother snatched the boy away and ran for help. The nurse had died instantly of a heart attack. Natalie took care of Stephen for the next four months while Betty and Bogey were away.

During their New York stopover, Gladys Hill interviewed them. She described how Betty was interrupted with a long-distance phone call she had placed to Stephen: 'In Lauren's conversation, the word "darling" was practically every other word. "What, darling? Yes, darling. Say that again, darling. Oh, darling ..."'

'Before Lauren hung up, Bogey made his contribution. He did not, so far as I know, address his son as "darling", although such was my amazement at hearing Humphrey Bogart reciting nursery rhymes that I couldn't be sure. Bogey and nursery rhymes would mix, you'd think, like beefsteak and chocolate sauce. But lo, as naturally as Mother Goose herself, Bogey was saying, "Baa, baa, black sheep, have you any——", then, "Simple Simon met a pie-man going to the——", then "Little Bo-peep has lost her sheep and doesn't know where to——". Soon Bogey returned to us, not looking the least sheepish, but wearing a broad grin. He

112

proudly proclaimed, "If you give him the first line or two of the nursery rhyme, he knows the rest of it. If you say it wrong, he stops you with an 'Oh, no!'"

'Taking out pictures, he said, "The image of his mother. I think Betty is beautiful. And she is also interesting looking—not a face you ever get tired of. I couldn't stand one of these Follies Girl faces ..."

'Bogey continues, "This marriage of ours is so right. The others were right, too—I mean, my previous marriages, all three of them—but things happened. They just, you might say, ran out. This marriage is, let's put it this way, *more* right. Betty's quite a gal, you know, quite a gal.

'"And it probably came—this marriage, I mean—at the right period in life for both of us. There are things I can give Betty which she would not have had otherwise and certainly there are things she can and does give me. In addition, I mean, to my son. She gave me, for instance, the hotfoot! Keeps me moving that is, mobile, alerted. I might not, as an example, have gone on this African safari, at all—probably be sitting off Catalina on my boat—if it wasn't for Betty's curiosity and sense of adventure. She has a *great* curiosity about everything in this world we live in from a dormouse to the Dark Continent. She wanted to see Africa. We're on our way to Africa.

'"Betty is the world's greatest backseat driver. She gives the orders. It takes an awful lot of time and strength to resist her which, as she's pretty capable, I do not attempt to do. ... To have found happiness in the world as it is today may be a kind of genius. My kind. I'll settle for that."' Later he added, 'Betty doesn't mind being my fourth wife. We go out more than most couples.'

The Bogarts landed in Cherbourg in March and immediately went to Paris. Betty had always wanted to see that city. French press interviews had Bogey saying, 'Betty and I always stick together. We're never apart—except for three hours she spends at the beauty parlor.'

'This is our delayed honeymoon,' Betty explained, saying that Bogey's only time spent in Europe before this was a short stint in Marseilles as a sailor in the First World War and the USO tour in the Second. 'Now he's bringing me along only to protect him from the jungle when they start shooting.'

Their suite at the elegant Ritz Hotel, they said, cost fifteen dollars a day because they were on a budget. 'I used to get forty dollars a week pocket money from Betty,' Bogey told Ken Smith, a British columnist who came to Paris to interview them, 'but she talked me out of half of that, so that our business manager would give her a full-time gardener.'

'And why not?' Betty interjected. 'Isn't he a better gardener than you? And at half the price.' Then she left the room for a few minutes.

Quickly, Bogey whispered, 'Don't tell anybody, but when I've spent my allowance, I write checks.'

To another interviewer, Betty revealed for the benefit of post-war Europeans, 'I think I've displayed a great deal of self-control in limiting myself to one coat, a dress, and a few sweaters. One can really go mad in those dress houses ...'

'And broke,' Bogey added. 'I find this a very expensive town.'

'You would,' she exclaimed. 'The way you throw around thousand-franc tips!'

They were making an issue of money because the local press had commented on his extravagant tipping. But, she admitted, she could not resist the bargains at the Flea Market. 'When I saw how inexpensive antiques were there, I really let myself go!'

While they were strolling around Paris, unrecognised for a change, Bogey kept taking pictures of Betty to send to Stephen. He told her, 'You're a Champs Elysée girl.'

When they arrived in London for his meeting with the producer, Sam Spiegel, three hundred fans were waiting on the platform at Victoria Station, and four burly policemen had to force a way through the crowd for the stars to get to their car. Wherever they went, during their fortnight's visit, admirers were close behind. The Coldstream Guards invited them to St James's Palace for cocktails and augmented the honour by asking them back for dinner.

Business matters, however, were not so agreeable. Spiegel informed Bogey that the production might have to be called off because the backers had withdrawn their financing. To save the project, Bogey invested in the film himself. And he, Hepburn and Huston deferred their salaries to take them out of the eventual profits, if any. Hepburn's only demand was that Spiegel fulfil his promise that he would pay her hotel bills. 'I don't mind doing the film for nothing,' she said, 'but I don't intend to pay money for the privilege.'

Soon the stars, Betty, the director and thirty-four British technicians departed for two months to remote areas of the Belgian Congo and Uganda to work in 'King Spiegel's Mines', as Bogey referred to the movie. Assisting them were Banyaro tribesmen who were not only helpers, but also performed as extras.

From the very start, Hepburn and Bogey acted like the characters they portrayed in the movie. In themselves, the names were allegorised personifications: Charlie Allnut was not quite all nutty, but looked at life through decidedly bloodshot eyes; Rose Sayer was a forthright sayer of truths concerning other people's rosy philosophies. When Hepburn—in real life—told Bogey her opinion of his drinking habits, he listened patiently, then told her to get a seat for him and pour the drinks. To his surprise, his brusqueness worked and Hepburn did as she was told.

'Kate talks a blue streak,' he revealed later. 'We listened for the first couple of days when she hit Africa and then began asking ourselves, "How affected can you be in the middle of Africa?" She used to say that everything was "divine". The goddam stinking natives were divine. "Oh, what a *divine* native," she'd say. "Oh, what a *divine* pile of manure!" You had to ask yourself, "Is this really the dame or is this something left over from *Woman of the Year*?"

'She does pretty much as she goddam pleases,' he laughed as he shook his head and continued to pay her his own peculiar form of tribute. 'She came in lugging a full-length mirror and a flock of toothbrushes. She brushed her teeth all the time and she habitually takes about four or five baths a day. She talks at you as though you were a microphone. I guess she was nervous, though, and scared of John and me. She lectured the hell out of us on temperance and the evils of drinking.

'She's actually kind of sweet and lovable, though, and she's absolutely honest and absolutely fair about her work. None of this late on the set or demanding close-ups or any of that kind of thing. She doesn't give a damn how she looks. She doesn't have to be waited on, either. You never pull up a chair for Kate. You tell her, "Kate, pull me up a chair, will ya, and while you're at it get one for yourself." I don't think she tries to be a character. I think she is one.'

In *King Rebel*, Huston said, 'For the film's early sequences, a camp had been built on the banks of the Ruiki, complete with bucket-showers and bamboo dining room. Lauren Bacall was the company cook, declaring herself an expert on python soup (which Bogey did not think was funny).'

A terrifying incident occurred that caused Huston to alter his intention of shooting a major part of the film in that sector of the Congo. While nearly everyone in camp was asleep one night, suddenly the torch-bearing natives began to howl.

'We were in our hut,' Betty recalled, 'and Bogey started to get out of bed. He put his foot on the ground and felt something moving; he slapped at his pajamas—and I could see that the floor of our hut was alive with ants. Since the legs of our bed stood in cans of kerosene, we were safe for the moment, but it was a ghastly feeling.'

The camp was in the path of an army of safari ants then devastating the countryside—a very real threat to everyone because of being meat eaters. Only fire could stop them. When Bogey began yelling orders to natives who were trying to burn out an attacking column, Hepburn came out of her quarters to reprimand him for carousing. His succinct reply was, 'Katie, old girl, ants.' The cast and crew were forced on to an old sidewheel paddleboat to avoid the possibility of being maimed by the insects.

After they moved to another jungle location, the boat developed a leak and went under, but, luckily, nobody was drowned. The natives worked five days to raise it, and then the English engineer who had kept the motor going just upped and quit. Huston took the crisis as a challenge, while Bogey celebrated the time off at least until he ran out of Scotch. Drink was his and Betty's way of protecting against the dysentery that beset everybody else in the production sooner or later. The Bogarts even brushed their teeth with Scotch.

Whenever Hepburn was not busy filming, she would use her time as efficiently as a schoolteacher on a cultural tour. Often she would venture into the jungle, protected by a couple of members of the crew, to seek out statuary and crafts from nearby villages. On days not spent in educational exploit, she would exercise by playing tennis with Betty. Because Betty preferred wearing tennis shorts, rather than slacks like Hepburn, the natives named her, 'Lady with a Two-piece'.

Throughout the gruelling shooting, Bogey worked and drank with equal intensity. All the while he complained about adverse conditions and Hepburn's 'damn cheerfulness'. After a few weeks, however, the actress's serenity succumbed to the rampage of illness that attacked not only her, but also most of the technical crew. Having fought sun, heat, jungle, insects and wildlife, the company finally surrendered to microbes and withdrew to London for the completion of the film.

As usual, Bogey thrived on constant arguments. Although Hepburn's moralistic outbursts may have antagonised him, he appreciated her restlessness as a show of strength. The attacks on his boozing may have been a reflection of her frustration with Spencer Tracey's imbibing. The admiration that Hepburn and Bogey had for Tracy, however, gave them a bond. Bogey thought Tracy was second only to himself as the best actor in movies. Tracy would say that he himself came first and Bogey was the runner-up. The interplay between Hepburn and Bogey, according to Huston, resulted in a picture 'better than we had written it, as human, as comprehending as we had any right to expect from any two actors'.

The ultimate recognition of Bogey's performance—and of his thirty years as an actor—came when he received the 1951 Academy Award. His competition was Marlon Brando for *A Streetcar Named Desire* and Montgomery Clift for *A Place in the Sun*, the leading exponents of the Method style of acting that was to influence the cinema for the next generation. Bogey did not believe he stood a chance of winning against these two.

When Bogey was named as the award winner, Betty let out a yell that resounded throughout the Pantages Theater. Giving Bogey a powerful shove, she shouted, 'It's you! Get up there and get it.' With the golden sceptre in his hands at last, he forgot the remark he was going to make. All he could do was turn to the audience and show how moved the unexpected victory had made him by delivering a simple thanks in a voice shaking with emotion. In the wings, he regained his composure and denied the validity of the award, calling it 'pure bunk' and claiming, 'You'd have to let all the candidates play the same role—then judge.'

Appropriately enough for the reigning monarch of Hollywood, the celebration afterwards was in the Crown Room of Romanoff's, and once again he received the accolades of his friends with understated gratitude. Later, he vowed he would never go after another award because an actor can ruin his career looking for a role of importance instead of just settling for 'meat and potatoes'. True to that limited objective, he played a righteous editor named Ed in his next project, *Deadline—USA.*

Betty continued to settle for her domestic role and did an encore in the maternity ward. Bogey's immediate reaction to her announcement of an expected second child was that he did not mind in the least. 'If you guarantee another one like Stephen,' he added.

Their daughter was born August 22, 1952.

'That night Bogey drove me to the hospital trying to look very casual, an old hand at it. Kind of nervous, though. A floor-pacer. But not for long. I have 'em like an Indian has 'em; just drop 'em,' Betty said, paraphrasing Bogey's dictum of the ideal birth. 'Two hours in labor,' she added. 'A breeze.'

'Before she was born, I don't think Bogey cared much which—boy or girl. Unless maybe he had a secret feeling that, with Steve and me so very close, he and a little girl might also be....

'Bogey had the baby christened Leslie, by the way—for Leslie Howard. They were together, you know, in *Petrified Forest.* They went through hell, of one kind or another, together. They were very close. I'd thought of naming the baby Tracy, if a girl. But Bogey very definitely thought of Leslie. That this is her name means something pretty special to him.'

'If it hadn't been for Leslie Howard,' Bogey explained, 'I might still be making up in New York dressing rooms. It's not for nothing my daughter is named Leslie.' The thought that he might have remained a stage actor did not appeal to Bogey because he felt that such a dedication demanded too great a sacrifice and offered no security. 'The Theatre doesn't support its people,' he would say.

A few weeks before Leslie was born, an article appeared in *The Saturday Evening Post* that reiterated Betty's determination to get a new home in town now that they had returned from Europe. 'I spent three years on that so-and-so yacht of his. I had to have

118

my first baby to escape. Now I'm pregnant again and we have got to get away from this mountain.'

Bogey resisted the move even though he realised that Betty didn't like living in the country but wanted rather to be right in the middle of everything. She kept complaining to him, 'There's no one around here for our son to play with, and you've got to watch him all the time or he'll run down the hill.'

It took an avalanche to finally convince Bogey that she might be right about the move. One night a torrential rain caused tons of mud and rocks to block the road and prevent Bogey from returning home. When he phoned Betty from a Beverly Hills bar to ask if all was well, she blew up and told him what she thought of the situation. At last, he admitted that they should be closer to town.

Soon they were living on Mapleton Drive in Holmby Hills, a suburb so posh that Bogey had once sworn he would never make his home there. He refused to have anything to do with the actual move and stayed away until it was over. Sidney Skolsky summed up the sumptuousness of their eleven-room, whitewashed, brick house by writing, 'She loves luxury.'

Betty crowed about her victory by admitting, 'Any house I've wanted, whether Bogey wanted it or not, whether he thought he could afford it or not, I've had. Take our home now, which we bought last June. Bogey didn't really want this house; didn't want to move from the little farmhouse we called home in Benedict Canyon. But while I was pregnant with Leslie, a new house, I told Bogey, was one of my pre-natal cravings. What, against such female-of-the-species tactics, could the poor guy do but just what he did do. It's a pretty big house and Bogey is well content in the eight-by-twelve cabin of his fifty-five-foot yawl. The house is of French Colonial architecture—and a mast against the sky is the only architecture that sends Bogey.' It has a swimming pool, in which he doesn't swim, a tennis court on which he doesn't play. It's pretty beautiful—and he's just as happy about it, and in it as ...' she laughed, 'as I am.'

Bogey's first reaction to the house after he had walked through it briefly was, 'Pretty big, isn't it?' Her explanation that it was great for a growing family drew the response that he did not intend to have any more children. The size of the house meant, he felt, that they would not have the money to decorate it properly. Despite her promise to use most of the furniture they already had and to do a room at a time when they could afford it, he called the place, 'Bacall's Folly'.

The view Mike Romanoff expressed to Ezra Goodman about Bogey's penury regarding their new home was, 'After Bogey began to earn large money, the fear of not having it worried him. The idea of buying a hundred-and-sixty-thousand-dollar house became a tremendous mental hazard.'

After some time, Betty came to understand Bogey's concern about money and thought it had to do with the realisation of his own mortality. 'When you have children you stop thinking of yourself,' she explained, 'and gradually the idea of security, security for the children comes to the fore. Bogey is now terribly conscious about having something to leave his children. I don't mean he wants to leave them a million dollars or anything like that. But in case anything should happen to us, he wants them taken care of. I also think he wants terribly much to have them, when they grow up, to be proud of his work.

'I guess maybe after another five years he'll call it quits. He'll be past sixty by then. But who knows? All I do know is that he's a wonderful and stimulating guy to live with.'

(*Inset*) Bogey. *Camera Press*

Bacall. *Camera Press. By Karsh of Ottawa*

(*Top*) Bacall's film debut opposite Bogey in
To Have and Have Not (1944). *Ronald Grant
collection/Warner Bros*

Confidential Agent (1945) with Charles Boyer.
Ronald Grant collection/Warner Bros

*(Top) The Big Sleep (1946). Ronald Grant
collection/Warner Bros*

*Dark Passage (1947). Ronald Grant collection/
Warner Bros*

(*Top*) *Key Largo* (1948). *Ronald Grant collection/Warner Bros*

(*Inset*) Bogey and Betty as they appeared in *Key Largo* (1948). *Camera Press*

Bright Leaf (1950) with Gary Cooper. *Ronald Grant collection/Warner Bros*

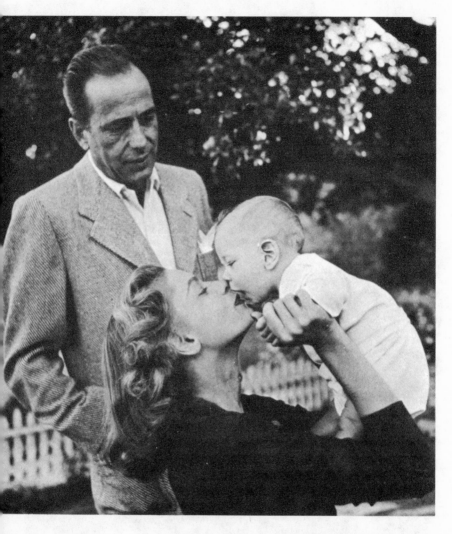

Mother and father with their first child,
Stephen. *Popperfoto*

How to Marry a Millionaire (1953). Cameron
Mitchell, Marilyn Monroe, Betty Grable and
Lauren Bacall. *Ronald Grant collection/20th
Century-Fox*

(*Top*) *Young Man with a Horn* (1950) starred
Doris Day, Kirk Douglas and Bacall. *Ronald
Grant collection/Warner Bros*

Winning an Oscar was child's play for Bogey
in 1952 for his part in *The African Queen*.
Popperfoto

(*Top*) Two-and-a-half-year-old Stephen takes a dislike to stubble-cheeked Bogey. *Keystone Press*

(*Right*) 'Poison Paradise' was how Katharine Hepburn described the Congo when she returned with Betty and Bogey from filming *The African Queen. Popperfoto*

(*Top*) Bogey and Betty were in the forefront
of the protest against the investigations of the
Un-American Activities Committee, 1947.
Popperfoto

In defence of a Panda—the toy which
involved Bogey in a legal action. He was
found not guilty of injuring fashion model
Robin Roberts. *Keystone Press*

(*Top*) Mr and Mrs Bogart switched from
Eisenhower to Stevenson for the Presidency,
1952. *Popperfoto*

Speeches and smiles, 1953. *Syndication
International*

The Bogart family was made complete when Leslie came along. *Syndication International*

The very relaxed Mr Bogart. *Syndication International*

Betty and Marilyn—beguiling
Bacall and marvellous Monroe.
Keystone Press

A couple of pals—Judy Garland
and Humphrey Bogart. *Keystone
Press*

A stroll in Portofino for the
Bogarts. Bogey was there to make
The Barefoot Contessa with Ava
Gardner (also in picture). *Keystone
Press*

A few days' holiday in Venice, 1954. *Keystone Press*

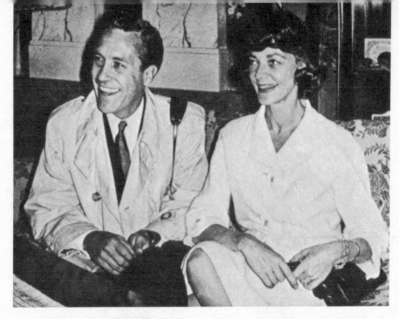

Widowed in 1957, Betty finally found a new man for her life: Jason Robards, Jnr, leading American actor. *Camera Press*

In London for *Applause*, Betty meets up with her eldest son Stephen and his wife Dale. Sam is on the right. *Syndication International*

Betty and her twelve-year-old son, Sam, the child of her marriage to Robards. *Syndication International*

op) Lauren and Leslie, 1968.
ystone Press

Bogey's influence continued to
spread after his death. Ringo Starr
is only one of his fans. *Camera
Press*

Lauren Bacall and Ingrid
Bergman in *Murder on the Orient
Express* (1974). *Syndication
International*

We're No Angels

A Star is Born was being made into a musical at Warner's in 1953 with the hope that the film would result in a rebirth of Judy Garland's stardom. The director was George Cukor, who did the original *What Price Hollywood?* two decades earlier. This time the movie would be a multi-million-dollar, three-hour monument to filmdom. The script was written by Moss Hart—the man who had told Betty to quit at the start of her career because, in his view, she would never be able to top herself after *her* star was born.

In *My First Hundred Years in Hollywood*, Jack Warner describes an incident that occurred when he tried to interfere in the casting of the male lead for the film. He had a brainstorm about who should play the part and called in the producer, Sid Luft, Judy's husband at the time. Without much fanfare, Warner announced that the actor he thought would be ideal for Norman Main was Humphrey Bogart.

Luft's reaction was decidedly negative. He wanted James Mason for the role and would accept no one else, not even—or especially— a star of Bogey's magnitude. Since Luft had Judy completely under his control and threatened to take her out of the movie if he did not get his way, Warner was forced to withdraw his suggestion and Bogey did not play the part that he had always felt was his real-life destiny.

By turning down Bogey for the picture, Luft betrayed the

pledge 'Never Rat on a Rat' that he had taken on the formation of the Rat Pack. Over a number of years, in addition to congregating for lunch in Bogey's booth at Romanoff's, his buddies would meet with him on an average of two or three evenings a week in an upstairs room of the restaurant or at his new Holmby Hills house. Beside the Bogarts and Romanoff, the regulars were Judy and Luft, Frank Sinatra, David and Hjordis Niven, Irving Lazar and James Van Heusen. One night, on seeing the entire modish yet motley crew gathered together at Romanoff's, Betty commented, 'I see the rat pack is all here.'

Being called the Rat Pack—or more specifically, the Holmby Hills Rat Pack—added to everyone's spirit of mischief as the evening progressed. Though Betty was given credit for coming up with the name, it was a variation on a description Bogey originated for another group with which he was associated. 'Just to keep the record clean,' he explained, 'I own one of those English racing cars, a Jaguar. Gary Cooper has one. Gable, Dick Powell, Al Jolson had one and so did Ray Milland until his back gave out. "The Middle-Aged Hot Rodders", we called ourselves or—another name, and I coined it—the "Beverly Hills Rat Traps".'

The next day an edict was issued to the newspapers officially announcing the existence of the organisation and naming Frank Sinatra, pack master; Judy Garland, first vice president; Sid Luft, cage master; Irving Lazar, recording secretary and treasurer. While Betty was den mother and Bogey only the rat in charge of public relations, it was understood that these two were the centre of all activities. The purpose of the Rat Pack, Bogey declared, was 'the relief of boredom and the perpetuation of independence. We admire ourselves and don't care for anyone else.'

What had been an informal gathering of night revellers surrounding Bogey soon became an organised band of favourites of the god. By declaring themselves a specific entity, they loved each other more for being so special, and their exclusiveness made them instant aristocracy. This self-proclaimed elitism, which they took with mock-seriousness, entitled them to membership in a crusade for pleasure.

The camaraderie expressed itself from dusk to dawn several nights a week in gatherings that made a ritual of the fun of drinking, talking and singing, occasionally interrupted by an argument or a fight that was quickly settled. Nothing was allowed to interfere with their determination to have the best time possible, except the obligations of work which, in turn, gave them the means and the need to continue this round. Reports of this enviable glamour-status club—unlike the forbidden orgies of early Hollywood or the forbidding snobbism of the Pickfair, San Simeon or English sets—appealed to the public of the ambitious fifties, and the Rat Pack was on its way to becoming a popular legend.

'Personal to LAUREN BACALL and others of the Holmby Hills Rat Pack' was the headline of Louella Parsons' column criticising their 'cute little group'. Annoyed because another columnist had scooped her on the announcement of the club's inception, she used a pretext to write: 'The very newspaper edition that carried your quotes, Baby, on your gang and how you are all having sweaters made up with rats on the back, was filled with a tragic story about a juvenile gang war in Los Angeles. Several teenage boys were stabbed. Eleven of them were arrested and turned over to juvenile authorities.

'So I am sure you can see my point, that it was a little shocking to turn over a few pages and read your facetious comments about your "adult delinquent" gang—even if it was all in fun.

'I am fully aware that you and your good pals meet only for social events or gay week-end expeditions to Sinatra's house in Palm Springs or to Las Vegas. It would all be very funny if it weren't for the fact that so many teenagers take everything done by movie stars with dead seriousness.

'And, believe me, there is *nothing funny* about juvenile gangs!

'If you and the other Rat Packers want to keep on with your harmless gang, it's all right. But I wouldn't give out any more publicity on it as something "cute" or "funny".

'You and Bogey and Frank and Judy and Sid are big kids now for such nonsense.'

Those sour grapes were mild compared to the Sour Apple Award of the Hollywood Women's Press Club that Bogey won as the Most Unco-operative Actor in 1952. But he found those bitter fruits easy to swallow for the very reason that they were given to him: his lofty position.

In the seven years since Betty had almost received the same citation, she had become more co-operative with the press to keep her name, if not her career, alive. Her success as a wife and failure as an actress were explored in soul-searching stories. Just when it seemed that none of those angles had been left unturned, a new development gave the Bacall publicity ball a push in a fresh direction.

Betty now signed her first contract since leaving Warner's three years before. It was with Twentieth Century Fox and they were paying her two thousand dollars a week to co-star with Marilyn Monroe and Betty Grable in *How to Marry a Millionaire*. In addition to the all-star cast, the film was newsworthy because it was the first film made in Cinemascope, although *The Robe*, completed later, was the initial one released in this wide-screen process.

Annoyed at being compared with Sinatra who had made his first film in a long time, *From Here to Eternity*, a year before, Betty told Sidney Skolsky, 'In this town if you go to Catalina after finishing a picture, your return is hailed as a try at a comeback.

'After *Bright Leaf* I took time off to have our second child and to take the stump in the presidential campaign. Now at my age [thirty], I'm making a comeback? Believe me, I've never been away—unless you count the times I've wished I could live in New York.'

In a bid for sympathy, she confessed to other reporters, 'My career has been funny. It got a lot of publicity at first. My second picture was the biggest flop and for some reason they blamed me. Ever since I've been trying to get back up.

'I've always wanted to work, but some subversive character got the word around that I didn't want to.' Then to make herself more desirable, she explained, 'I always had offers. Either for crummy pictures I didn't want to do, or else they wanted me to play heavies. I don't think I'm the heavy type. Really I don't.

'It's hard to say what brought about the rebirth of my career. Certainly timing has a lot to do with anyone's success. And the element of getting older and maturing is a factor. There's no doubt that I'm a better actress than I used to be, which is not saying much.

'It's not because I kept busy acting because I didn't. But I think radio had a lot to do with it. Bogey and I did a series and I learned a great deal.'

The need to resume her career was intensified, according to her friends, when she realised that Bogey would be away much of the time and she could not always leave the children for long periods in order to go along with him. His projected schedule for the next few years had become heavier since winning the Oscar. Some of his pictures were to be made abroad, a tactic that was becoming increasingly popular with producers to save on costs and taxes while enhancing production values with authentic backgrounds. Working on his own productions as well as percentage deals meant that he had to be concerned for the box-office and available for promotional tours. Since Bogey was entirely involved in going from one picture to another, Betty had either to accept being an accessory to his activities or to decide to revive her own professional life in whatever manner possible and proper. Not only was her status as an actress at stake, but also her standing as an individual, a spouse with spirit of her own.

The last time Betty had been off the screen for a while, she had returned in a film she had been insisting she wanted to do for two years, *Young Man with a Horn*. Once again, after a long lay off, she chose her own property and worked on seeing it realised. Like many a tempting movie morsel who became aware her seductive-ness was going stale, Betty decided that her hardening crust would seem crisp in a hot comedy. The physical allure was transformed to an appeal of the mind through wit. When she heard that her friend Nunnally Johnson was looking for a funny film to produce, she suggested an adaptation of Zoë Aikens's *The Greeks Had a Word for It*, a thirties film that had starred Ina Claire and Lilyan Tashman. Just one third of that story went into the new movie. An equal amount came from a recent unsuccessful play called *Loco*, and Nunnally Johnson supplied the rest. In piecing the picture together, he even had to purchase the title. The results made Betty hope that her ambition of being like Lombard might be realised. 'If I don't go over in this,' she declared, 'I'll give up because I don't think I could find a better part.'

A 'fat diet' was necessary for Betty so that she would not look too gaunt next to Grable and Monroe who in turn, according to publicity releases, took off some poundage in order not to appear too curvaceous in Cinemascope. The return to work resulted in another kind of loss that gave Betty great satisfaction. 'As I walked toward the stage that first day, I could sense the old feeling taking hold of me,' she described. 'I actually thought I was going to have a stroke. But the instant I put my hand on the door to open it, the quivering legs were suddenly steady and all the old fright fell away forever like an old coat I'd never wear again.

'Since then I've tried to figure out what happened and why. Could it be because I'm older? Has some magic change been taking place inside my mind that I haven't even known about? Or aren't we meant to understand how we grow and develop and mature. But perhaps it's enough to say that I'm thankful the miracle has happened to me and that I'll never go through the old panic anymore.' Contentment with her new contract was given as another reason for her increased sense of security.

Unglamorous though it was, Betty asked the studio to put a refrigerator in her dressing room so she could bring sandwiches and salads from home every day. She preferred to lie down during her lunch hour, eating, reading or napping. Such details about her were being circulated in the press again, and Sidney Skolsky reconfirmed her importance by publishing, 'She sleeps in pajamas or nothing in an oversized bed. Avoids fresh air. A firm believer in pillow talk.'

During the making of Betty's film, Bogey was filming *Beat the Devil* in Italy. This was the first time he had left her alone for a lengthy period. The separation lasted a long four and a half months as her studio was taking time in experimenting with the use of Cinemascope for intimate scenes. 'He didn't like my staying in California, working on my picture, while he was in Europe working on his,' she recounted. 'I think Bogey would be very happy if I didn't work. Just stayed at home all the time. Or made a home whithersoever he might be. As when I traipsed along to Africa, made *The African Queen* safari with him, washed his clothes, cooked for the cast and crew. This suited Bogey down to the last tsetse fly. He was prouder of me then, this I know, than he ever is when he sees me on the screen. I was in a woman's place, wasn't I?'

Her recollection of Bogey's behaviour while they were apart differs from his. 'He *loathes* writing, can't bear to write a letter,' she said, and explained that, in his view, it would be too conventional to do so, but he *was* concerned enough to write occasionally and to make phone calls. Her version of a typical call went like this:

' "Hello, honey, how are you?" he would start.

126

' "I'm fine."
' "How are the kids?"
' "They're fine."
' "I miss you," he would inevitably say.
' "I miss *you*." '

Laughing about the conversation, she told a reporter, 'At home such a brilliant interchange would drive Bogey out into the night. But when he's not at home and I am, anything, I take it, is better than nothing.'

As Bogey recounted it, he was not as tender and was remiss in contacting her. 'When I went to Italy, I left Miss Bacall in Hollywood starting in the movie,' he said. 'She hadn't heard from me in months. "What happened?" she cabled. "Are you all right?"

'The reason I hadn't written or phoned is that it takes a letter written in Novello a week to leave Italy, let alone to get to California. And, to phone, it's necessary to stand in the lobby of the hotel and scream, "*Pronto, pronto*", at the top of your lungs into the phone for a half hour. After operators half way across the world echo, "*Pronto*", you finally get a connection. Everybody hears everybody's business in Italy.'

The habit of conveying facts in different ways gave the Bogarts, like others in Hollywood, a Pirandello quality which often made any claim questionable. They followed a specific line of image-building when divulging basic information in interviews. Details, though, were manipulated for effect. All their self-exposure for publication did, however, unconsciously reveal some measure of wish fulfilment—whether expressed in self-abnegation or self-glorification. So while not every fact may be verifiable, the accumulation of material in print did express their motivation. In the future, looking back at what had happened at that time, distortions would prevail for the sake of preserving a memory in a way that would have significance for the person they had become. Originally, publicity men may have been responsible for many irresponsible statements the Bogarts were supposed to have made. But the couple did have the ultimate authority over what was given out for publication. And they did not make an issue of refuting questionable quotes. This was particularly disconcerting for the public to whom the Bogarts were such self-proclaimed champions of veracity. Yet their silence at such times spoke for them.

'Bogey has a theory: the most important thing in the world is to tell the truth,' she would say. 'And that no matter what the reaction, it made no difference. At least he's been honest. He's told the truth. I go along with that up to a point, not *his* point.

'My husband has a habit of getting right to the heart of the matter with one salty, honest, devastating crack. This doesn't sit well with lots of people. The truth hurts them. When I call Bogey on this tactic, his invariable answer is, "Well, it's the truth, isn't it?"

'"I don't care if it's the truth or not," I say. "You don't have to tell the truth. Everyone isn't interested in hearing the truth. As a matter of fact few people are. If they ask you for the truth, then tell them. Otherwise, don't." But Bogey's a man of enormous integrity and when he feels he's right in principle you can't argue him out of it.'

Despite such proclamations, Bogey put out, within a few weeks of each other, two versions of how *Beat the Devil* was first conceived as a movie property. In September 1953 he wrote in *Look* magazine, 'Somebody lent me a novel called *Beat the Devil*. I told Huston he was sure to like it.' By November 28 that year, he was by-lining an article for publication in which he said, 'John tossed a book over to me, "We might make a picture of this."' Considering the results, no wonder Bogey changed his mind about who was responsible for originating the film.

An irrefutable truth was used as a joke in Betty's new movie. In reply to William Powell's protests of being too old for her, she, as a fortune hunter, tries to convince him that she prefers more mature men. She lists some examples of the venerable whom she admires, concluding with, 'and what's his name, that old fellow in *The African Queen*'.

This interchange between fact and fiction continued into a feature story she wrote for *Look* to account for her taste in men while promoting her film. The caption in red type boldly proclaimed 'I Hate Young Men'. Betty revealed why men over forty were so captivating to her and the reasons why their juniors could not compete.

The list of men she liked best contained older ones exclusively because, Betty explained, 'I must have been born too late, or they were born too early, or my nose was to the grindstone too young in my life and I missed some of the good ones, but I find that the men alive in the world today that capture my imagination most were all born at the turn of the century.' She did not include any actors among her choices because they were on too many other lists and she thought she would look in different areas. 'Besides, this will keep peace in my house and keep Bogart from turning into Bogart.' Her preferences were based on the qualities she looked for most in a man: eyes that seem honest, imagination to prevent boredom, a sense of humour, humility and dignity.

With those traits as her criteria, she named as her favourites: Adlai Stevenson for being the politest person she knew; Robert Sherwood for making her feel good; Nunnally Johnson, her best friend, for his wit; Alastair Cooke for being an Englishman; Louis Bromfield for his courage, and John Huston for living the life many people would like to live and cannot. All these men, for her, had character, creativity, concern and non-conformity in common. Betty's summation was that in the battle of the sexes men lost the war because 'there were too few like these'.

The article was so widely discussed that years later Ezra Goodman reminded Mike Romanoff of it during his interview for *Time*. The restaurateur revealed that Betty did not know any of the six men she mentioned very well. What motivated her, he said, was that she 'loves to pass as an intellectual, knowing politics and literature. She's taken on a certain color from Bogey. It is feminine aggressiveness in a pleasant way, the feminine counterpart of his aggressiveness.'

The opinion of this friend who knew her well was that the closeness Betty was able to enjoy with Adlai Stevenson prompted her to work for him. The intimacy was more important than the issues he stood for because it satisfied her need to be a public figure.

Her activity on Stevenson's behalf during the 1952 presidential campaign began a few months before the birth of Leslie. Impressed by his speech on accepting the nomination, she immediately volunteered to make appearances for him. Originally she, like Bogey, had been for Eisenhower. Once she made the switch, she placed Stevenson literature around the house to pique Bogey's curiosity. Gradually, through her manœuvring, he became interested in the Democratic candidate, even though liberalism was then considered dangerous among people of his echelon in Hollywood. Bogey's total conversion came when Betty, without as much as a by-your-leave, prepared to travel to San Francisco for a Stevenson rally. Angry at first because she had not asked his permission to go, Bogey relented on seeing his pregnant wife packing to leave. He decided to join her and embrace her cause.

Age and marriage were the two topics they were continually asked to pontificate on for publicity purposes. Such pomposity— they had more interests, and were more interesting, than just those two subjects—could well have inspired them, using their sense of humour and sharp perspective on matters, to synthesise all the banality into one of their fun home movies.

The opening of such a factual film would have Betty setting the tone by showing off her home and stating, 'My advice for would-be wives is to marry a man a few years older. And not because women are supposed to mature earlier either.

'I don't think they do and, for this reason, successful marriages call for a lot of patience on the part of the husband. Couples the same age are too evenly matched. Unless they absolutely adore doing a number of things together, they'll have a tough time of it.'

Juxtapose this with a contrary interview showing Betty on the go while recanting: 'Bogey doesn't have the interests I have—going places, travelling, meeting new people. He's definitely content to live in his home or live on his boat. That's not for me. He says I was great and did everything he wanted until I got him in my clutches.'

Abrupt cut to Betty standing over Bogey who is snoozing on the lounger beside the swimming pool. She complains that she married him at a difficult time, when he had given up golf because he felt he was as good as he would ever be—and it offered him no challenge. She admits that for three years she has tried unsuccessfully to make him take up the sport again and concludes with, 'I realized very early in the game that I can never change him, that a wife has to make most of the adjustments in a marriage, especially to an older man.' Betty dives into the pool.

Dolly in on Bogey who awakes and says, 'You can enjoy life no matter how old you are. I'm not a flaming youth any more. I'm irritable and I'm not an easy man to handle and I'm grateful for the wonderful job Miss Bacall has done handling me.' As Betty submerges Bette Davis emerges and he tells her he would rather spend a week with Betty 'than a lifetime with any other woman'.

Now Davis goes under and Betty comes out to caress Bogey and state, 'If I'd married a younger man, he wouldn't have put up with me. I'd have probably killed him—or we'd have killed each other.'

Wipe to a series of other situations in which Betty continues to fondle Bogey while speaking without a break: 'It often amuses me, and always annoys me when people speak, as they do about the girl who marries an "older man". The inference being heartfelt pity for the poor young thing ... Nuts! It's the other way around. Tell you why, I'm no bed of roses—I get all steamed up about things, imbued with ideas.

'Now, although he'd rather have me with him, he goes off on the boat weekends with the guys, while I stay at home, where I want to be, play with the kids, play tennis. Bat the ball around with James Mason, Stewart Granger and Jean Simmons—lots of tennis people about. I don't know how he puts up with me.'

Quick cut to Betty and Bogey shouting at each other. They suddenly stop and she turns to camera to explain, 'My husband loves to argue, but won't allow himself to be drawn into controversy simply for the sake of arguing. He and I don't have arguments; we have discussions.' A usual harbinger of a stormy session, she admits, is his prefacing a statement with 'Look here' and starting to sound like Bogey of the movies.

Zoom in on Bogey as he takes over the scene to explain, 'Actors and actresses have a hard time staying married to each other. Their differences usually develop into something more intense than they started out to be. You find you are playing a dramatic scene. And some of the arguments I've had in my time in married life have gone on long after either of us remembered what the tiff was about.'

Trucking shot following Bogey as he crosses over desk to write an article entitled 'Life Begins at 40'. He turns to camera and elucidates that as a paragon of fifties' fulfilment—family, fortune, fame and friends—he has the right to advise anyone approaching middle age. According to his beliefs, there are four reasons why the mature is preferred as a lover. First, he is more experienced, knows more, has seen and read more. Second, he knows how to court a woman. Third, he is not as fickle as his juniors. Fourth, he offers security of character. Most women prefer a man they have confidence in, he says, to one who merely amuses them. As proof, he quotes John Adams's comment on Ben Franklin, 'At the age of seventy-odd, Franklin had neither lost his love of beauty or his taste for it.' His final conclusion, as the film ends in a clinch with Betty, is, 'The young romantic is over-confident, over-eager and over-stimulated.'

Over-anxious himself to have Betty join him in Rome during the shooting of *Beat the Devil*, Bogey sent Darryl F. Zanuck cables that indicated his fury. 'You've had her long enough,' he wrote. 'I demand that you release her.' The minute her film was completed, Betty rushed over for the last month of production. Earl Wilson recalled the statement Bogey had made before he went to Italy about movie stars who are supposed to fall in love with their leading men and the actor wound up with, 'So maybe Miss Bacall will be coming over there sooner than expected.' The columnist now kidded about her rush to get there as quickly as she could. 'She has the right idea,' he wrote. 'Never leave the bums out of your sight!'

Always ready to provoke controversy, Bogey at first paid his co-star Gina Lollobrigida the compliment, 'She makes Marilyn Monroe look like Shirley Temple.' Then he shocked Italians by saying that Betty, despite her angularity, had it all over Gina and her curves when it really came to being a woman.

Part of the film had been made in London and while there without Betty, Bogey had surrounded himself by the very type of person he disliked most: freeloaders. Because he was lonely and, above all, hated to eat by himself, he had not minded paying for the attention of spongers. Their numbers, according to reports Betty heard, 'equalled the cast of a DeMille epic'.

A London paper told how reluctantly Bogey played at being a roué while he was there. Alone with a friend, Bogey had asked, 'Do you know a pretty doll I could take to dinner tonight? I need some diversion.'

A name was mentioned and Bogey's response was, 'Not that one. She likes older men.'

So his friend suggested someone else and this time the actor replied, 'Not that one. She's an actress and I hate actresses. Always wanting to talk about their goddam careers.'

The result, predictably enough, was that Bogey took no one out and phoned some newly acquired pals to play poker instead. And while the game was going on, he found the time to call Betty in Hollywood.

The only lasting friend he made during the filming was Truman Capote. The writer, who collaborated on the script with Huston, surprised Bogey by besting him in Indian wrestling. Capote's wit was also disarming. When Betty arrived, she, too, became fascinated with Capote and Bogey was proud of the way they got along together.

The film itself was a loser. Starting with an inept melodramatic script, Huston had had to call in Capote to make the shortcomings of the plot seem intentional by turning it into a satire. Before shooting began, Bogey had been in a car accident. Once again the focus of his injury was oral. He had to have his tongue stitched together and his teeth fixed. The disaster of the film, however, made the profits he expected from the four hundred thousand dollars he invested seem questionable. If anyone asked him what he thought about *Beat the Devil* after it became a pseudo-intellectual cult movie, he would answer, 'Only phonies think it's funny!'

Jack Warner's explanation for the cataclysmic results was, 'I think they shot it through beer-bottle glass instead of lenses.'

Bogey redeemed himself with some of his fans later that year by doing *The Caine Mutiny*. Although he earned himself an Academy Award nomination for his Captain Queeg, he was quoted as saying, 'I don't think *The Caine Mutiny* is so hot. They added too much of a pointless love story to it.'

For the location shots on that film, Betty tagged along and took Stephen. 'When we went to Pearl Harbor,' she recalled, 'more than one gossip columnist hinted at how many times Bogey would be thrown out of Hawaiian bars. They were wrong. When he wasn't before the cameras, he was at the beach with his family, teaching young Steve, our five-year-old son, to swim.'

Betty gave her own interpretation of Tolstoy's 'Happy families are all alike' by stating, 'Our home is no different from any other when it comes to recognizing father as lord of the manor. When Bogey's away, I tell Steve I'm the boss, but that Daddy will take over again when he gets back. So what happens? Humphrey comes home and Steve asks him if he can do or have something, intent on getting a definite decision from the boss. He gets confused when father says he'd better ask mother.

'Humphrey never visibly succumbs to any female's charms, with the exception of our daughter, Leslie. Her father—who was never one for holding Steve on his knee and left that sort of thing to me for the first couple of years—hovers around her, ready to interpret her slightest wish as a command.

'Leslie's like me—she has a good sense of humor. I'd say that's an important ingredient of a successful marriage. It works when all else fails.'

Bogey expressed a dislike for men who never cut loose from their mothers' apron strings, probably because of his lack of love for—and from—his own mother. A contradiction was that one of his best friends, Clifton Webb, was never without his mother. Yet Bogey declared, 'You should treat kids like birds. When they can fly, push them out of the nest and let them go it alone.'

Betty observed, 'However, I have noticed him regarding our daughter with a faraway look in his eyes and I have an idea that this is one bird whose wings would get clipped if she tries to fly too early.'

Always protective toward Leslie, he would often side with her when there were disagreements between her and Stephen. He did not believe in coddling the boy and he would try his best not to seem menacing. 'I saw Bogey cry,' Betty recalled, 'when he first saw Stephen in his schoolroom. I think the impact of fatherhood had caught up with him.'

Yet Bogey refused to give in totally to fatherly sentiment. 'He claims to be above the usual clichés of parenthood,' Betty said. For Stephen's first Christmas, they had him posed for their greeting card picture holding a bottle of Scotch as big as himself.

'Once Bogey was invited to attend the Christmas play at Stephen's school,' Betty remembered. 'He erupted violently. "Not on your life!" he shouted emphatically. "Why should I get hooked into some dull affair with a lot of brats? Just because I was foolish enough to get involved in a family, that doesn't mean I'm going to have my life dictated for me." He went to the performance. And he had a great time, though he would never admit it.'

The attempt to be casual with Stephen disguised Bogey's genuine concern for the child. When Steve had a hernia, Bogey

134

was so upset that, as soon as the doctor arrived, he vomited. Betty remained overnight at the Cedars of Lebanon Hospital with her son and told reporters, 'Stephen is all right now and improving so rapidly that I fear he will be spoiled when I take him home.'

Alone with his son Bogey was always tense because he did not know what to do with the youngster. 'But I love him,' he would say. 'I hope he knows that.'

Stephen had a habit of calling everyone 'Blubber Head' or else 'Mr Dog Do In The Pants'. This created some worry when Edward R. Murrow was interviewing the Bogart family in their own home for the *Person to Person* television show. Betty had already made her television debut on the Ed Sullivan show reciting *Casey at the Bat*. Bogey's initiation in the medium had been on Jack Benny's programme, in spite of him vowing he would never appear on television. Now they were both concerned that, during the impromptu interview, Stephen might call Murrow by one of his pet names. Unexpectedly, it was Leslie who created the embarrassment. She was not used to seeing her father in his toupee since he never wore it around the house—Betty found the hair piece 'ticklish'. Confused, the child pointed her finger to Bogey's head and announced to the nation that her father had on a 'hair hat'.

'I suppose our Steve is as much a monster as any little boy, but he makes me fold up like an accordion,' Betty said in *Look* when the boy was five and a half and Leslie was two. 'Leslie, who's a dish, has the same effect on Bogey. Our favorite game with the children is to tell them to do something—and wait while they don't do it.

'Steve likes to ride ponies, but Leslie, being female, prefers a Jaguar. Indoors, Steve is usually quiet with his books, but Leslie is a clown and a mimic, and loves to match making faces with Bogey.' Leslie's ability at mime recalled the talent Betty had displayed when she was the same age.

'Neither child has ever seen us on the screen,' Betty revealed. 'They don't know what we do.'

For the first time in nearly a decade, Betty was creating some excitement in cinemas. After stealing *How to Marry a Millionaire* from Grable and Monroe, she topped both June Allyson and Arlene Dahl for acting honours in her next film. Most critics considered that performance as the sympathetic wife of Fred MacMurray in

135

Woman's World to be her finest. For a change, she was getting raves that said, 'She has become the actress everyone has been waiting for since her first film.' The trade papers proclaimed, 'Bogey should be proud of her.'

As her principal champion and critic, Bogey would go over Betty's parts with her but not, strangely enough, until after having seen them realised on the screen. Only after she had created her performance by herself would he condemn or praise so that she could have confidence in correct choices and learn from possible mistakes. In private, he would tell her that despite her recent successes, she was no actress and would have to train herself to become one. Critical appraisal was all that was forthcoming; pride in her, as Betty had earlier realised, was conversely reserved for her homelier role in life.

In an interview with Gladys Hill, she confessed, 'If I didn't have any ambition, it would be better, speaking seriously, much better for Bogey. I'd like it better for him, too. But I'm not the kind of a girl who could ever enjoy those luncheons with the girls. I've worked all my life. Work and myself go hand in hand. And while he may regret this, and I'm sure he does, Bogey understands.' The press recognised this too when they pointed out, 'Though Bogey wants her to be a housewife, she remains an actress as well because of her ego and to prove she is as important as her friends.'

Betty reassumed her status as a star—if not important at the box-office, at least able to hold her own against some of the competition—by upping her salary from the forty thousand dollars she received for her last film to seventy thousand. For strategic purposes she let it be known that it made no difference if the studios met her price or not because she could always stay home with her family and forget about acting. The independence worked and Metro Goldwyn Mayer hired her for the first time to play in another all-star film, *The Cobweb*. And she had the satisfaction of being asked back by Warner's to do *Blood Alley*.

'Oh, it's grand to be pursued again,' she exclaimed. 'Lord knows it has been long enough since that has happened. That three-year stretch was the longest period. But I wasn't exactly idle.' While glorying in her progress, she became critical of Bogey and said, 'He's in a rut. Well, he takes his lunch to work, and he takes the same darned thing every day—deviled ham sandwiches.'

Never settling for status quo, Betty tried to keep Bogey hopping. 'Lauren has ordered a swimming pool,' columnist Frank Farrell wrote, 'and Bogart's throwing a fit. Last time he agreed to let her recover a living room chair, she had the whole house redecorated to match it.'

As if acting, interior decorating, and being a housewife and mother were not enough, she claimed to be writing a novel. 'I am schooled to work,' she said. 'I could never stop, no matter what, I work better under pressure.'

The effect of her schedule on her husband was described to a reporter: 'When both Bogey and I are working, it's great. It's fine when he's working and I'm not. It gets a little grim, though, when I'm working and Bogey isn't. He gets restless hanging around.'

For all his seeming encouragement while she was being ignored by the studios, Bogey's attitude changed once her career became active again. Even though he was in constant demand, he was afraid that each picture would be his last. The has-been image of *A Star is Born* never ceased to haunt him. The situation of being off work himself and his wife being on call alarmed him. As Betty prepared to leave for the day, he would accuse her of selfishly putting her public before their children. And, if those recriminations were not enough to make Betty feel guilty, he would pick out some flaw in the running of the household to make her realise how necessary it was to stay home—he would, in Betty's words, 'raise Cain' if there were so much as a wrinkle in the bed sheets.

The reason for his petulance was soon dispelled when the rush for her services ended. Again Betty had made the mistake of playing parts without bite. Cast as the standard sincere Hollywood heroine, she came over as bland and uninteresting. Once again Charles Boyer proved a jinx for her in *The Cobweb* when she played the only normal, but the least intriguing, woman in this film about a mental institution. And in *Blood Alley* Betty showed she could not merely be used as a pretty prop in a he-man adventure. According to her own observations about actors always having to climb steps, she had made progress in *How to Marry a Millionaire* and *Woman's World*, but had endured setbacks in her last two efforts. They were not completely worthless to her, however, because seeming busy was vital to an actor, according to Bogey.

As an explanation for making so many pictures himself, Bogey said, 'Frank Sinatra recently told me work is therapy.' He took the cure for whatever ailed him by keeping up his own busy pace. After Europe for *Beat the Devil* and Hawaii for *The Caine Mutiny*, he stopped off in Hollywood to do *Sabrina* and returned to the continent to appear with Sinatra's wife, Ava Gardner, in *The Barefoot Contessa*. Now he was back home again and acting a little too devilish to be acceptable in a minor item called *We're No Angels*.

Still he found time to be Betty's best publicity agent. 'Most of the actresses in Hollywood are the dullest broads in town,' he announced. 'Ninety-nine percent have no appeal for me whatsoever. Make that ninety-nine-point-nine percent. That goes for Marilyn Monroe, Jane Russell, Audrey Hepburn and Gina Lollobrigida. The only actress in town who has true allure is Lauren Bacall.' To him, although she was 'plankish', that did not matter because he was not 'a bosom man' anyway. She has 'just plain everything', he declared.

Betty also approved of her own looks. She called the wardrobe women, hairdressers and make-up men, 'The Wrecking Crew', and refused to wear falsies. 'If you don't be yourself, you wind up being *nothing*,' she stated. 'Look at Lombard. She never needed the bosom gimmick.' She also quoted Katharine Hepburn who had told her, 'If you're flat-chested, you're flat-chested. There are things you can't do anything about.' Bogey, however, needed the enhancement of lifts because he was her height, five feet eight and a half inches; he also wore a toupee and his teeth were capped to reinforce his screen image.

Because he was outspoken, Bogey grabbed a great deal of type-space for himself. As far as other actors were concerned, he expounded, 'I don't approve of the John Waynes and the Gary Coopers saying, "Shucks, I ain't no actor." If they aren't actors, what are they getting paid for?' He was particularly annoyed when the studio tried to make Tony Curtis seem ordinary. Bogey felt, 'Who wants to see the kid next door?'

Never reluctant to express himself about the behaviour of other stars, he said of Anne Baxter's cigar-smoking publicity gimmick, 'Somebody should smoke Anne Baxter.' The one actress he never faulted was Ingrid Bergman because she was, to him, 'the only lady in Hollywood'. Years later she would say, 'I only kissed him. I never really knew him.'

Critical of his own movies, he called *Sabrina* 'a crock'. His opinion of his co-star Audrey Hepburn was, 'She's all right—if you don't mind a dozen "takes".' His stealing her away from young William Holden in the film caused some controversy, so Bogey stated to the press, 'The talk that I shouldn't get the girl is kind of insulting. I don't give a damn whether I get the girl in a movie. One of the things Hollywood does is bury you after you reach the age of Tony Curtis.' Referring to his own marriage, he declared, 'So if in real life it comes true, why not the movies?'

His view of Hollywood morals was widely circulated: 'As long as they spell your name right and you're not accused of taking dope you're all right in Hollywood.' Betty's opinion, though, was that the name of Hollywood had been so besmirched by scandal that it should be changed.

Usually, however, Betty agreed with what Bogey said. His published statements denouncing females provoked the expected antagonism, and Betty did not help when she tried to explain, 'He frequently remarks that he doesn't trust women at all, declaring they are a cunning bunch whose prime purpose in life is to charm men and pick their pockets at the same time. He hates groups of women with a purpose or a mission, women who wear corsets, and women who wear too much lipstick.

'I guess I am the only one about whom he makes an exception.'

Bogey boasted that he considered Betty 'a pal'. Later he elaborated on that by saying, 'In my opinion, what qualifies her for this elevated estimation is that she has no affectation. You can like her, which is more important than love.'

As for his view of himself, Bogey confessed, 'The challengers will never overtake me now. It takes a long time to develop a repulsive character like mine. You don't get to be the Boris Karloff of the supper clubs overnight. You've got to work at it.' This self-effacing trait helped him avoid becoming a target for other people's comments.

A star of his stature with such an outrageous record of behaviour was the ideal subject for scandal magazines. Above all, they would try to diminish him by showing him not to be the hero the public imagined he was. A headline in *Confidential* once read,

'What Made Bogart Run?' and the sub-head was, 'An 18-year-old pimply-faced kid pinched Lauren Bacall's bottom at one of those Hollywood parties, Bogey saw it all and what he did about it had the whole town snickering ...'

The scene took place, according to the writer John Griffith, at a 1954 New Year's Eve party in the North Bedford Drive, Beverly Hills home of the scenarist Charles Lederer and his wife, actress Anne Shirley. Bogey told the reporter that he 'remembered most of the principals but wasn't absolutely positive on the action' because he had gotten an 'ample load on'.

Two young Canadian Air Force cadets crashed the party and became drunk. Everyone tried to ignore their unruly behaviour as they went around nipping the derrières of the women guests. When they did it to Betty, she let out a startled shriek. Bogey, who witnessed the action, put down his drink and crossed over to grab the offending cadet by the sleeve. Everyone was hushed, waiting for a fight.

'Now see here, sonny, what do you think you're trying to pull here?' Bogey snarled.

Not intimidated, the cadet looked Bogey right in the eye and shouted, 'Why don't you go to hell!'

In fear, not caring that the élite of Hollywood was looking on, Bogey rushed to one of the bathrooms and locked himself in. 'Efforts to bring Bogart back out to stand his ground were useless,' Griffith claimed. 'Outside, the air cadets had returned to the bar and were beating each other over the shoulders with laughter. Finally, Lederer called the police who drove around and dragged the kids off to jail. ... As the youngsters were being hustled out of the house, Bogart opened the bathroom door, stretched out a trembling finger and shouted: "*Out!*"'

The party quickly came to an end.

The sensation-seeking press was not kind to Betty either. The *New York Enquirer* reported how she had used one of her diamond earrings to cut the arm of a young lady she found going through her purse at a party.

Betty also proved a formidable opponent when some of her neighbours, writer Cy Howard, TV MC Art Linkletter, Charles Correll of Amos and Andy, and architect Welton Becket took the Bogarts to court because of the barking of their three boxers. The plaintiffs alleged that she had ignored their pleas to keep the dogs quiet.

Betty's reply to Howard's protests that he could not eat dinner because of the noise was, 'Don't eat then.'

To his claim that the sound of the dogs made guests nervous, she responded, 'Don't have guests. What do you expect me to do, kill the dogs?' Then she said to the press, 'Mr Howard says some-body should cut out their vocal cords, but I think everybody would be happier if Mr Howard removed his own. I think Mr Howard is making more noise than the dogs.'

Most of the time the stories that were published about Betty concerned the skill she showed in making Bogey less erratic without altering his uniqueness. Constantly there would be reminders printed that proclaimed, 'Despite her many talents, she is best known as the woman who made Humphrey Bogart behave.' Capitalising on that claim to fame for publicity, she advised, 'It is foolish to change the man you're married to. It'll make him worse. If a man has been drinking a little bit, it doesn't pay to disagree with him. It only means you'll be up all night.'

Betty was admired for her candour in admitting her problems in coping with 'the ugliest handsome man I ever met', as she called him. 'Humphrey thinks I handle him carefully,' was her usual opener. 'He's right. If I hadn't we wouldn't have lasted long enough for him to carry me across the threshold. The years have been anything but dull. Maybe that's why I've been so happy. I can forgive anything except dullness.'

Occasionally, she portrayed herself as the difficult one, as in an interview with columnist Hal Boyle when she exclaimed, 'To think I've given that guy one third of my active life! But I'm tougher to live with than he is. I'm more selfish. He's very patient with me.'

Betty's happiness with Bogey, she told Gladys Hill, was the result of the two kinds of security that he gave her: 'I never had anything until I met him. I've had everything since! The things you can touch, you know. He has spoiled me, I guess, to quite a degree by never depriving me of anything I want to have or want to do.

'The things you can touch, yes. But aside from these, of much more importance than these, I've had another sense of security. The feeling of home. Bogey cares about his home, cares about keeping it safe, keeping it intact. Every man thinks of kicking over the traces at one time or another, so it's said, of letting the eye rove, the feet stray. Bogey may think about it, who knows, but he would never do anything about it. As far as he's concerned his life is set. This is what I mean when I speak of security. I haven't the fears or jealousies, or need to have.'

Taking credit for what she felt was due to her, Betty stated, 'In recent years he's had a steady run of hit pictures and he points out that his confident progress has coincided with success in marriage. His film future appears even brighter and when he quits acting he's going to be a director. A good one. I'll see to that.'

Before even attempting to make that prediction come true, there were other aims which had priority. 'We plan to work together in pictures again,' she said, 'but not until producers come to the conclusion that we've both outgrown the action-romance rut they had us in before.'

After seven years television gave them the professional reunion they wanted. They were signed for the May 29, 1955, NBC *Producer's Showcase*. Before the show, an eager executive exclaimed, 'Mr Bogart, I've just talked with our office and they have just completed an audience survey and from all indications it appears that you will have the largest viewing audience in television history!' This elicited a smile from Bogey. The young man continued, 'What do you think of that?' As Bogey walked away, he muttered, 'I don't give a damn if the whole world watches.'

For the first time since her screen debut, Betty received better notices than Bogey did. The play was an hour-and-a-half adaptation of *The Petrified Forest*, also starring Henry Fonda. Turning back time twenty years, Bogey was once again Duke Mantee, but without the strange fascination that made his original performance memorable. Since he was now a star, he was expected to be the main character, but the part had been written as a catalyst for the leads. Critics, therefore, wrote of their disappointment, but Bogey achieved what he wanted. His upcoming picture was to be *The Desperate Hours* in which he played the role of a gangster who holds a group of people hostage. And the primary reason for this television revival was to build public acceptance of him in the film part. Taking the role which Bette Davis had played in the film, Betty received praise qualified by declarations that not much had been expected of her. The compliments in her reviews—'Surprised us with a neatly turned portrayal', or 'Keeps improving all the time, was a revelation'—all implied anticipation of inadequacy, just as the fault found with Bogey was based on the anticipation of much more.

An announced appearance of both of them in a television version of F. Scott Fitzgerald's *The Last Tycoon* never came about. But Betty was invited to appear on *The Donald O'Connor Show* and *The Seventy-Fifth Anniversary of Light* without Bogey.

In addition to the entertainment pages that year, Bogey made the real estate news columns by consummating a deal in partnership with Don Hartman, head of production at Paramount. They acquired a great deal of property in the vicinity of Disneyland Park, just outside of Los Angeles, for the construction of drive-in restaurants, motels, gas stations and sports facilities.

Travelling also had the Bogarts in the news. They were constantly on personal appearance tours or taking trips to New York. 'We trek to our old home town,' she explained, 'for a look at the shows and a few evenings at "21" and other night spots whenever we can. We shed our usually bucolic, lazy life for a fling at the bright lights and old friends. Manhattan seems to give us a shot in the arm after busy days at the studio and languorous week-ends in Hollywood.'

During time spent in London, Betty tried to make Bogey jealous one night in a night club by continuing to dance with another partner for more than half-an-hour. After ignoring Bogey's signals that he wanted to dance with her, she confided to her friend, 'He'll appreciate me more when he gets me. Anyway, he's no Arthur Murray.'

That was Betty's way of putting her philosophy of being aloof into action. Describing her technique, she said, 'It's simple. Make it appear that you're not trying to hold him. Let him think he's got all the freedom he wants—but don't give him too much. Invisible chains last longer.'

The attachment was reciprocal, but he was more obvious about it. On *The Barefoot Contessa* jaunt she went abroad with him so that he would have none of the impatient waiting he had experienced during *Beat the Devil*. 'When Betty told me she was going to Italy with me,' he said, 'I knew it wasn't because she was jealous of Ava Gardner. I knew because she told me she *was* jealous. What she actually wanted I didn't find out until I was in Paris on Bastille Day when all the couturier shops were closed. Betty had them open up just for her. I realized then that she went to Rome to live like a queen while I worked like a slave. Then she waited for Paris and a chance to spend the sweat off my artistic brow.'

If she bought him something extra like cuff links, he would exclaim, 'Gosh, Butch, but you know I have a pair.' Her comment on that reaction was, 'He also has one watch, one cigarette lighter, one belt, and figures one of each is enough for any man.'

Before she went on her Paris shopping spree, they rented a boat in Portofino, where the picture was being made, and explored the coves, taking films of the scenery. Then, when they came to Paris and stayed up until 3 a.m. in a night club, Betty became angry at Bogey's ordering yet another drink. 'Either you send it back,' she warned, 'or I'll have a double and we'll both got sloshed!' She got her way, but her ability to control him made him refer to her as, 'that interfering doll I'm married to'. She would retaliate with 'that bum actor who happens to be the father of my children'.

Name-calling was so much a part of their relationship that when the Friar's Club threw a stag-razz luncheon for Bogey, Betty sent a recording as a joke because she was annoyed that the entertainers' club would not allow women in to hear their ribald humour. On the transcription, which later became a bootlegged underground collectors' item, she used profanity to describe what she thought of the members for preventing her from attending. Addressing herself to Bogey, she added, 'What can a Friar say that you haven't already called me?'

Then to show she was one of the boys, she told risqué stories. One time, she said, before their marriage, Bogey was going with a very possessive girl. After he walked out on the lady, she went to the window and yelled, 'Hump-freeee! Hump-free!' And she was trampled to death by twenty-two sailors.

Betty claimed that the constant trading of witticisms with Bogey helped sharpen her to put across the wickedly sophisticated humour of Elvira in the TV production of *Blithe Spirit* with Noël Coward and Claudette Colbert. The offer to do the part came when she and Bogey went to Las Vegas for Coward's American night-club debut. Bogey had known Coward since the twenties and Betty was first introduced to him in the fifties. During their visit to his dressing room after the performance, Coward suggested she play the role in the television special. Terrified and flattered, she said that either she would sign immediately or give him a chance to think it over.

In answer to her probing of whether he thought she was right for the part, Coward laughed it off as a display of insecurity. 'Of course, darling,' he reassured her. 'Forget your fears. We'll have a divine time. Just think of the party afterwards.'

The party was given three months before the show. Betty made it to welcome Coward to Hollywood and to celebrate the birthday of Tony Martin as well as the anniversary of Claudette Colbert and Dr Joel Pressman. This gala event was contrary to the intimate gatherings that Betty said they preferred. 'We usually enjoy small, informal dinner parties rather than big show affairs where nobody has a chance to talk to anyone,' she declared. 'We do two blowouts each year—one on our wedding anniversary and another on Christmas Eve. One of the few times I have known Bogey to get trussed up in dinner clothes willingly was for the brilliant shindig our friends the Danny Kayes gave Larry and Vivien Olivier on their arrival in Hollywood. Too bad Bogey doesn't care about dressing because he really looks good in a tuxedo.'

To make Betty relax about playing the ghost of a first wife who comes back to haunt the second spouse, Bogey began tormenting her with silly jokes like, 'These ghoulish things remind me of you', 'That's the spirit', and 'The ghostess with the mostess'. Such fun-making always delighted him and she forced herself to submit to his game, no matter how tiresome it became. 'I hate people who can't take a little ribbing at their own expense,' he expounded. 'I like to rib. I *have* to rib.' Some of his victims rationalised his verbal attacks with the explanation that he needed to needle to make his boredom bearable.

But Bogey's fun-making could not diminish her elation at bringing off the Coward coup. *Blithe Spirit* was Bogey's kind of play— pure entertainment—and he agreed with Coward's contention, 'Since the war a terrible pall of significance has fallen over plays. Now a hero must be a tramp or a drunk or a juvenile delinquent.'

After the show, Betty could have been mistaken for one of those three types. She could not find a shower in Hollywood's newly built Television City and had to drive home wearing her ghostly grey and lavender make-up. The next morning, though, the reviews made her glow. Again, she had proved her flair for comedy. The part, of course, was flamboyant, but as an actress she could shine in a flashy role and would become drab when required to play an ordinary person.

Bogey's career had come full circle. Returning to the Duke Mantee type of character in the film *The Desperate Hours*, he was told by the critics that he was getting too old for that kind of role. Several reviews stated that he was less ominous than Paul Newman who originated the part on the stage because Bogey lacked the volatility of youth, constantly threatening to explode.

In that movie, as if to underline the has-been Norman Main fate that age could hold for him as an actor, he was finally co-starred with Fredric March, the originator of the part in *A Star is Born*.

Written on the Wind

'If two people love each other, there can be no happy end; one must die before the other.'

That conclusion by Ernest Hemingway, whose creativity first brought Betty and Bogey together, practically prophesied the outcome of their relationship. The growing together that had flourished since Bogey began sharing his 'Have' with the 'Have-Not' Betty was destined to end eventually. And she, who had become a 'Have', returned to being a 'Have Not', but with a sense of loss that meant being lost.

In the quarter-of-a-million-dollar, French Provincial living room that the Bogarts had not yet finished furnishing, but had filled with art by Picasso and Dufy as well as with Betty's collection of antiques, two trophies represented Bogey's greatest triumphs. Prominently and permanently displayed were his golden Oscar for *The African Queen* and the silver cup he was allowed to keep for winning the Channel Island race four consecutive times with his beloved *Santana*.

A third and more significant keepsake was brought out for show only on their anniversaries and occasionally for publicity poses. It was the bride-and-groom decoration from their wedding cake, which they still kept under a glass dome. 'The toughest couple in Hollywood', as they were often called, still prized this plastic memento for the sake of sentiment.

147

A fourth souvenir of his accomplishments was a decoration in the den. A cheque for his part in the sale of Santana Productions for over a million dollars was photocopied and framed as a reminder of his progress since his marriage to Betty. This wall-hanging showed how far he had come from the days with Mayo when they had tacked over the bar the Algonquin Hotel bill for furniture breakage during their honeymoon. The facsimile of the three-quarters-of-a-million-dollar cheque, as it was realised after taxes, he felt, represented a legacy 'for Betty and the kids'.

And now at fifty-seven, Bogey was dying of cancer.

Betty had once said, 'Bogey lives on forty-five cigarettes a day.' On screen he never seemed to be without that trademark dangling from his lips. This habit, that seemed so important to his life, proved to be the cause of his death.

Like the great actor he was, Bogey played the final act with panache. Every day at cocktail time, during his last year, he sat in the living room for a couple of hours, surrounded by friends, and gave the finest performance of his lifetime. He pretended not to be in pain, played his own doctor by improvising a rationale for smoking and drinking, and still acted as if he were capable of living it up.

If Bogey's courage in his confrontation with cancer gave inspiration to others, his spiting of suffering re-enforced his own spirit. As always, he had a magnetic way of turning a negative situation into a positive force. Getting out of his sick bed to go on, he would change into the same costume every day: an 'I-don't-give-a-damn' scarlet velvet smoking jacket and grey Dak slacks. His only complaint was that the pants were too big for him. 'I must put on some weight,' he would say, trying to make light of his loss of fifty pounds as a result of the cobalt treatments.

Resembling a god in a Greek play, he would descend to the floor below in a *deus ex machina*: the household dumbwaiter with the top removed so that he could sit inside, a device he found humiliating to use. Then he would transfer to his wheelchair, and roll into the living room to await the entrance of his supporting cast, which consisted of some of the most celebrated actors and actresses in Hollywood. The regulars were Katharine Hepburn, Spencer Tracy, Frank Sinatra, David Niven and Richard Burton. The Freeloaders, he liked to call them just to seem contrary and not overly-grateful

148

for the constant company. Among the missing were several once-close companions who could not bear to see Bogey fading. He respected their feelings and tried unsuccessfully to make Betty understand. She would busy herself directing his entertainment. As soon as Bogey became fatigued, she would ring down the curtain for the night.

Still intent on being counted among the living, he was incensed at the 'ghoul' columnists and 'vampire' reporters who would make passing references to his illness or write their own versions of his premature burial. Dorothy Kilgallen particularly angered him by describing how he had been taken late one night to the eighth floor of the Los Angeles Memorial Hospital for some mysterious operation to be performed on him. Riled, he issued a vehement press release which noted that the hospital did not go that high and that the eighth floor sounded like the mental ward.

During the cocktail scene, the only reference to his condition was an occasional explosion in his strange forced voice at the reports concerning his illness. Otherwise, the dialogue usually consisted of actor-talk about parts, promotions and personalities, their own or others.

Bogey boasted that he was still making the film pages. He was a leading contender for the 1956 Cannes Film Festival Best Actor of the Year award for *The Harder They Fall*. His name also appeared in the columns because Harry Cohen announced that he had bought *The Good Shepherd* for Bogey and was holding the property until the actor would be well again. Although that seemed like a magnanimous gesture made to encourage the actor, the hard-bitten head of Columbia was not above using that device to avert any depressive effect Bogey's ailment might have on the box-office for his last movie.

'I made seventy-five films,' Bogey would say. 'I claim one more than Tracy.' Maintaining his average of two or three pictures a year, he had gone almost immediately from *The Left Hand of God* into the filming of Budd Schulberg's novel about racketeers in boxing. In the short interval between those productions, he and Betty went to New York to relax. As was inevitable, he also publicised his forthcoming picture and made Leonard Lyons's column with a story about the difficulty in casting the pivotal character of the fighter who was similar to the huge Primo Carnera.

149

'We had two men each six feet, ten inches,' Bogey claimed, 'but they lost out when my seven-year-old son, Stevie, said they weren't big enough to scare him.'

'Bogey exaggerates,' Betty interrupted. 'To give you an example, that seven-year-old son of ours is six years old.'

While working on the movie, a cough and huskiness he had neglected for some time became more pronounced. Three years before, Ezra Goodman had noted, 'There were rumors around Hollywood, in certain places, that Bogart was not too well. He spoke in a guttural voice. He seemed to have trouble walking sometimes. Obviously, Lauren Bacall knew this. Miss Bacall, or Mrs Bogart, however, did not take this and other matters too seriously.'

There was gossip, as well, during the making of *The Harder They Fall*, that the gruffness of Bogey's voice on the sound track was excessive and necessitated calling in an impersonator, Paul Frees, to redub some of the scenes. When shooting was completed the day before Christmas, Bogey's intention was to start his next movie right after the holiday week. He was to return to Warner's and make his first film with Betty in eight years, *Melville Goodwin, USA*, based on John P. Marquand's novel. She was cast as an aggressive writer, a role similar to the one he had just played.

Just before New Year, he was prodded by Betty and his friends into going to Dr Maynard Brandasma to find out what was causing the irritation in his throat. A biopsy was performed and the growth he had in his oesophagus was diagnosed as malignant.

On March 4, 1956, Bogey was in Good Samaritan Hospital for major surgery. The operation, performed by the noted surgeon, Dr John Jones, took eight hours. Two inches of Bogey's oesophagus was removed. His stomach was raised twelve inches. And one rib was discarded.

After the surgery had been performed, Dr Jones told Betty, 'I hope that the operation has checked the cancer. But only time will tell.'

For the three weeks of his convalescence, Betty moved into the hospital to spend as much time as she could with him, aware of his aversion to being alone, especially at this time. Every afternoon she would go home to see the children, but she would return to Bogey as quickly as possible.

'She's one of the great women,' he later acknowledged to a

friend. 'When I was in the hospital, she was never away from my side for more than an hour. There aren't many women like that.'

As a patient, Bogey was impossible. He still tried to exercise his independence and behave as though nothing was wrong by continuing with his liquor and cigarettes, albeit moderately. Once he woke in the middle of the night with a coughing spell that opened his stitches.

On his arrival home, he let the press know that illness would not prevent him from showing his annoyance at their practices. 'What the hell have they got against cancer?' he asked in a statement prepared in protest against the reports of his operation that made no mention of his ailment. 'It's a perfectly respectable disease—not like having a venereal disease.'

Never for one moment would he admit to anyone—perhaps not even to himself—that he would not conquer his cancer. Nurses looked after him night and day, freeing Betty to accept the lead in *Written on the Wind* a few weeks after his return home. At the studio, she was besieged with inquiries about Bogey's health. She would always give the same cheerful reply: 'He's doing fine, thank you. Doing fine.'

The controlled anxiety she felt about Bogey showed itself in her taut performance. Betty looked drawn and uninvolved in the melodramatics of the film. Obviously, she was preoccupied by her personal tragedy. Besides, neither she nor her co-star Rock Hudson stood a chance since the second leads had the more provocative roles. Robert Stack, in the performance of his lifetime, played a wild millionaire drunk. And Dorothy Malone—who had bested Betty before in *The Big Sleep*—was so outstanding as Stack's nymphomaniac sister that she won the supporting actress's Academy Award. Against such incandescent competition, Betty's cool could not hold its own.

Finer actresses, stronger personalities and greater beauties had come and gone in the dozen years of Betty's fame. Now some columnists began to intimate that had she been known only as Lauren Bacall, without Bogart added to it, her name would, in truth, have been written on the wind.

Bogey knew that no matter how the public may be manipulated for a while, they cannot be forced to want to see someone continuously over the years, and so he expressed his faith in Betty's

151

endurance to Louella Parsons: 'This is a great woman! My Betty is a good wife, a fine mother and a wonderful actress. She'll last longer than most of the dames on the screen because,' touching his heart, 'she's got it *here*.'

Betty's constant concern and devotion prompted Bogey to comment, 'She's my wife—so she stays home and takes care of me. Maybe that's the way you tell the ladies from the broads in this town.'

Bedside duties prevented Betty from helping Adlai Stevenson as much as she would have liked in his second bid for the presidency. Even those limited activities, however, were enough to provoke a feud with avid Republican Hedda Hopper. According to Earl Wilson, the disagreement began at a fashion show in New York for Mamie Eisenhower. Although it was a Republican affair, Stevenson's sister, Mrs 'Buffy' Ives, attended. When Mrs Ives met Hedda, she asked the columnist for advice on what to do about some of the Hollywood celebrities who were 'working for and hurting my brother'.

'Get rid of Dore Schary, Leonard Spigelgass, and Mr and Mrs Humphrey Bogart,' was Hedda's suggestion.

Mrs Ives replied, 'Maybe I can eliminate those last two, but not the first.'

Reports of the exchange came to Betty's attention and she told Earl Wilson, 'I think Hedda ought to shut up for a change. It's OK as long as you're on her side, but it's sure as hell not OK when you're not on her side.

'I know Mrs Ives and she's always welcomed Hollywood help. Hedda's probably making this up as she goes along. She's giving herself more importance than she rates. If she tries to tell me any of this, I'll let her have it because I can be pretty unattractive, too. The funny part of this is that Hedda's been trying to make it up with me for a year and keeps asking why I'm mad at her.'

Wilson's column on the fracas ended with, 'Bogart, who's been ill, stayed out of the battle, deciding to let the girls fight alone.'

Not working again, Betty constantly hovered around Bogey and this annoyed him. If she did not go out occasionally, he told her, he would feel that the end was near. Usually, she ignored his protests about the necessity for her to distract herself. On rare occasions, because Bogey would insist, she would dine out with friends. When her birthday came, he kept saying, 'Go and have some fun. I feel fine.' So she joined the Romanoffs for Frank Sinatra's opening at the Sands Hotel in Las Vegas. Following the show, Sinatra hosted a birthday party for her.

For some time, Sinatra had been a fixture in the Bogart household. And he became even more so once Bogey fell ill. In the three-way friendship, Bogey was the wiseacre, and Betty and Sinatra the wisecrackers.

One night Bogey invited six novice actors to his home for a professional discourse. Until the end, Betty and Sinatra respected Bogey's domination of the evening.

In response to one young actor's description of the Stanislavsky method, Bogey said, 'If you'll pardon the expression, you've got me completely screwed up. But I know this: The audience is always a little ahead of you. If a guy points a gun at you, the audience knows you're afraid. You don't have to make faces. You just have to believe that you are the person you're playing and what is happening is happening to you.'

Later, Bogey's statement that he was against the star system made Sinatra, who had been quiet throughout the session, let out with, 'Watch it, Bogey.'

The sage reprimanded, 'Quiet, boy.'

Winding up the evening, Bogey warned the beginners, 'Personally I think you're all in a hell of a mess—wanting to be actors. But keep trying, and it *may* happen.' The prediction was to come true for only one out of the six tyros present: Dennis Hopper.

Though Betty did not interrupt during the entire time, she could not resist retorting, 'You mean they may turn out like you? God forbid!'

Bogey's reply was, 'Pay no attention to Miss Bacall.'

'Pay no attention to Mr Bogart,' Sinatra intervened and closed the meeting.

Another assignment drew Betty away from Bogey's side. For his last film as head of MGM, Dore Schary was to remake the Tracy–Hepburn hit *Woman of the Year* with such a completely new script that, except for the barest outline of the plot, it would be unrecognisable. The film, *Designing Woman*, was the second that Betty would make with Vincente Minnelli who had directed her in *The Cobweb*.

Originally Grace Kelly was to play the part of the designer who reconciles her life-style with marriage to a sportswriter. Kelly, who had also played Hepburn's role in the remake of *The Philadelphia Story* as *High Society*, became unavailable because of her marriage to Prince Rainier of Monaco. When the nuptials were announced, Bogey thought that it was just a publicity stunt for the release of Kelly's movie, *The Swan*, in which she played royalty. Disagreeing with him and most of the sceptics in Hollywood, Betty believed that the engagement was legitimate. Two weeks before the ceremony took place, Betty told a columnist, 'Bogey even paid up the five dollars he bet me. And he's the last one to admit anything.'

Now she was to profit even more from Kelly's marriage. Her satisfaction in being cast as the replacement was increased because she beat Doris Day for the part. And it was a coup to have as her co-star Gregory Peck who took over from the previously announced male lead, Jimmy Stewart. There was talk, though, that the script would have to be re-written to suit her and Betty protested, 'Do you think there'd have to be changes because I have two heads and Miss Kelly only has one!'

Her presence in *Written on the Wind*, only a few months earlier, was so overlooked that she felt obliged to state on starting this new film, 'It's not a come-back, but a resumption of activity.'

Finally, in this, her thirteenth picture in twelve years, she was being treated as a star who did not require an all-star cast, heavy supporting players or an overpowering male lead. She was playing opposite and was considered equal to an actor of major magnitude, Gregory Peck. Moreover, there was not a scene-stealing subsidiary in sight, except maybe Dolores Gray, who could be considered musical relief. Not to be outdone by Gray's curves, Betty shed her inhibitions by appearing for the first time on screen in a bathing suit, showing her appealing boyish body.

On a dock location at Newport Beach, the cast was amazed to see the *Santana* approaching. With the help of David Niven, the ailing Bogey had made the trip as a surprise for Betty.

Although Bogey would be the last to concede the fact, it now seemed recovery was impossible because the cancer had reappeared and spread from the region immediately below his mouth to encompass other areas. The loss of weight from half a year of radiation at the Los Angeles Tumor Institute made another operation imperative. Surgery was performed at St John's Hospital to remove the scar tissue in the hope that his appetite would improve and his pain would diminish. Home again after a week, Bogey was no better.

Longing to go aboard the *Santana* once again, he took his son along and was joined by some friends for a couple of days' sailing to Balboa and Catalina. Most of the time he stayed in the cockpit alone, enjoying his scotch and cigarettes, studying the sea and sky and sleeping intermittently.

As he skimmed along in his yacht—not like the destroyed Norman Main who drowned himself in that same ocean—memories of other voyages could not help but flood in on him. His father helping to cultivate his taste to be a sailor and then himself running off to sea to die ... his own escape to the navy ... *Sluggy* and the slugging ... Betty and the loving ... the boats in their first and last pictures together, as well as in *The African Queen* and *The Caine Mutiny* ... trips to and from Europe for work and play ... the immeasurable pleasures of the *Santana*. His metaphoric belief that to be submerged would be his ultimate destiny, as foreshadowed in *A Star is Born*, was unrealised because imagining such a fate made him keep his head above water and remain a star until the end.

When he disembarked, he did not know that this would be his farewell to the *Santana*. He planned on going out on the yacht again in a few weeks, but his condition became worse and his activities were more restricted.

Until the last weekend, he still gave the impression that he believed he would be cured. He continued to be his 'brave self', as Truman Capote described Bogey's invincible front. Never ceasing his outrage at ominous items about himself, Bogey called a New York reporter to say, 'I'm feeling fine and not in danger of dying. My treatment was completed two weeks ago and was successful. I plan to do a picture in March.'

On the morning of Friday, January 11, a year after the onset of his illness, he held a meeting with his lawyers to prepare suits against several newspapers which had reported that his death was imminent. By that afternoon, he was feeling so weak that his parting with those who called sounded final. On Saturday night, the last of his friends to leave him were the closest, Spencer Tracy and Katharine Hepburn. After Hepburn kissed him, Bogey said a meaningful goodbye to both to let them know he sensed approaching death.

Betty decided to spend the night in Bogey's room because he was having difficulty breathing. Instead of Bogey kissing her and saying, 'Good night,' as usual, according to a report by Dr Michael Flynn, this time he put his hand on her arm and murmured brusquely, 'Goodbye, kid.'

'It was the worst night he'd had,' Dr Flynn stated.

The next morning Bogey said his last words to Betty: 'Take the kids to Sunday school, bring me the papers and hurry back.'

On her return home a quarter of an hour later, she was told by the nurse that Bogey had fallen into a coma and that the doctor had been called. Betty broke down, but snapped out of it quickly. Her ability to spring back under tension once caused Bogey to describe her as 'steel with curves'. As long as she was with him she had always been able to disguise her insecurities. And during his illness she had learned a great deal about controlling emotions and seeming sturdy. Now with the prospect of having no one to lean on and with children of her own needing her, Betty would have to be the sole source of strength for the first time in her life.

After more than fifteen hours in coma, Bogey died that Monday morning, January 14, 1957, at ten minutes past two—only nine days before his fifty-eighth birthday.

So that the blow would be softened for the children, Betty made them follow their usual routine by going to school. The funeral arrangements were to be the simplest possible and she suggested that, instead of flowers, contributions be sent to the American Cancer Society.

That Thursday on all the movie lots in Hollywood a minute of silence was observed while services were held at All Saints Episcopal Church in Beverly Hills. Outside, three thousand people stood in mourning. Inside, the famous of Hollywood paid homage to Bogey.

The only close friend missing was Frank Sinatra who was in New York for a booking at the Copacabana. On hearing of Bogey's passing, he had sat stupefied in the lounge of the night club and Jerry Lewis volunteered to go on for him. Then Sinatra locked himself in his room for twenty-four hours, not wishing to speak to anyone except Betty. When he called her to say that he was coming to the funeral, she told him that it would mean a loss to the Copa and said, 'You gave Bogey your deep friendship when he needed it; during his lifetime.'

No casket was on the altar because Bogey's wish was to be cremated. In its place was a reminder of the thing he loved most from the one he loved most: the model of the *Santana* that Betty had given him when he had first bought the boat. The eulogy delivered by John Huston expressed the sentiment everyone felt; there would never again be the likes of Bogey.

Then, while his ashes were being placed in Forest Lawn Cemetery on a hill overlooking Hollywood, Betty had a few friends in their home for drinks—just as Bogey would have wanted.

Of all the tributes published in newspapers throughout the world, the most penetrating analysis was written by his friend Alastair Cooke for *The Guardian*: 'It would be tempting—and the French will be tempted—to write of the Bogart character as the archetype of the Outsider, but he packed in fact the more explosive social threat of the Insider gone sour. He was, in short, a romantic hero, inconceivable in any time but ours.'

At the time his mortal remains were being interred, it was impossible to imagine how his spirit would endure in this world. Only Betty could be absolute in the belief that even after death he would continue to be 'a romantic hero'. The gold whistle she placed in his urn was a token of their eternal connection.

I'll Never Smile Again

Eight months to the day after Bogey's death, the marriage of Betty to Frank Sinatra was forecast.

'Miss Bacall has already distinguished herself as the woman who tamed Bogart,' wrote columnist Thomas Wiseman in London's *Evening Standard*. 'She converted him to domesticity. Under her influence he became as mellowed as the scotch he liked to drink. When she marries Sinatra, Miss Bacall will be taking on an even tougher assignment. It will be like trying to mellow wood alcohol.

'I understand that Sinatra is anxious to keep his marriage plans secret and that he will probably deny that he has any intention of marrying Miss Bacall. You can take his denials with a pinch of salt.'

The expected repudiation of this first newspaper story of their proposed attachment was not forthcoming, which increased speculation about the wedding date. Both Betty and Sinatra would reply, 'No comment,' to reporters pursuing them for a statement. On one occasion, however, she said, laughing, 'Let 'em ask him.'

The excitement caused by the report recalled a similar happening that had resulted when another London newsman scooped the world by predicting that she would marry Bogey. As before, because the man with whom she was involved was still married, the Hollywood gossip columnists had not indicated the seriousness of their relationship until now. It was a tribute to their love of the Bogarts and their respect for her loyalty during his illness. Since

158

the first shot was fired, however, open season was declared and the couple was fair game for newsmen.

The story was published while Ava Gardner was visiting London soon after securing her Mexican divorce from Sinatra. The legality of the decree, Ava admitted, 'would not stand up even in the Siberian salt mines'. Sinatra had not contested the proceedings, but for long after the decree was issued—the day after Independence Day, 1957—continued to profess his love.

Only three months earlier, while Ava was involved with Walter Chiari, she had asked Sinatra for a Mexican divorce and he had replied by wire, 'I wish you every happiness and will do nothing to stand in your way.' As a result, Ava waited several weeks before going to Mexico. Now she went through with getting the divorce, unlike the time five years earlier when she had sat in Reno for six weeks and never got round to picking up the Nevada legal papers.

Ava had summed up her feelings about Sinatra once by telling Bogey, 'This is a real difficult person to live with—this guy.'

The friendship between the Bogarts and Sinatra had begun more than five years before. On their first encounter at the Players Restaurant in Hollywood, Bogey had poked fun at Sinatra by challenging The Voice to try his swoon-making talents on a tough guy. Retaining his composure, Sinatra had explained quietly that he was saving his vocal chords for his opening the following week. Bogey became intrigued because he found he could not provoke Sinatra into an argument. And though Sinatra was considered a wise-guy, he regarded Bogey as a wise man. This new friend, Sinatra felt, could refute the motto that hung on a wall in the singer-turned actor's office, a sentiment he lived by: 'Nobody knows the trouble I've seen. And believe me, *nobody cares*.' Bogey was somebody who had overcome problems of his own and could be concerned about those of a friend. Alone after the break-up with Ava, Sinatra enjoyed the privilege of turning to Bogey and depending on him and his wife for those bad moments he had. Soon he shared good times with both of them. Bogey and Sinatra had a father–son relationship and Betty played surrogate mother for what turned out to be one big, happy family for several years.

Both physically and philosophically there was a great similarity between the two men. They shared shortness, thinness and toupee-wearing in common. Though not particularly handsome, they were overwhelmingly attractive to women. They were bonded as buddies by sharing the same outlook on success in show business, the company of toughs, the pleasures of drink and a sense of humour. Above all, both concealed their vulnerability except when their empathy was aroused by those in need. Sinatra was obviously trying to do a 'Bogey' on-screen as well by playing roles like *The Detective*. But in real life his preoccupation with the pursuit of women was un-Bogey-like. In other drives toward pleasure the twenty-year age discrepancy made the younger appear to be a hedonist while the older seemed only self-indulgent. The main difference between them, however, was that Bogey had been born a gentleman, whereas Sinatra had had to work at being one.

From the moment Sinatra had been introduced into the Bogart household, there had been gossip of an emotional attachment between him and Betty. Except for her platonic relationship with Leonard Bernstein, this was the only other time that Betty's name had been linked with another man while Bogey was alive. Several years before, her excitement over the musician's creative brilliance had been misinterpreted, she claimed. Her feelings had led to an extremely close friendship, according to Betty, that was an antidote to the stagnation of Hollywood life. The shock to some people was that when Bernstein had come to town, Bogey had gone away aboard the *Santana*, leaving Betty alone to spend the weekend expressing her love of genius.

Four years before Bogey died, Betty was 'palsy walsy, if that was the word, with Frank Sinatra. Bogart didn't seem to care— but there was no doubt he knew about it, too,' according to Ezra Goodman's research for the *Time* article in 1953 that resulted in the book, *Bogey—the Good-Bad Guy*.

'Sinatra was a character. I had done a *Time* magazine cover about him,' Goodman wrote. 'Frankie boy liked to pal around with the wives of some of his cronies. For instance, there was one eminent songstress who had once been an eminent child star of the movies.

'Bogey didn't seem to care. Maybe he knew he was in bad shape and maybe even dying. He spent his time before the cameras, at Romanoff's and on his boat.

'He was philosophical about it all.

'My information, duly annotated and pinpointed was relayed

to *Time* magazine in New York on the magazine's own teletype system. It was promptly classified and locked up.'

A couple of years after Goodman's 'facts' were filed away, Betty's opinion of Sinatra was published in *Woman's Home Companion*: 'While he's with you, he adores you. He's charming and witty and fun. And he's a wonderful person to have as a friend. When Bogey and I are in New York, for example, he stops by the house every day or so to check on the children, to be sure they're okay. But that boyish quality fools you. Frank's strong, don't think he isn't. You may get the idea that he wants to lean on you but actually he wants to be boss.'

A power struggle between him and Ava was an important factor in their break-up because toward the end his career was on the rise once more and he wanted to be master at home again, too. Now it seemed as though they were still competing. While she was making news with her European affairs, he wound up in the headlines with Betty. Even Frankie's frankness to reporters was out of character. But Sinatra was trying to prove that he no longer missed Ava.

Once, long before, at a party, Ava had commented to Bogey about Sinatra's self-protective ability. 'Don't worry about that little man,' she had said, pointing to Sinatra on the dance floor with Betty. 'He'll be around when you and I are dead and forgotten.'

Although now there was talk that Betty was getting Sinatra on the rebound, others believed he had been fond of her for a long while and this was the first time they had both been free to express their feelings for one another. He had been her escort for years, playing proxy for Bogey when he was working or sailing. Pictures of Betty and Sinatra enjoying themselves together or even kissing were a staple in newspapers and magazines long before anyone actually hinted at a romance. So the public came to appreciate their 'companionship'. Once, Betty had served as a go-between for him and his wife by carrying an orange-coconut birthday cake that Sinatra wanted delivered to Ava as a peace offering while she was shooting *The Barefoot Contessa* in Spain. On that film, Bogey, being of the opinion that she was not a capable actress, had deliberately fluffed his lines on occasion so that scenes had to be re-shot until he felt her performance was worthy.

One night when Bogey was busy, according to a regular routine, Sinatra took Betty to a party. This time the volatile singer became

161

involved in a fiery argument with a couple of guests and was annoyed by the way Betty watched him.

When he confronted her about the look he interpreted as reproving, she elucidated: 'Listen, Frank, I'm not staring. I'm only using my two eyes.'

Nonplussed, he exclaimed, 'Yeah? Well, any dame with class has three!'

The ridiculousness of his remark broke them both up. Later, he paid her what he considered the ultimate compliment, 'She's a million laughs.'

Magazines were not above publishing posthumous reports describing Bogey in his illness telling Sinatra, 'I'm worried about this broad of mine. She ought to be getting away from the house a little. She's been cooped up much too much. How about taking her out now and then, Frank? It would do her good.' Stories also appeared which claimed that 'Bogey's deathbed wish was that Sinatra would be his successor with Betty'.

The consideration that Sinatra showed to Betty while Bogey was ailing continued after his death. Sinatra was always known as a man who could be depended on in time of trial, even though his behaviour under other circumstances was sometimes difficult for some people to understand or anticipate. When he had made that phone call to Betty from New York to console her, he had suggested that after the funeral she should get away with the children to his home in Palm Springs. She did take him up on his offer and spent a few weeks there. Then she had returned home to face the responsibilities of being single again.

Betty had become a statistic. On contemplating her new position as one of the seven million widows in America at that time and the most eligible in Hollywood, she stated, 'I lived one complete life with a beginning, a middle and an end.'

The legacy which was publicised as being a million dollars was closer to eight hundred and fifty thousand. 'After taxes, Bogey's estate will total only around six hundred thousand dollars,' a columnist who knew her reported. 'His widow will draw an income of four per cent per year—or twenty four thousand dollars. However, there's a catch, Bogey's will stipulates that when the couple's two children reach the age of twenty-one they will get an equal share of the four per cent. Betty's annual income from the estate will amount to only eight thousand dollars.' That is why Betty was often forced to admit, 'I work because I can't afford not to. I'm not independently wealthy,' even though some people thought it was a bid for sympathy.

To justify the extravagance of continuing to live in the Holmby Hills house, she told Lolly that she had to stay because 'I love every inch of it. Bogey and I planned it together. I want the children to have a real home where they can take roots.'

Most of the time she was alone with the children. Every day she would spend hours filling scrapbooks with clippings about Bogey so that the youngsters would be able to see and read what the world thought of their father when they grew older. She would also try to answer personally some of the thousands of condolences she received. 'As I read some of these letters which refer to him as the nearest thing to a saint walking the earth,' she revealed, 'I think how amused and cynical about that he would be. I can just hear him saying, "Tell 'em they're crazy in the head. I don't want to be thought of as a goodie." He would be quite insulting about it outwardly—and inwardly he'd be so very pleased.'

Even his old antagonist, Jack Warner, became emotional about Bogey after he was gone. 'I really liked this ornery cuss,' he admitted in his biography, 'because he had a heart under the crust, and I had a hard time shaking off the blues when Bogey died. And Betty knew it. After the funeral, she sent me this note: "Dear Jack, So many thanks for your contribution and all your thoughts of Bogey and me. It's surely the end of an era for both of us, and I don't see how anything in the future can be quite as good. With all the ups and downs we had together, I am sure we were lucky to have any part of Bogey's life. Betty." Yes, Betty, we were lucky. We had a friend.'

In *A Star is Born*, there is a scene that is the turning point for the widow of Norman Main. After his death, Vicki Lester retreats into herself. Then she is told that such an attitude is a betrayal of Main's intent in life and death. The one who reminds her of that and inspires Vicki to go on was the grandmother in the Janet Gaynor version and a friend in the Judy Garland remake. In real life, Betty's mother flew in from New York to give her that encouragement.

'Life goes so fast; you lose the best of it before you know,' was

163

Betty's feeling immediately after Bogey died. But with the help of her mother, Betty was able to function once again without showing her sorrow.

Soon she attended the first party since her widowhood. The event was the launching of the publicity campaign for *Designing Woman*. Besieged by reporters, she was asked about her new way of life. To rumours that she was changing her professional name to Lauren Bogart, she replied, 'That's a good one. Bogey would choke on his drink wherever he is, if he heard that. He made a big mark on his own. It would be hopeless for anyone to carry on for him.'

Inquiries about dating brought the response, 'When you have been protected for years and years, you are worried about going out into the forest with all the wolves. But luckily I'm bigger than most of them.'

Three months after becoming a widow, her attitude had changed—perhaps because of the attention Sinatra was paying. Her answer to Louella Parsons's question about ever wanting another husband was, 'It's much too soon to talk about such a possibility, but I have no complex about marrying. How could I when my marriage to Bogey was such a good one? I think it is a tribute to the many happy years together that I feel as I do about being married.' When asked about what she would do if the Hollywood Lotharios started pursuing her, she replied, 'If one of them does, I'll clobber him. But, seriously, my children are the most important thing in my life these days. My grief will be with me for a long, long time.' The interview ended with Betty saying, 'I only wish that Bogey could have lived to see *Designing Woman*. I think it is the best thing I have done and he was so interested in my career.'

To further promote the film, Betty want on a publicity jaunt to Chicago, Washington DC, Boston and New York. The tour, she declared, was for 'therapy', otherwise she would have 'cracked up' over Bogey. She let the reporters know this was the first time in twelve years that she had liked herself in a film. 'I think this one will finally establish me, but, let's face it, I'll never win any awards. And I don't care. I'm not the competitive kind of actress.'

While she was in New York, before the picture was to open at the Radio City Music Hall in May, Walter Winchell printed an item in his column that read, 'Lauren Bacall is making it her business to visit all the people who were "mean" to Humphrey Bogart during his lifetime. She's personally telling them off—one by one ...'

'Lauren Bacall has lost her voice,' another columnist reported, 'because of the frantic pace she kept in New York that allowed her only an average of four or five hours sleep a night.'

The children were taken along on the tour. And with the help of the writer Quentin Reynolds, they did the sights of New York from the Statue of Liberty to the Empire State building. While at the circus, they witnessed one tiger clawing another to death. The children screamed and Betty cried, although the clowns tried to comfort her.

When she turned down a chance to plug her movie on the Ed Sullivan show, she stated, 'I refused to go on and stand there with egg on my face. After all, I'm an actress. I don't sing or dance, and if you can't perform you shouldn't be on.' Those reasons had not prevented her from making a television appearance on the same programme half a dozen years earlier. The comment by *The New York Herald Tribune* TV columnist on her reaction, however, paid her the usual compliment: 'Yes, Lauren learned well under the training of the late Humphrey Bogart.'

Betty's performance made Hedda Hopper write, 'Lauren is so good in *Designing Woman* Metro is looking high and low for another property for her. I don't know whether they could buy the rights from Warner's for *Dark Victory*, which starred Bette Davis, but I feel sure Bacall could act the pants off it.' Betty never got the chance to take over her idol's role, for Susan Hayward starred in the remake called *Stolen Hours*, filmed in England several years later. Hayward also took over Betty's part when *Melville Goodwin, USA* was finally made with Kirk Douglas substituting for Bogey. The film was retitled *Top Secret Affair* to disassociate it from the deceased actor.

As soon as the London story of the possible marriage to Sinatra was out, Lolly wrote, 'At first when I saw them together many times at various bistros, I thought at the beginning Frankie was comforting her. They were never seen alone at first and we kept it out of the columns.'

Early in the courtship, they were entertained privately by married couples like Lucille Ball and Desi Arnaz or the Sam Goldwyns. The première of Sinatra's film, *The Joker is Wild*, at the El Portal Theater in Las Vegas was the occasion for their first venture out in public together. They flew down with a group of other stars. Afterwards, they caught the El Rancho Hotel show, starring Joe E. Lewis whose life Sinatra had portrayed in the movie. Never stopping, Sinatra hosted a party at the Sands Hotel that lasted until dawn. The next day, at three-thirty in the afternoon, they returned to Hollywood, having seemed inseparable the entire time.

A few weeks later he threw a party and she was the only un-attached woman there. After an interval of another few weeks, he started taking her out alone. The first function they attended as a couple without an entourage was a party given by Clifton Webb. Because Webb was one of Bogey's closest friends it seemed as if their relationship was being sanctioned.

From then on they were constantly on the go together. Usually they were seen at Romanoff's or Villa Capri. Once he escorted her to the Slate Brothers night club five nights in a row. Sometimes they had dinner together every night in the week.

On finishing *Pal Joey*, Sinatra took Betty for a five-day cruise aboard a rented hundred-and-two-foot yacht, the *Celeste*, that was nearly twice as big as the *Santana*. Sinatra helped Betty overcome her usual aversion to boats by making the trip festive instead of the sailing chore that Bogey's voyages had been. With Mike and Gloria Romanoff and Mr and Mrs Mervyn LeRoy along as chaperones, they went from San Pedro down the California coast to Coronado. Sinatra was most attentive to Betty's every wish, sometimes even anticipating her needs, like fetching her a terry towelling robe so that she would not be cold in her swimsuit. His tender considerations made it obvious to his guests how far their relationship had progressed.

Originally Sinatra confessed that he took out Betty because 'She is lonely since Bogey left us—I'm a lonesome guy, too.'

Betty confirmed his explanation by admitting, 'I always gave the impression of being the gal whom nothing fazes. But my emotions were never that secure. I felt safe with Bogey. He was the only man in my life, from birth on, that I had felt safe with. Life had been so secure and solid, and then you are alone.'

In the beginning it seemed, figuratively speaking, that their loss moved them to duet the old Sinatra favourite *I'll Never Smile*

Again, but now they were singing another tune. With Bogey gone and the Rat Pack dispersed, Betty no longer represented a mother figure. Yet he would tease her by having Mother written in cream on her birthday cake that she cut with the help of him and Kim Novak. Despite the constant and obvious display of closeness, those who knew Sinatra best were sceptical about his marrying her. The main reason, they said, was Sinatra's continual concern for the son and two daughters he had by his first wife, Nancy. Ava had tried to come between them, but she finally had to admit, 'You can't compete with three children.'

Betty's description of her feelings towards Sinatra was, 'I have dated others. They just don't get as much publicity. I think I date Frank more often than other men because I am happy with him. I enjoy myself. We laugh and bubble a little at what we see and hear. And he is so full of surprises. Nothing pleases him more than to see a look of consternation on my face.

'For example, quite often we'll go out on a date and I'll ask Frank where we're going. With an absolutely poker face, he'll answer, "Oh, why don't we just have dinner at the Capri and see a play." I'll agree.

'Twenty minutes later, we go into the Villa Capri and he steers me straight to the private dining room. He opens the door. I walk in and fifty people whom I haven't seen in ages look up and say, "Hi, Betty! Long time, no see." You couldn't possibly know what that means to me.'

One night they were involved in an adventurous incident. While they were at Slate's, a heckler provoked one of the brothers who owned the night club and a fight broke out. To avoid becoming involved in the free-for-all that suddenly surrounded them, Sinatra grabbed Betty by the arm and headed her toward the rear exit. On his trying to open the back door, the burglar alarm was set off. They pushed through the turmoil that had by now become contagious and finally made it to the entrance. Police arrived just as Betty and Sinatra jumped into his Italian sports car and made their getaway.

Like a couple of teenagers, they would wear shorts and T-shirts while driving around Hollywood in his new ten-thousand-dollar car. Occasionally they would have parties for a small group of intimates or just one other couple like Bing Crosby and his May–

December, bride-to-be Kathy. Sinatra would busy himself with the barbecue and spaghetti, while Betty would make the salad. Sometimes in her happiness, she would burst out in song, but laughingly she admitted, 'Frank says I sing like Tallulah Bankhead, off-key—but loud.'

Still anxious to exercise her acting talents, she told an interviewer for an Australian women's weekly, 'Any day now the right script will come along and I'll be back at work. I wish I could work six months of every year and loaf the rest of the time. But I won't plan for that. I refuse to plan for anything. Why should I know in advance about tomorrow? I like it to be a surprise, anyway, not be the product of a pattern. All I know is I would like to travel. I would like to go abroad.

'We've stayed in Europe on three occasions, Bogey and I, and each time it was great. We liked London most. When they offer me a picture there next, I'll come to stay at least half a year so I can place Stephen in an English school. I love English schools. I would like a flat in Mayfair. I've found there's nothing wrong with living in the Dorchester.

'But I won't plan. There's plenty of time for everything. No hurry. This, I suppose, is the great advantage of still being young. I've been married half my life. You can't dismiss that with a shrug of the shoulders, can you? And I have no such intention. But I won't arrange my future, either.'

Although she never did *Dark Victory*, she was, in another remake, to play the part of a woman who' dies. Twentieth Century Fox granted Betty's wish to work again by assigning her to a new version of *Sentimental Journey*. At first the film was to be called *Our Love* and was intended to co-star Anthony Franciosa. Later they changed the title to *The Gift of Love* and Robert Stack was cast, in this tear-jerker, as the husband whom she comes back to haunt. There is a scene in which the child they have adopted is taken aboard a rowing boat and pretends she is floating down a river in Africa—evoking memories of *The African Queen*.

The first day on the set, Betty revealed, she felt as 'nervous as I can possibly be. This is the first time I've started a picture without having Bogey say, "Good luck, Baby." It's kinda tough, you know. It's been eight months since I did *Designing Woman*. Think of all the things that happened in that time.

'I'm glad to be going back to work. It gives me something to keep myself busy, and I need that desperately. All I've had to do is sit and think. If I hadn't had the children, I would have been in really bad shape. I'd like to go right into another picture if I can find one. I think work is good for me. You have theatre in New York and lots of things to do. Hollywood is no place for a single woman.'

Later she added, 'It's just that there are a lot more hours in the day alone, now, and there has to be something important to do in all that time. And acting is necessary to me. I remember Bogey used to say, "If you're an actor, you must act."'

Though she and Bogey had formed Mapleton Productions, she admitted, 'I have no interest in producing. I just love to act, and I'm happy to have the man have the biggest part.'

In an attempt to start a new life, she announced during October, 'I'm going to sell the house. It keeps alive the memories of his last year when Bogey was no longer Bogey. It was not in every way the best of the twelve years we were married.

'I am not trying to disassociate myself with the past, but this house has ceased to be a pleasure to me. I can't live here unless I want to live in the past. I don't want to forget Bogey—I never will—but the vitality which was so much a part of him left in that year and I find myself re-living it all over again. I owe it to Bogey as well as the two children and myself to look forward to the future.'

The break with the days of her marriage became even more essential when she realised that three other people who were in the wedding party were dead: Louis Bromfield, his wife and George Hawkins. She stated, 'I'm fighting to stay alive.'

The *Santana* was put up for sale as well. Once she had freed herself of those attachments, she told a reporter from *Newsweek*, 'I don't even belong to any movie company. I only belong to me and I'm delighted. I'll never make any long-term plans. They just don't work out. When Bogey and I bought the house in 1952, I said I had all I ever wanted—a beautiful home, two children, I'm working. But it got loused up and I found myself with a lot of belongings I didn't want anymore.

'The day Bogey died I looked at my kids and said, "By God, these two make it worthwhile." I love children. I think I'll have some

169

more. Guess I better get married first. Ring-a-ding-ding. My son, he's a gasser. My daughter, when she's around men she swings her hips. What instinct. I've forgotten it myself. Guess I'll have to borrow some of it from her.'

The five-year-old girl's playful seductiveness made Betty comment, 'I'm just a little worried about Leslie. The other day when my agent came to call, she met him at the door wiggling her hips and saying in a sultry tone, "Come on in the house and visit us." She'd never met Miss West and I have no idea where she picked it up.'

The children were still unaware of Betty's profession. 'To this day,' she said, 'Leslie and Stephen know only that I go to the studio in the morning to work, whereas some women go to work in offices.'

The recollection of how she felt at the same age as Leslie when she had lost her father—albeit by divorce—prompted Betty to say, 'The little one misses him without sadness, but the boy is different. It is taking him a long time adjusting himself. And he has need of a father more and more. This is my great problem. They meet other children, all of whom have home, mother and father. That's why we have to get out of here. I mean this house. Without Bogey, it is not the same. Sure, it's beautiful. But we'll never have it back the way it was, and these memories are hard on a child. I don't want to forget the past or any part of it. But I think it would be easier for all of us to begin a new life in new surroundings.'

At Hallowe'en time, Betty planned a party for one hundred and ten guests. When people wondered if the purpose of the festivities was an announcement of her engagement to Sinatra, she let it be known, 'That's the most ridiculous thing I ever heard. I am leaving my big house and am moving into a smaller house in Bel Air so I want to leave in a blaze of glory. Don't you think it's about time I entertain? I have been living off other people too long and I think I should be a hostess instead of a guest for a change.'

Concerning her new residence on Bellagio Road, she said, 'Fortunately, I only had to move a few blocks to the home I am now renting. It's smaller and I am glad. Never again do I want a big one. Let us look at it this way. My whole world is changed. I just can't live that way anymore. That part of my life is over and I would like my friends to remember that.'

At the same time that she moved, Sinatra sold his Palm Springs home and bought a huge estate there that had belonged to Al Jolson. The coincidence of her compacting and his enlarging their respective residences gave rise to further speculation about the imminence of their betrothal.

Her usual answer to such guesswork was, 'That's crazy' or 'That's the maddest.' And Sinatra would put off reporters with, 'We're not ready for marriage yet.' Once he divulged his philosophy in terms befitting the star of *The Joker is Wild*: 'Love is like a game of poker. The girl if she wants to win a hand that may affect her whole life should be careful not to show her cards before the guy shows his.'

Taking a cue from his line, Betty said, 'I've seen a lot of Frankie, that's no secret. He's a special friend. But I have a lot of special friends. I've seen other men too.' Yet she neglected to mention their names. A moment later, she added, 'I'm not quite as strong as I thought I was. I can't be alone all the time.'

Unable to keep up the pretence perpetually, she replied to the question of who was her favourite date: 'Number one, Sinatra. Number two, Sinatra. Number three, Sinatra.'

On the first night back from ten days in Europe shooting scenes for his new movie *Kings Go Forth*, Sinatra's date was former girlfriend Peggy Connolly. They went to a night club and later that week they were seen together in Palm Springs. Like many of the girls he escorted before Betty, Peggy bore a striking resemblance to Ava. His intimates believed that Sinatra was unhappy, even though he was at the height of his career once again earning four million dollars a year, because his second success cost him Ava, just as his first triumph made it impossible to continue his marriage to Nancy.

As soon as he returned to Beverly Hills, he called Betty and invited her out to dinner. The following night she was hostess at his party after attending the fights. From then on, they were rarely apart.

The frequency of their dating made columnist Frank Collins question whether the reason for her seeing so much of Sinatra was an attempt to alter his ways *before* heading for the altar. At first she laughed and then said seriously, 'Any woman who tries to change a man, particularly after he's reached his thirties, is a fool. The only thing she can do is make him worse.

171

'His views, his attitudes, his habits, his ideas, everything you know about him are part of him. Now you either love him as he is, or you don't love him at all. You can't love parts of a man and ignore the rest.

'I was married twelve years to a guy I still think is the finest man I have ever known. But you may be surprised to learn that I was tougher to live with than he was. Yet I am not overly sophisticated and I would feel very uncomfortable being regarded as one of those emancipated women who wants to go it alone. I hate loneliness,' she said, admitting the same dislike that Bogey had.

Concluding the Collins interview, she stated, 'Everybody wants to know if I am going to marry again, and mainly whether I am going to marry Frank. "When are you going to announce your engagement to Mr Sinatra?" they all ask coyly. They should know right now that I am not the announcing type.'

They did announce, however, that they would make a film together. And Betty divulged that she kept a picture of Sinatra in her den.

Just when it seemed they would soon be wed, they had a blow-up. Ava had fallen from a horse in a bullring at a friend's estate in Spain. A scarred face as well as permanent paralysis of her lip and right cheek appeared inevitable. And so she flew to New York for surgery. In hysterics, Ava called Sinatra because she knew he could always be depended on in a crisis. Quickly he came to his ex-wife's side to bolster her courage.

'Betty hit the roof,' Lolly reported.

While Sinatra was away, Betty dined out one night with Spencer Tracy. A reporter approached her to ask, 'Where's Frankie?'

'Frankie who?' she exploded. 'I'm not his keeper. Who knows where he is? Or who cares?'

Within a short while, Ava recovered completely and went back to Europe without requiring any operation. Sinatra returned to Hollywood for a reconciliation with Betty. Their constant changes of heart earned them the same on-again-off-again reputation Ava and Frankie had shared.

Once more the press put an alert on her and she announced, 'The papers say Frank and I are going to get married. They've done everything—predicted the time and the place. There's nothing left for me to say.'

Soon it was Betty's turn to travel again. At the beginning of

February 1958, she went on a publicity junket to the East Coast for *The Gift of Love*. The reviews acknowledged that Betty's controlled performance cut the cloying quality of the story. Her gallantry in the face of a personal bereavement reverberated in the portrayal of a doomed woman. But her acting was not enough. The film needed all the exploitation she could contribute.

Newspaper space was made available to her at the expense of her privacy. In Boston, all the papers reported her declaration: 'Palship is my watchword for the year,' indicating that there had been a rift with Sinatra. In New York, she told the reporters what they wanted to hear about her possible remarriage, but she did not refer to any specific prospect: 'Once you've been married, then the routine of going out on dates becomes something just for fifteen-year-olds. Those fights in taxicabs or cars going home. They are too much for me. If I thought I was never going to get married again, I'd retire from the human race right now.'

Previously, her marriage-counselling had always proved newsworthy, but, on this tour, widow-advising was the stance she took in her message to the media: 'Children need a man in the house, the influence of a father. That's particularly true of a boy—he needs the sound of a man's voice. It's bad for a boy to be surrounded by women, one of the worst things in the world. They can grow up thinking women run the world, and, then, boy, have you got a problem.

'I don't think a man can be a mother and father to a child, nor can a woman. You just do the best you can, but don't think it is easy. It's a little easier with a girl, but girls need daddies. They have crushes on their fathers and they give their fathers a different kind of emotion than their mothers.

'There's nothing you can do about it until you have a husband. No outside man can influence the children—he's not around enough and he doesn't have a position in the household. As for my children—they will have a father eventually, but it may take thirty or forty years.'

Continuing to explore the need of a husband for herself and a father for her children, as though bidding for Sinatra's help, Betty said, 'You can't live almost your whole adult life—in my case from age twenty to thirty-two—with a man you love without it becoming a way of life. All of a sudden there you are faced with a big adjustment to make. I don't think I've made it yet, and I don't think I ever will. When you marry young and well, you find it is the only way to live. You may think you wish you were free to do this or that when you're married, but when you're free you don't do those things. It's no fun alone.

'Whenever there's a woman on the loose, there are characters that come around to see what's new. But ever since I was fifteen I couldn't see going out for the sake of having a date.'

Despite being busy with interviews and theatre-going during her two-week jaunt, she still missed Sinatra and so he came to join her. This reunion could have duplicated the rendezvous in Gotham she had had with Bogey at the beginning, except that Sinatra spoiled everything by provoking a fight with her at The Colony.

Their bumpy relationship reached a new high a few weeks later. Under the headline that made the front pages of papers across the country, 'SINATRA AND BACALL TO MARRY,' Lolly wrote, 'Frank Sinatra is going to marry Lauren Bacall! This isn't if, and, or maybe. He was overheard by several persons asking her to marry him at the Imperial Gardens where they were having dinner.

'So I faced Betty with the story at the Noël Coward party Zsa Zsa Gabor gave at her home. At first Betty tried the usual hedge and said, "Why don't you telephone Frank in Florida?"

'Then, she finally admitted he had asked her to marry him. And you'll say yes, I told her. "Of course," she answered. She was beaming with happiness.

'Agent Irving Lazar, who is a friend of both, was her escort at the party, said, "Don't you dare say I told you this, but since you know. Yes, it's true—they'll marry."

'Betty joins Frank in Chicago to go to the fights March 25. They leave the next day for New York, then they head for Palm Springs.'

Besieged by other reporters as a result of that story, Betty declared, 'Any further statement has to come from Mr Sinatra.'

The Voice said nothing. The Rat, as he was affectionately known to his intimates, was 'scared' because Betty had backed him into a corner by exposing his intentions. This upset was complicated by her annoyance with him over Brigitte Bardot. As part of the publicity build-up for a movie, *Paris by Night*, that he was to make with the French sex-pot, intimations of a future assignation between them were promulgated. Naturally jealous, Betty tried to talk him out of doing the film. On hearing this, Bardot commented, 'Miss Bacall is no fool. I would do the same. Sinatra and I will make interesting chemistry together.'

Gossip had it that the competition made Betty even more aggressive about her marital future with Sinatra. Compounding her anxiety was a statement he made to reporters when the French seductress suddenly married Jacques Charier: 'You tell Brigitte Bardot that she broke my heart when she got married. She was one chick I really wanted to meet.'

Almost immediately afterwards Brigitte separated from her husband, then invited Sinatra—via the press—to come to France. She awaited his arrival because, she predicted, 'We will make lovely sparks together.'

In spite of Betty's objections, Sinatra accepted Brigitte's offer. But on his return from France, he and Betty were reunited and the movie was never made. The entire episode made Betty realise her precarious position and she decided not to be victimised by pretending to be passive. But this time her aggressiveness did not succeed.

'Pushy broads' were Sinatra's nemesis. Though she had held herself back until now, Betty's old wilfulness was aroused. And she ended the affair while they were dining out one night by breaking a wine glass over Sinatra's head.

His only reaction was to call over the owner of the restaurant and say, 'Make her apologise for breaking your glass.'

She exclaimed, 'I won't apologise. I'm glad I did it.'

Her futile attempt to get a rise out of him failed and caused their break-up. And that pun is an indication of the many levels of meaning her gesture had. The incident was reminiscent of the time in another restaurant when she was three and had gloated over having forced her father to order ice cream for her. She said then, 'I get anything I want, Daddy.' So her frustration now was expressed in a child-like way. The method she chose to show her disappointment in not marrying Sinatra was a reminder of the Hebrew wedding custom of breaking a glass at a wedding. The use of a wine glass, which is an English translation of her adopted name Weinstein—or Bacal in Rumanian—could be interpreted as an act of throwing herself at him. The deed was similar to the action of Dolores Gray in *Designing Woman* when she is informed by her boyfriend, Gregory Peck, while they are eating out, that he has married Betty. Dolores dumps his plate of ravioli in his lap.

Later Betty enters and witnesses his discomfort as the hot dish burns his groin. Dolores, still on the rampage, runs into Peck at a fashion show that Betty is conducting. Again Dolores menaces his masculinity by threatening, while Betty watches, to sear his genitals with the hot tea she is pouring. The real-life act was cooler. Betty did not strike below the belt, but aimed for the part of the body that gave her trouble: Sinatra's head.

Within a few weeks, Betty showed up at the Villa Capri with someone else. When asked where Sinatra was, she answered, 'I'm not his keeper.' As for their future dating, she said, 'Oh, I may see him casually, but there never was anything between us. That talk all started in the newspapers.'

A few months later the schism between them was so complete that when their liaison was brought up, she screamed, 'Never mention me again in the same breath with Frank Sinatra.' To emphasise her disdain for the singer, she avoided going with her friends to his Las Vegas opening and instead went alone to his competitor Dean Martin's first night in a Hollywood night club.

The following winter, Betty showed up at Judy Garland's opening party in the Grove's Regency Room with playwright Leonard Gershe while Frankie arrived with the night-club owner Jack Entrater. By then, there was no further point to be made and Betty and Sinatra casually acknowledged each other. During the entire evening she socialised with everyone else. Press photographers had her pose hugging Rock Hudson. Meanwhile, Sinatra provoked a gag tussle with Jerry Lewis and wound up with his buddy Entrater at the Beverly Wilshire Hotel drugstore having lox and bagels at three in the morning.

His off-handedness eventually caused Betty to make the observation: 'You've got to have your head off your shoulders to get involved with a man like Sinatra. But I did. It was a bad time.'

Years later, when she remembered this interlude, she was kind. 'We had our so-called romance at the wrong time,' she surmised. 'I was still half-crazy with grief over Bogey.'

The public's fascination with this romance lingered. Nearly a decade later, a feature of Roy Newsquist's interview with Betty for *McCall's* was her explanation of the outcome of the affair: 'Sinatra was definitely a part of my life. He practically lived at our house (four or five years); he was there five or six days a week. He was a fixture in my life. Then after Bogey died, I eventually did get involved with him on a boy-girl basis so-to-speak. It worked out marvelously for a while—at least until the press went absolutely mad and drove both of us mad. The press made it impossible. They were trying to back us into a corner.

'I remember asking one of the wire service reporters, a fellow I've known for many years and whom I like very much, "How long are you going to keep it up?" And he said, "I'm afraid we're going to keep it up until you either do or you don't." In other words, the press was going to keep at us until they either made it impossible for us to see each other or we got married. Chances are we would do either for the wrong reasons, simply because we were so harassed. It was front page stuff every other day. Frank is really put off by that sort of thing; he runs for his life. I was very uncomfortable. I found it an undignified way to live. So as a result of what the press had done, we didn't see each other anymore. And I just couldn't function in Hollywood anymore.'

This last statement echoed what Betty had said soon after the attachment to Sinatra was severed: 'I have no life in Hollywood anymore.'

Back from a four-week European trip she took with her friend Slim to forget the emotional upset, Betty declared, 'My life has changed in the past couple of months.' The new perspective she gained from going abroad made her realise, 'Hollywood is a town of couples—married, divorced, romantic—and I felt like a third wheel and more alone than ever.' Of the more than twenty friends she once had, she believed that only six remained loyal. Most of the original group were also close to Sinatra. When the break came with her, they chose to side with the singer. Sinatra revived The Rat Pack with different members who were more hedonistic and called it The Clan.

Feeling as though she had caught herself in a trap of her own making, she said, 'I didn't have the courage to move away. And then when I moved into a new house, I chose one in the same neighborhood—can you beat that?'

Aware also that she had lost her place socially and had no real standing in her profession, Betty had to seek a new environment in order to go on. The opportunity to do so came while she was visiting London. She was offered a chance to appear in a film opposite one of Britain's most popular actors, Kenneth More. Flattered, but uncertain about making her first film in another country, she was not convinced until Vivien Leigh and Laurence Olivier threw a party for two hundred guests in her honour.

'Everyone in the theatrical and social world was there. I kept pinching myself to see if I were the same girl who once would have fainted at the thought of even meeting the Oliviers. You can imagine what this did to build up my morale—to be accepted on my own, without Bogey, for the first time.'

This impressed Betty so much that she told a London reporter of her readiness to exchange Hollywood, 'where flesh is cheap and people forget too quickly', for England 'where people have something to say and are willing to listen to what I think'.

Now she was ready to abandon everything familiar. 'Bogey always told me not to relive the past,' she explained, 'that nothing good could come from it. And he was right. He was always right.' The unfulfilment in her relations with Sinatra forced her into re-evaluation of herself. What had happened made her recall that Bogey had once said, 'Live each moment as well as you can, one moment at a time and perhaps when you put all the moments together you'll have something worth remembering.' Bogey was obviously still her mentor.

As for allowing anyone else to share her future, she confessed, 'I'm thirty-four and too young to retire from life. I'm not ready to sit back and become a spectator.'

With a changed perspective, she was later able to tell *Time*, 'Being a widow is no picnic, you lose your place. I had to go on because of my children, and I had to because of my own sense of survival. Bogey's belief was always that if one mourns too long, one mourns for oneself rather than for the one who's gone. Life is for the living. It's all cliché, but it's true.'

Looking back, she admitted, 'I couldn't cope except by getting out of Hollywood completely. I was a bitter young woman.' The business of being Bogey's widow 'was a humiliating way to live'.

Once the British film was completed, her intention was to set up her future home in New York. After fifteen years of having devoted herself to filmdom, Betty decided to return to the place from where she started in order to make a new beginning.

So ended the dream that became impossible.

Big Fish, Little Fish

'You ask if this revival of Bogey is necrophilic?' Betty said. 'Well, you're damned right. That is the one man I'm necrophilic about.'

The Bogey cult began even before he died. In the summer of 1956, the Brattle Theater in Cambridge, Massachusetts, booked *Beat the Devil*, which by then had been around for two years. The long-haired audience from the summer student population of Radcliffe and the Massachusetts Institute of Technology became so enraptured that the theatre booked a package of old Warner Brothers' films the following summer. Among them was *Casablanca* which turned out to be the biggest hit of all. Then the Brattle started showing Bogey's films one at a time and this led to screening them in groups. A Bogey festival was initiated that became a regular attraction at exam-time. It was as though Bogey's boldness could inspire the students to leap over this hurdle of conformity.

Exhibitors across the country caught the Brattle fever and soon it spread throughout the world. France made immediate claim to the Bogey craze. The actor was the perfect existential hero. As Alastair Cooke predicted, the French made the definitive pronouncement on the actor. André Bazin, the illustrious Parisian critic and one of the most important influences on the New Wave directors, wrote: 'Bogart is a man with a past. When he comes into a film it is already "the morning after", his face scarred by what he has seen, and his step heavy from all that he has learned, having

179

ten times triumphed over death, he will survive for us one more time.'

The zeal for Bogey-ography became even more relentless as the sixties progressed toward new freedoms, and the young discarded outmoded ideas. Through his image of non-conformity and being outside society, Bogey became a representative of a time beyond his time. Even by enduring he was continuing the death and resurrection that was his film fate. No actor other than Bogey became more idolised after he was gone than while he was alive.

Betty's explanation for this phenomenon was, 'I think it's due to what Bogey was as a man. I'm very proud of it, and I think his children are proud of it, because it came from the young people themselves, was not promoted, it was a perfectly natural evolvement. I think that fifty years from now, a hundred years from, the same thing will happen. Bogey was an extraordinary man. And the qualities he had as a man, his kind of purity of thought—and he did have that—came out in every part he played. He was in some rotten movies, and he survived them all. I think there is so little that is really solid in this world to identify with, and Bogey is solid. Bogey was a solid man. He was sure of what he believed in and sure of his way of life. I think that's the big secret, and kids sense that. It's something very tangible to hold on to.'

With Bogey's image becoming all-pervasive, Betty was forced to write guidelines for her own persona. Calling the list *This is Me from A to Z* when it was published in a magazine, she compiled such characteristics as:

> 'I Love: my children, desert air, rainy nights, music, except Hawaiian, imagination, black, talking to myself. I Fear: being alone in the house at night, being a flop as a person and as an actress, speeding, height. I'm Sentimental: about all occasions, many things I associate with Bogey. But I'm determined not to remain attached to them for that reason alone. I'm Impulsive: not so much in actions but in speech. I'm Neat. I Burn: at lateness and inquisitiveness. I'm Brave: when I did my scarf dance. I was twelve and had made

up my mind I was going to be a dancer. It was at camp and I was a smash that day. I Dress: to please men and myself, simply. I'm Pig Headed. I Laugh: at myself and wit. I'm Proud: of my children, the improvement in my work and my zest for learning. I Regret: my face and every morning I'm getting to like it less and less. I'm Embarrassed: by husbands and wives arguing in public.'I Sleep: erratically and not as well as I used to. I'm Bored: by afternoon and people who pour their problems on you. I'm Superstitious: about walking under ladders and three on a match. I Hope: not to live alone the rest of my life. I don't like living alone.'

Intent on making the most of her stay in London, Betty arrived with twenty-seven suitcases, a cook and a nanny for the children. She leased a flat for six months, and enrolled Leslie and Stephen in the American school in Regent's Park.

In the film she was making, called *Northwest Frontier*—and renamed *Flame Over India* in America, so as not to be taken for a Western—Betty played the uncharacteristic role of a governess at the turn of the century. The first month of filming was on location in and around the city of Jaipur, India. The strangeness was stimulating, but the heat exhausting. Sometimes she had to work in temperatures that went up to 116 degrees. Her make-up would melt within twenty minutes, even though she applied chamois-covered icebags to her face between scenes. When lunch was eaten out of doors, she had to fight off flies to get at the food. Later, working in the deserted city of Amber was fascinating because the only inhabitants were wild monkeys. The entire time, she kept taking photographs and ciné film to show the children later. Before leaving, Betty told an interviewer that she would like to return for a vacation 'to study comparative religions'.

After a few more weeks of shooting in London, the company went to Spain to use the Sierra Nevada near Granada as background. While in the tiny village of Izolloz, all the shops closed one day because a public holiday had been declared in honour of the producer who was bringing money to the town and they named it: *El Fiesta de Ingles Señor Rank*. During the filming of a scene in Guidix, an even smaller village, Betty had to sing the traditional Eton Boating Song and soon every native picked up the melody but used Spanish words that carried suggestive innuendos.

Betty found she was helped by being the only American in the cast and working in different surroundings. 'It got me out into the world again,' she said. 'I've discovered that I can take more than I thought I could—and that's good. I can adapt and adjust to new places and people better than I knew. Also, I'm aware of becoming professionally mature and that's a wonderful feeling. As an actress, I believe I've grown up—at thirty-four.'

Continuing in the same vein, she declared, 'If you want a philosophy from me, I guess this is it: I believe I have to use every moment to grow and develop.

'A well-known Hollywood actress arrived in London last week saying that she was proud to feel twelve years old still. Heavens, that's a sad remark. I'd hate to feel twelve years old on the first day I was thirteen. Now I'm thirty-four and I hope I sound every day of it. Next year I want to be thirty-five, with that extra year of experience to live with. And I hope if I teach them nothing else, I get that point over to my children.'

After the production was completed, she stayed on in London to enjoy the social scene with her newly acquired friends, and was presented to the Queen Mother and Princess Margaret at the Royal Film Performance. Not completely happy, however, she admitted to the press: 'I guess you could say that my life at the moment is just a search for a man. But that is a fine reflection on Bogey.' She begged reporters not to force the issue as they had with Sinatra. 'Human nature being what it is,' she said, 'I'm almost bound to meet some men. Please, please don't expect a romance every time I'm out with a man. One day I may like one well enough—though I'm choosey—and we may decide he can put up with me. When that happens, I promise I'll tell you ... but until then, let's forget it.'

While she was at an American Embassy dinner party one night, burglars climbed through a bedroom window of her third-floor flat and stole more than fifteen thousand dollars worth of jewellery.

This was the second robbery she had had in twelve years, and though the loot was recovered within a few days without the thieves being caught, she told Art Buchwald, 'I've had a pretty bad two years, and so I decided at the time of the robbery that this was par for the course. Things had been tapering off as far as sheer disasters were concerned, but a robbery like this helps to keep a person on her toes and not fall into the trap that everything is going to be all right.'

After nearly nine months abroad, Betty received an offer to appear in her first leading role on Broadway. Once again, it was Slim who was instrumental in opening up a new facet to Betty's life and career. Now married to the successful stage and movie producer, Leland Haywood, Slim suggested that he cast Betty in *Goodbye Charlie*. Once again, as in *Blithe Spirit* and *The Gift of Love*, Betty would play a ghost, but this time the role was of a man shot for being a womaniser who comes back reincarnated as a beautiful girl.

Even though fifteen years had passed since Slim had brought Betty to the attention of Howard Hawks, the benefactress told columnist Frank Farrell, 'Mr Hawks and the late Humphrey Bogart simultaneously fell in love with Miss Bacall. She had to choose between the director and the actor at the end of the picture they did together.' Obviously, there was no animosity between the ladies and they remained close through the years.

Another friend was also involved in the offer of the play to Betty. Joan, the wife of the playwright George Axelrod, was an old Julia Richmond chum. The entire project seemed like a family reunion.

Yet Betty admitted that when they suggested that she take the part, 'I didn't sleep for days. There was this awful fear—actors have more fears than people realize—can I do it? Then, one afternoon, I suddenly decided. The thing, which is so important in all our lives, was right. Now was the time. My life was better than it had been in three years. The time was right.'

Expounding on why she felt she had to work in the theatre, she explained, 'Every once in a while you should shake up your life a little bit. There comes a time when you have to stop kidding yourself along. Have you been selling yourself a bill of goods about your so-called talent or haven't you? I believe in gambling. It's easy to go to a roulette table and toss away fifty bucks. I would rather gamble on a larger scale. I believe in gambling with your life. I don't think it's good to play it safe for too long. So you take the big plunge and a whole new life opens up.'

To demonstrate her faith in the show, Betty invested twelve per cent of the eighty-thousand-dollar production cost while George Axelrod and Leland Haywood put up the rest. Sydney Chaplin was Haywood's choice for the lead opposite Betty. But the actor, who was in Paris, said, 'Leland, I'm having a good time. I don't even want to think of working.'

When Axelrod came to London, he told Betty of Chaplin's reaction. She suggested, 'Well, let's have him over,' and put in a call to Paris.

That evening, Chaplin arrived and Axelrod read the play to him until dawn. By the time Axelrod left at ten that morning, he was able to take back with him a contract signed by Chaplin. A few days later, Betty followed the playwright to New York.

The show toured for eight weeks in Pittsburgh, Detroit, Cleveland, Baltimore and Philadelphia. 'I wanted to get as far away as possible,' Betty stated, 'from the usual try-out places like New Haven and Boston. I was nervous about being on the stage again. It's no good to have everyone you know coming and giving you advice. I thought it was better to sweat it out far, far away. I also wanted as long a time as possible to practice.'

While in Detroit, Betty met the radio interviewer, Shirley Eder, at a party held in honour of the cast. When Eder mentioned that she was heard on the air five times a day, Betty explained, 'I can't think of anything more loathsome.' In retaliation, Eder compared Betty to Christine Jorgensen because of the sex-change she portrayed in the show. Just as they were about to come to blows, it was reported, 'Joe Pasternak's Hungarian cooking was served and saved that opening night.'

The show itself needed more rescuing than that. The second act had been re-written five times and was still in trouble. No money would be lost, however, because fifty-five thousand dollars was made on the road, and fifty-four thousand was paid in a pre-production movie deal that could net up to three hundred thousand dollars. The high price the film company was willing to pay was due to the success of Axelrod's *The Seven-Year Itch*. There was a three-hundred-thousand-dollar advance sale at the box-office.

'It's funny,' Betty mused, 'when I was pounding producers' doors on Broadway, ushering and all the rest—I had only one dream. To be a star on Broadway. Now it's fifteen years later. And here I am, on Broadway. And soon my name will be on a marquee after all.'

Her name was by itself above the title, a billing she had never achieved in the movies, which she now regarded as a lesser medium.

On December 16, 1959, at the Lyceum Theater in New York, the play opened. It was almost hello and goodbye, Charlie. Slightly embarrassed, her old friends David Niven, Sammy Davis, Jnr, Moss Hart, Rita Gam, Anatole Litvak and Sam Spiegel came backstage and tried to act as though the misfortune had not occurred. Adlai Stevenson also showed up even though he had seen the show several times out of town. Feeling awkward, he tried a feeble joke: 'Well, we're behind the footlights, aren't we?' Stevenson kissed Betty, but refused to be photographed giving her a hug. All of them went to the opening night party to await the first reviews. The critics kissed off the play but embraced Betty. The dean of them all, Brooks Atkinson of *The New York Times*, wrote, 'If this is the kind of part she wants to play, she can take satisfaction in realising that she is playing it as well as anyone could, Lon Chaney and Mae West not excepted.'

After 109 performances the play closed. Later Betty was able to say to Tom Meehan in *The Saturday Evening Post*, 'It was no picnic but in one sense it was good for my ego, which was plenty low, pal. I discovered that I was a Broadway box-office draw. People kept buying tickets mainly to see me, I'm not afraid to admit, and that was nice.'

Describing the entire theatrical experience to Howard Thompson in *The Sunday New York Times*, she said, 'My ego soared to know that people wanted to see me and that I could sustain a stage performance even scared to death. We actually played for three-and-a-half months, too. I kept telling myself Jack Lemmon only ran a month in his.'

If Betty's talent could not keep her in the theatrical spotlight, she could always depend on her knack for publicity to restore her to centre stage. According to Romanoff her great satisfaction, anyway, was to be in the public eye. This unique gift for gaining attention was noted by Ted Lewis, a Washington columnist for *The New York Daily News*. Fifteen years after the picture of Truman and Betty was published, he wrote, 'But for the death of F. D. R., it is probable that Harry Truman would be remembered today only as the Vice President who played a piano with Lauren Bacall seated on top of it with her lovely gams hovering over high C.'

For the third time in a row, a major love affair was to put Betty in the headlines. During the past year she had been seeing several men without creating any fuss in the papers. Even though she had been romantically linked with Adlai Stevenson, very few people put much credence in it. The same opinion was expressed regarding her so-called relationship with Rock Hudson that the fan magazines said was broken up when Betty met her co-star Sydney Chaplin. No one was particularly impressed, either, when she was photographed being escorted by Christopher Plummer to the opening of his ex-wife Tammy Grimes's show *The Unsinkable Molly Brown*. Nor did anyone seem really to care when Danton Walker printed in his column: 'Very decorative couple at the new Chien Vert restaurant, Lauren Bacall and Met Opera conductor Thomas Schippers. Talk is that they'll marry this summer in Italy.' Stories like that did not have the drama that had made Betty one of the most discussed women of her time.

Betty stated her objective to Radie Harris: 'I want my next husband to be someone closer to my age, not only for the children, but also for me ... I can finally look at Bogey on TV and not be sad ... And now all I want is a one-woman man ... I believe in the togetherness of love that builds a home and a family. I was lucky enough to find it once and I hope I will again.'

That Christmas Betty got her wish. During the week after the opening of *Goodbye Charlie*, she went to Roddy McDowell's huge holiday party feeling sad because the third anniversary of Bogey's death was nearing and she was still alone. She was about to leave when a man entered who was considered the successor to Bogey by everyone who ever saw him. He stopped her and reminded her of his name: Jason Robards, Jnr.

'We hit it off immediately,' Betty confessed, 'and then a few days later I ran into Jason again at Lee Strasberg's annual New Year's Eve bash. And from that night on, well—one thing led to another.'

They really got to know each other at the parties, but they had met before. A year earlier, she had been offered the lead opposite him in the stage version of *The Disenchanted*, a fictionalised biography of F. Scott Fitzgerald. Like Bogey's last movie, this play was also based on a novel by Budd Schulberg. Her agent turned down the part for her. On the opening night of the show, she went backstage with some friends who knew Robards. Betty said nothing more than a polite hello and a slight compliment on his performance in *The Disenchanted*.

Now they were completely enchanted with each other. But Robards was in a situation similar to that of Bogey and Sinatra when Betty entered the picture: he was already married ... and to an actress. Only a few weeks before, he had wed his second wife, Rachel Taylor. Again the scandalous elements existed for an explosion of newsprint.

Soon an item appeared in the papers that revealed, 'Must be love for Bacall and Robards, Jnr, staging battles royal in the best Bogart and Methot tradition ... like in a Manhattan saloon the other night when Jason reportedly threw something at Betty and she stomped out.'

Not only was Robards's behaviour considered reminiscent of Bogart's (even their names were similar), but there was also a sameness in their personalities and status as actors. Betty, as a novice in the theatre, became involved with the celebrated stage actor, just as she had fallen for Bogey when she started out in movies. Aside from not being physically imposing, the two men both had rugged charm. And they were boozers as well, who floundered early in their lives until acting gave them a purpose.

'I went into the Navy. It was before the war, and I wanted to go to sea and travel. When the war was over, and I had been in the Navy for seven years, I didn't know what to do. For a while I considered staying in for twenty years and retiring when I was thirty-seven. But what would I do if I got out? I'd only a high-school education, and I didn't want to go back and bum around.'

This excerpt from the author's interview with Robards in his book, *The Off-Broadway Experience*, could almost have been written about Bogey, but he was talking about being in the Navy during World War II. And he was only thirty-nine when the thirty-five-year-old Betty came into his life.

As the actor who eventually became the leading interpreter of

Eugene O'Neill roles, Robards's choice of career was strangely inspired. 'By accident, I picked up a play in the ship's library aboard the cruiser on which I was stationed,' Robards continued in the interview. 'I thought it was a novel, but I found out that *Strange Interlude* by Eugene O'Neill was a dramatic work. I became excited by the style of people speaking their thoughts, and that triggered something that must have been lying dormant within myself that I didn't even know was there. Something that I had probably shut off all through my childhood.'

The influence of the sea on Robards, through being a sailor and becoming an actor because of the ocean-oriented O'Neill, gave him a shared experience with Bogart. Robards's parental preference for his famous actor-father was matched by Bogart's early closeness to his illustrious doctor-father.

Also like Bogart, Robards's first wife was an actress with whom he had worked. Bogart's struggles during the Depression were almost duplicated by the early days as an actor that Robards described in the author's history: 'A lot of times I came close to losing my faith. I was even forced to seek empty bottles in trash cans, so that I could return them to the supermarket for nickels. This way I was able to get together as much as a dollar and a half on some weekends. And, with this, we could buy a lot of meat at the wholesale meat market over which we lived. The stew we made from it would last us for a week. That's the way we got along, raising a family while trying to stay in the theatre.'

The part of Hickey in the Off-Broadway production of O'Neill's *The Iceman Cometh*, that brought recognition to Robards, can be equated to Bogey's Duke Mantee role that made him famous on Broadway. Both actors portrayed murderers who controlled the lives of people in public gathering places.

As actors, their one big difference was that Bogart came to his full realisation in films while Robards achieved his greatest distinction in the theatre. Because of this, Bogart was a heroic figure who was immortal while Robards, often associated with tragedy, was involved in work considered ephemeral, even though he was constantly on Broadway. His latest hit was *Toys in the Attic*.

'MISSUS SAYS JASON TOYED IN BACALL ATTIC' shouted the headlines of the October 19, 1960 *New York Daily News* and the story read:

'Broadway star Jason Robards, Jnr and Lauren Bacall committed adultery up in Lauren's apartment at 1 W. 72nd Street during early morning hours last July and August, according to Mrs Robards' divorce papers on file yesterday in Supreme Court.

'The papers filed by blonde Rachel Taylor Robards of 153 E. 51st St., herself an actress, disclosed that while Lauren is named as co-respondent, there was no messy business of a raiding party. Instead, Rachel is relying on the testimony of persons present in Lauren's apartment at various times.'

Soon afterwards Rachel must have had misgivings because the accusation against Betty was dropped and her name was cleared. Apparently the wife became 'convinced that Lauren did not date Jason until their marriage was doomed'. And Betty never was served with papers, nor was she involved in the litigation.

For weeks prior to the instigation of legal action, Betty and Robards had made the front pages. The newspapers revelled in a story of Robards being hauled off to police court. One morning at 3.40 he smacked into a parked car on Sixty-eighth Street and Central Park West, near where Betty lived. Robards was about to flee, according to the report, when a patrolman who had heard the crash speedily drove in to investigate. As one paper put it: 'He made Jason—who was after the golden Bacall's fleece—pull over and arrested him. Jason was allowed to call a lawyer. Patrolman Walsh said that Jason "staggered from his car and was intoxicated".' Even though the damage to both cars was extensive, Robards's lawyer convinced the magistrate that the actor should be released on a hundred-dollar bail.

During the time the divorce action was changed to a separation agreement because Rachel lacked the proof of adultery required for a New York divorce, Robards was also having other difficulties. One morning at about 4, he and Betty were starting to get out of a taxi in front of her apartment when they spotted a reporter and photographer waiting for them.

Robards pushed her back into the cab and warned, 'Watch out. Don't get out.'

As Betty slumped down, she exclaimed, 'Oh, God!'

Robards shouted to the newsmen, 'You're not getting any pictures,' while Betty dashed up to her apartment. Robards chased the interlopers down the street and smashed the camera. Enraged,

189

they threatened Robards with police action. The actor knew he was in trouble enough already, and so he relented. Apologising, he took the gentlemen of the press back to Betty's house for an interview on the street and even asked her to come down and join in.

Betty claimed that she and Robards had done nothing to be ashamed of. 'I've lived my life with some dignity and with some integrity. Jason's paid enough for what he *hasn't* done.'

Robards burst out, 'I'll do anything for this woman.'

As punishment for his philandering, Rachel wanted Robards to increase his separation payments of one hundred dollars a week to four hundred, but Supreme Court Justice Thomas A. Aurelio denied the request pending the trial. Robards felt vindicated and announced, 'My answer to my wife's charges is a complete denial, and the facts speak for themselves in that the judge awarded my wife no more than I had been giving her voluntarily.'

Though Rachel did not get a Mexican divorce until April 1961, as early as January the newspapers carried the story that Robards 'will marry Lauren sometime this year'. Despite her misgivings about returning to Hollywood, Betty accompanied Robards when he made his film debut in *By Love Possessed*. They did not linger in her old surroundings too long because Robards had to head back to New York for rehearsal in his new show *Big Fish, Little Fish*. In this watered-down comedy, he played a seemingly strong character to whom parasites cling before he finally exposes his own weakness. The play proved to be just as weak and did not last long.

Starting in May, their frustrated attempts to get married in Europe had all the international amusement of a couple being pursued from country to country by legal technicalities so ridiculous that they could be personified by the Keystone cops. In London, where they had gone because he was making the film version of F. Scott Fitzgerald's *Tender is the Night*, they were refused a marriage licence because Mexican divorces are not recognised in England. In Rome, too, the ceremony was prohibited. And in Vienna the following month, an issue was made by the government about their desire to take the vows there. In spite of a personal appeal to Justice Minister Christian Broada, they could not go ahead with their plans because Betty was unable to produce Bogey's death certificate and Robards lacked certification of his divorce.

'I am afraid they are taking such things too lightly,' announced Dr Viktor Hoyers, an official of the Justice Ministry. 'For me, Hollywood stars are in no way different from Frau Mayer or Herr Mueller. Stars, too, have to comply with Austrian laws.'

The agent for Betty and Robards, Peter Witt, retaliated with, 'Apparently Vienna is not so romantic as the two artists had hoped. It seems that the authorities in Vienna have heard nothing of the American adage "Everybody loves a lover".'

Giving up, Robards returned to the States alone from Brussels and she followed from Paris the next day. He went on to Hollywood to finish his film while she stayed in New York for a few days to send the children off to camp. Then on July 4, 1961, they were finally able to get married in Ensanada, Mexico.

On December 17 of the same year, at 8.15 in the morning, Betty arrived at Harkness Pavilion, Columbia-Presbyterian Medical Center in New York, accompanied by Robards. At 2.35 that afternoon their son was born. The 'premature baby', as Betty called him, was named Sam Prideaux Robards after one of Jason's favourite cousins.

'He's an absolute smash,' Betty declared about her new son. 'I'm afraid I'm absolutely besotted about him.' Now that she had the three children she had always wanted, she confessed to a friend, 'I've had all the babies I'm going to have and I can't wait to get back to work.'

For a while it seemed her only job was to defend Robards from being taken for Bogey. 'Jason and Bogey have only two things in common,' she would say to the press, 'talent and me.' Getting specific, she would continue, 'I was trained for marriage by Bogey. Now I'm married to someone of my own generation. There's nothing alike about them. At a distance, there's the same kind of head and coloring, but they're not the same kind of actors and they're totally different characters.'

To help reinforce Robards's credentials without relying on Bogey's credits, she told Helen Markel in a *Redbook* interview, entitled *What is a Man?*: 'I was trained in a marriage in which a man is a man and a woman is a woman.

'Before I ever knew Jason I was impressed by his ability as an actor, his capacity to convey emotion. He did not have to keep saying he was a man. *He was*. I hope that our new son, Sam

191

Prideaux Robards, will, like his father, be so secure in his masculinity that he will have no need to go around proving it.

'The men who embody my personal requirements for masculinity have little in common with each other except one overriding characteristic—none of them has ever learned to play it safe. Jason is first and last himself which is the only way a man can be: Dedicated to his craft—and he *is* the best. He is gentle. Undeterred by trivia, such as the need to have everyone love him. He is totally honest. Also, irritating, demanding, unpredictable, vulnerable, impatient, funny, egocentric, extravagant, exhausting and exciting.

'He is a man ...'

Asked by Hedda how she managed to give the impression that her husband is King and, at the same time, keep her own personality, Betty replied, 'Sheer genius. I think a man should run things and if he doesn't I don't feel the marriage is any good. Jason knows I think he comes first, so I'm ahead before I start. After that, the children come first; but to me, Jason comes before the children.

'Steve at fourteen, looks and gestures and even walks like Bogey, goes to non-military Milton Academy and wants to be a biologist while Leslie goes to Lycée Française. They and Jason's children are close.'

Betty did not end the interview without giving a plug for her husband: 'Jason is a great actor and maybe Hollywood will eventually appreciate him.'

Robards's own description of himself revealed that, outside of the theatre, he had hardly any major interests. His main concern, he said, was his family. 'I've got six children—two stepchildren and four of my own. Two boys—almost fifteen. Two girls twelve and eleven. A boy six. And an infant. I spent last summer with all the kids. I was busy ... fishing, playing ball ... It's like running a summer camp. At one time, we had nine cats and a dog. I love pussy cats. They remind me of my wife. She's a pussy cat. Meeting my present wife is the greatest thing that ever happened to me. She's loyal, honest ... basically very much for the family. She's a great mother.'

Again not satisfied with the domestic role, Betty ventured into television despite her saying, 'I've never been fond of the thought that anyone could turn me off!' Surrendering, she made her first appearance on a filmed series, the Dr Kildare show. Afterwards, although she had just been named 'Young American Legend' by *Vogue*, Betty joined the vogue of old American legends from the Warner days like Bette Davis, Joan Crawford, Olivia de Haviland and Mary Astor and made a freak film. At first, when she went into *Shock Treatment*—that came complete with a mad scene for her—Betty described her feelings to Hedda, 'This is one of the most difficult parts I've ever attempted. I decided to play it as best I could, and not look at any part of the picture until it's done, and I've learned that when I attempted something people said I couldn't do, I did it better than I expected.' After the release, an embarrassed Betty confessed, 'I never saw the movie. I mean, it was bad enough making it without having to see it.'

Apologies also had to be made for her next effort. She appeared in *Sex and the Single Girl* with Natalie Wood, Tony Curtis and Henry Fonda, all of them looking as if they had been locked into leers in order to get their suggestive lines across. The script, based on the title of Helen Gurley Brown's best-selling book, was devised by the prestigious Joseph Heller of *Catch 22* and later writer of the experimental play that was to star Robards called *We Bombed in New Haven*. Betty's picture bombed everywhere. But she was furious for other reasons as well. She thought her role would be more prominent and both Betty and Fonda were ready to sue when they realised that the cutting of the film made them come off as supporting players. Also, Betty was annoyed that she seemed to be much more mature in the film than she had expected.

'Three cheers for the old folks at home,' was how Bosley Crowther saluted Betty and Fonda at the end of his review. This infuriated her and she issued a statement to the press that she was not ready to be considered a veteran, especially since Tony Curtis, who was a year younger than her, was playing the juvenile. Her attack was similar to the remark Bogey had made about having the right to win the girl in *Sabrina* even though he was not Tony Curtis's age. Curtis, in London to make a film, replied to her via the newspapers: 'Miss Bacall is griping because she looks like a skinny middle-aged woman. I believe Miss Bacall is forty-one, or perhaps more. How long can she keep on being a forty-year-old teenager?'

Infinitely more gallant during the making of the movie together, Tony had been concerned about her smoking habits. Every time he saw her with a cigarette on the set, he would say, 'Well, it's your life,' or 'You're trifling with death,' or 'So you have a death wish.' Betty cut down from two packs to a couple of cigarettes a day by the time the picture was through. As she tossed away a supply of cigarettes, she said, 'Tony haunts me.' For her, kicking the habit was only temporary, while the stand Tony took proved ironic for him many years later. While heading the 'I Quit' anti-smoking campaign for the American Cancer Society, he was picked up in London on a marijuana charge.

'They always say I'm making a comeback,' Betty told Sheilah Graham on the release of the movie. 'The fact is that I've never been away, except for two years. I took off after *Goodbye Charlie* on Broadway of my own choice to have our baby. I've recently finished this film in Hollywood where I stayed alone in a hotel— and never again.

'I was miserable without my family. Jason couldn't be with me because he was and still is in *After the Fall*. It was more fun last summer when I did *Shock Treatment* and we all lived in a beautiful house at the beach. It was great for the children. It was total bliss. One thing I do miss in New York is the beach—that divine Malibu ... My career has never been easy. I hope this picture is successful. I haven't been in a successful movie lately.'

Since her wish was not granted, she was no longer very choosey and turned again to television. She appeared in *A Dozen Deadly Roses* with Walter Matthau and Robert Alda, in *Double Jeopardy*, and even went on a quiz show, *The Price is Right*. While playing a has-been singer in an episode for a series, *Mr Broadway*, she was called upon to do a few songs. When the producer David Susskind attempted to have another voice dubbed in, she instituted a suit against him for three million dollars. 'I shall stand convicted of not being able to perform even the part of a singer on the skids,' she complained. 'My reputation and career are in obvious peril.' The producer agreed to allow her voice to be used and she dropped her suit. 'I'm so damned sick and tired of actors being pushed around,' she stated, 'particularly by people of no talent like Mr Susskind. I think my singing is the best thing in this show.' The producer replied, 'If she's a singer, I'm a—oh, never mind.'

Betty finally did have a chance to sing seriously on the Danny Kaye Show when she joined Kaye and Robards for a trio. While she was becoming more and more anxious about her career again, her husband was in great demand by both stage and films, especially after his big hit, *A Thousand Clowns*, in which, fortunately, she had invested.

And the fame of her late husband was ever-expanding.

A friend felt that when Betty tried 'to look out the windshield there were always things in the rear-view mirror that got in her way'. Now all she was seeing was the reflection of what she tried to put behind her. In addition to theatres constantly reviving Bogey's films, television played them relentlessly, and also presented documentaries on his life. Stories and books were creating a mythology that was influencing a new age. Because he made the greatest number of film classics of any actor and since his character was a contemporary inspiration, colleges began offering courses such as the one at California State College, *Humphrey Bogart; the Man and His Times*.

Bogey's Baby lived with this ghost in the very building where *Rosemary's Baby* was filmed, The Dakota. While visiting their home, the author noticed many pictures of celebrities, but Bogey was not represented. Nevertheless, a huge ceiling fan, straight out of *Casablanca*, was being installed in the kitchen. The eleven-room apartment was as large as Betty's Holmby Hills house and was hers before this second marriage. It reflected her taste for antiques. Books and art were everywhere, and photographs and scripts as well. On one of the mantelpieces stood figurines of stage characters. Above another fireplace was a porcelain statuette of a girl, a gift from Robards to Betty. The focal point in the library was a cast-iron lion, a reminder of his zodiacal sign, which Betty had given him. The only obvious memento of her time with Bogey, aside from some of the furnishings that had been in their home, was a leather-bound script of *Key Largo* that had imprinted in gold: 'The Bogarts—Betty and Humphrey'.

The apartment was so huge that a burglar jemmied open the front door one night between 5.00 and 5.30 in mid-October 1962, without being noticed either by the nurse, the cook or their beagle, Benjamin. Only Leslie got a peek at him just before he made off with a dozen pieces of jewellery worth over six thousand dollars from her mother's dresser. As with the London robbery, Betty later managed to retrieve her jewels.

More troublesome to Betty was the feeling that she was missing out on her career. She had learned so much more about acting as a result of being in a Broadway show, improving as a professional with increased resources in performance, yet nothing was happening. She was announced for a movie, *Faster and Faster*, with her husband and Shelley Winters, but like the one she was supposed to do with Sinatra, it never materialised. She began taking voice tuition to play *Mame* without ever being seriously considered for the part. She intended to go on the road for a summer tour of *Lady in the Dark* and that fell through. The only recognition she received during this period was an alumni award by the American Academy of Dramatic Arts in 1964 that she shared with her husband for outstanding achievement.

Her actual standing in the profession at this time was summed up by Ray Hagen when he entitled her career story, which he wrote for the April 1964 issue of *Films in Review*, 'Lauren Bacall—Became A Star Via Her First Picture And First Husband'.

Finally, Betty burst out to Hedda, 'I want to be part of the entertainment world but I never had the urge to give up my soul to play a part. I'd love to do certain things, but when people don't see you for six months or a year they figure automatically that you're either dead or a hundred-and-twelve-years-old. I started with a generation of actors two or three decades older than I was, so many people identify me with that age group. Now I'm faced with getting them to realize I'm not so ancient. I'm not ready to play the mother of twenty-five-year-olds because I'm not a lot more than that myself.'

Ironically, she was soon cast as the stepmother of a girl of that very age. It was in a star-studded detective picture so exploitive of her presence that Bosley Crowther opened his review by writing, 'Bogey's back and Baby's got him.' Though the film was well received, all the critics picked up on the Chandler-like plot and the Hawks-like direction, with Betty doing her bit to underline Paul Newman's interpretation of her deceased husband. Originally the picture was called *The Moving Target*, but the title was changed to *Harper* because Newman had had recent successes in two other films with capital H in the title: *The Hustler* and *Hud*. Like all the major young actors in the world, from Jean Paul Belmondo in nearly all of his films, to Albert Finney in *Gumshoe*, Newman had

196

to put in his bid for the Bogey crown. Although she received star billing, Betty's part could be described as a walk-on, except that she was in a wheelchair. She looked and acted as embittered as she probably felt about being cast only for the apparent purpose of giving Newman authentication in the Bogey sweepstakes.

Since her best publicity agent had died, Betty continued in his tradition. She entered the controversy of the East–West life styles, with her views depending on where she was being interviewed. Before she left for Hollywood to do *Harper*, she told the New York-oriented *Cue* magazine that she was not completely in love with the city because of the pace, the danger, the ugly glass buildings on Park Avenue and the killing of tradition. However, she preferred living in Gotham because 'the old buildings give the feeling of solidity that still exists. But I long to step out of my living room and put my feet on the soil. Life is about fifty per cent easier physically in California. There, though, you get caught in your own circle. And Hollywood is more interested in money than art. In the city you're in touch with more varied aspects of life. I like walking around at dusk or late at night on Fifth Avenue or in the snow or skating with your kids in Central Park. I adore hot chestnuts and shopping at Bloomingdale's for food or pots and pans— I'm mad about gadgets.' She admitted that she did not have the patience she used to have for clothes shopping. Instead of running all over town trying to find bargains, she would simply go to Norman Norrell's to choose her wardrobe. Entertaining was not as extensive as she would prefer because her husband was in the theatre and he did not like being 'social'. Though she and Robards were high on the list of the 'in' people in New York, she admitted to her chagrin that she had lived everywhere in the city in her lifetime except the smart East Side of Manhattan.

But when she arrived in Hollywood, she told Sheilah Graham, 'I can't stand New York anymore. It's taken me a long time to realize I can't stand New York's way of life anymore. It's a killer.' Betty was alone in Malibu while Jason was in Gotham preparing *The Devils*. 'I like it here. I like not dressing up. I like wearing no shoes. I like the openness of the sea. He has signed to do the play for a year and that will be it for a long time. He has served his time in the theatre.

'I feel I have never done what I'm capable of doing. I guess it was laziness, but now I know I want to work. I've had a lot of clearing up in my mind—all different pulls. I've cut myself in many directions for too many years. I have to re-identify myself with young producers so I can play young women. Of course, I couldn't stay here all the time. It gets a bit boring and there's nothing like New York in winter.'

Suddenly out of the blue California sky under which she was languishing after *Harper*, a script was flown to Betty that was to bring about a big change for her. David Merrick had contacted her agent about Betty playing the lead in the American version of a French comedy hit, *Cactus Flower*, and they sent it to her. Her description of how she felt was, 'By last summer, six weeks or so before *Cactus Flower* came along, I was in the real doldrums. I was about as low as I'd ever been, but then, July 14, 1965, I went lower, all the way to the bottom of the roller coaster. Adlai Stevenson died.' Applying the same imagery to the rest of her life, she said, 'I sure took the long way around, a long delay. I travelled by roller coaster on which the highs were as high as any-one could go. And the lows! Oh, those lows were lower than anyone should ever have to go—ten degrees below Hell!' Almost resigned, she added, 'Two blood-curdling years but I learned a lot.'

Betty was goaded into action by *Cactus Flower* and flew back immediately to sign for the show. Grasping the opportunity quickly was necessary because she was feeling desperate about recent events. 'It hasn't always been happy,' she was impelled to say. 'Everything seems to come at once. I had seven years, begin-ning with Bogey's illness which I wouldn't wish on anyone. It happens that way until you don't believe anything more can happen. I believe that life goes in cycles and that if we didn't have the dark side, we might not be able to appreciate the light.'

Not until much later did she let it be known that the adjustment to being without Bogey and the disappointment with her career were not her only troubles. The reverberations of her despair also came from the echoing hollowness of her life with Robards. 'What I need is somebody to take care of me. But where to find him? I'm just not enough unto myself,' she confessed to interviewer Leonard Thornton long after she and Robards split. 'It was worse years ago. Then I really used to go mad. Which is why I made mistakes. After Bogey's death I wanted things to go on just as before.

'It took a long time for me to realize that marrying someone else just wasn't the answer. I married badly and was more alone than when I was alone. I knew for five years that I was going to divorce him, but I wasn't ready emotionally to do it. So I waited.'

While waiting for the break, Betty put up a strong image of marital bliss although their careers often kept them apart. She was not used to their going separate ways, especially after the extreme closeness she had shared with Bogey. When she went into rehearsal for *Cactus Flower*, she had to face the problems of this important venture alone in New York because Robards was in Boston for the opening of the torturous tragedy of *The Devils*. During the seventy-five-performance run of his show on Broadway, she was concerned with the try-out tour for hers.

Before going on the road, she was asked about her ability to combine the roles of wife, mother and actress. 'I don't know that I'm too successful at it right now,' she replied. 'But I think that if you're in this business, you have to be in it all the way. It's a commitment. It's a rough business, you know. It's tough to get to the top, and tough to stay there. People—producers—get to think of you in only one kind of role. When you're at the top and not working, they think you don't want to be. They forget about you. And then, there aren't many right scripts. You have to have those words in front of you to speak them. Actors can't make them up. Being in theatre is a commitment ... It's not easy on our children ... While I'm in Washington, I don't know what Sam will do, but I'll cry.'

'Out of town is designed to rid the world of actors,' Betty told Gereon Zimmermann of *Look*, describing how tense she was during the pre-Broadway tour and facing the critics, 'I was a basket case in New York after Washington and Philadelphia. Your whole life depends on seven fellows in an audience. It is a converging into one horrible experience.'

Reinforcement came from David Merrick who did not, this time, live up to his notoriety as a difficult producer. His description of the attitude he took toward her was, 'There are a lot of great stars sitting around without work. I treated her as a major star from the beginning.'

And Abe Burrows, who did the American adaptation of the farce, helped her by offering personal as well as professional understanding. As he told Zimmermann: 'I rewrote for Betty's rhythms, her inflections.

'Years ago Bogart was the star, and overshadowed her. Betty is a vulnerable person. She gives the *illusion* of overpowering strength. In the play, you can see she can be *hurt*. It's very tough when a woman seems strong, she's not helped in life as she should be, and it's not just a matter of opening car doors for her. Betty is not that strong. People are always waiting to kill a star. She was terribly frightened on the opening night.'

At the Broadway première, December 4, 1965, Betty converted the energy aroused by fear to make a high-voltage connection with the audience. So electrifying was this experience for her that she quickly wiped out all memory of Hollywood ambitions and substituted the more appropriate new recollection: 'From as early as I can remember, I've been wildly stagestruck. As a kid, I never even considered being in the movies, a second-rate medium, I thought ... My dream was to star in a Broadway hit, to be another Katherine Cornell.' Gone was the memory of lusting after the glories of Bette Davis and Carole Lombard and, in its stead, she had the hope that Bacall and Robards could live up to Earl Wilson calling them, 'Broadway's new Lunt and Fontaine'. Urged by the columnist to do a show with her husband, she responded, 'We just haven't found a script.' But they did work together for two days doing a coffee commercial that paid them two hundred thousand dollars.

As an awakened virgin, Betty was miscast in *Cactus Flower*. There was too much flower when she was supposed to be the cactus. Her innate beauty came across no matter how subdued it was at the beginning. And her model-like chicness made even drab clothes look smart. But the audience enjoyed seeing the real Betty about to burst forth like the Cinderella she was in life. So for the first time in twenty years Bacall was having a ball in her honour.

'I've waited for this for forty thousand years,' Betty exclaimed in *Look*, and expressed hundreds of variations of that theme in the newspapers and magazines that once again began begging her for interviews. 'I mustn't be limited now. I'm going the route. You only go around one time, right? I'm out to kill all of the people and myself at the same time!' was the way she expressed her glee to Zimmermann while she was at a furrier buying a mink and an ermine at the same time. So as not to seem too greedy, she told him that her old mink was going to her mother. 'Now this is my moment,' she went on. 'Lots of things have come into focus for me. I was a star right away, but it was always Bogey and Baby. That took over, just as it should have, all my personal life. I was never thought of as an *actress* out there. I kept a warm and friendly house where people had a good time, and they thought I was always having a good time, too. But they were mistaken.' She also brought up the difficulties of having an early success and being married to an older husband, and said, 'I never had any of that flotsam-and-jetsam time as a kid. I was never associated with my own generation, but I wanted to be identified with it, to find my own identity.' Then she contradicted all her previous claims about preferring mature men by admitting, 'I only mind that I lost my own youth in the association with the older set.'

Though Robards was considered by Betty and everyone else as 'the greatest stage actor in America', he was recovering from the latest in a series of flop plays while she was blossoming in her second starring role on stage. Of course, she was co-starring with the ever-popular Barry Nelson and she had yet to have a vehicle of her own which she carried totally, but right now she was the hit of the family. At the beginning of the marriage it looked as if she were going to act out the same reverse pattern of *A Star is Born* that she had followed with Bogey. Now, since she was the one being more celebrated, he was being forced to play Norman Main. His realisation of this, while between shows, was implied when he said to Zimmermann, 'At seven every evening, I get the urge to go to the theater, to work.' He conceded, '*Cactus Flower* gave Betty the lift, the boost she needed. This brings her right up there again. All those years, it must have been tough for her.' Later, while the show was having a run longer than any of his had, he told the author, 'I don't see how Betty could enjoy what she's doing, saying those same lines night after night.'

Except for a one-week vacation, Betty never missed one of the more than nine hundred performances the show ran on Broadway because, as David Merrick put it, 'She is delirious with joy about being in a hit.' Betty said it another way: 'Because of the play, I just feel a great freedom. It is just that the play and my own timing,

201

you know, or the time in my life have coincided—they have converged, and a most horrible explosion has taken place. I've always wanted to be a star on Broadway. One reason is that in this business you meet people you ordinarily would not meet. But you yourself have to be successful, or forget it.' Betty virtually reiterated Romanoff's conclusion of ten years earlier that her real motivation was for recognition among the celebrated.

While the comedy kept on going, she was always saying, 'This is more fun than I've had in ten years. Something is here I never had before in my whole life and some people never find. I'm standing on my own two feet. And this has nothing to do with a good marriage and my children and my love. That's a fine other department.'

About mid-point in the show's stay, *Time* featured Betty on the cover for the story 'The Pleasures and Perils of Middle Age'. She was chosen as 'the personification of the command generation' which consisted of those between forty and sixty, and made up more than a fifth of the nation's population during that period. Her annoyance with Tony Curtis only a year before about being considered a member of the older set was forgotten as she expounded on the perils of drifting into the crisis of purposelessness that afflicts many women in their middle years. 'I lost sight of myself as a woman, as an actress—even in my friendships I was neglectful,' she said, baring herself to *Time*. 'I knew I wasn't functioning well. I became run down physically. When you have the responsibility of a husband and children, you also have responsibility to yourself. If you neglect yourself, you are actually neglecting them. It's unfair to all.' On realising this, she told herself, 'Damn it, straighten up! Pull yourself together and *point* yourself in the right direction and MOVE!' The move was back to work.

Time made Betty sound like Bogey when she was quoted as saying, 'I love the ocean—it's one of the last free places on earth.' Gone seemed to be the former loathing of the sea she had had while Bogey was alive.

'Betty Bacall has also learned the ultimate wisdom of the middle years, to live in the here and now,' the article continued. Inspiration was given in Betty's own words: 'There are things in life that are pretty rotten. The part that's good you've got to enjoy while you have it.'

As a final inquiry, *Time* asked her what she was going to do with the next twenty years. The response echoed the message of Tennessee Williams's heroines: 'Try to survive—for openers.' Her immediate hope, however, was, if she survived the *Cactus Flower* role, to do a musical.

Now that she was considered popular again, her television appearances were only on specials, the all-celebrity *Star Salute* and hosting a show on social dancing with John Forsythe, *The Light Fantastic*, which was rather more light than fantastic.

Now that she had come through what she considered the worst period she had ever experienced, Betty was able to say, 'I hate people who can't cope with life's difficulties. I don't hate anything, but what I really mean is that I get impatient. If you are going to deal with life, you have to deal with it as it is. So I get impatient with people who don't do it that way, but just beef about it ... which, of course, I *have* been known to do. I *have* been known to complain now and then.'

This time she did not speak about what was really bothering her. She kept the disillusionment of her second marriage to herself. The effect of Bogey on their relationship was so over-rationalised that it could have been interpreted as a cover-up for the trouble his memory was causing.

'It's tough. Bogey is a living ghost,' Betty told Zimmermann. 'Jason doesn't complain about it. You're rising above a surprisingly strong personality, someone who isn't here, but is. What I have with Jason is different. My past is too full, too powerful to get away from. I can't quite get away from it. From another point of view, the past is fresh and productive. It helps, the past does, but it hinders too. It is an awkward thing, a strange and unusual situation. Widows and widowers—they never forget the past. You put it in a different place. Then, it revived of itself. God, I've been submerged in the past. It is the now that counts. Yesterday is part of *now*, and tomorrow becomes now—too soon.'

One night at a party, the editor of an important magazine carried on so profusely about Bogey, and ignored Robards so completely, that Betty finally screamed, 'Bug off, Buster.' This scene was often repeated with slight variations.

The Bogey cultists were on the uprise and, as a living part of his existence, Betty was forced to say in *The Saturday Review of*

Literature, 'Here I am married to Jason Robards, a very talented actor and there is enormous interest in Bogey all around us. It must be tough on Jason, yet I can't ignore or lessen this thing that has grown up around Bogey. One has children to give something to. They are entitled to know about their father. For a man to be kept alive by so many people he must be unique. I would never have to apologize for that. I'm certain it's very tough on Jason's ego, and I hope he understands.

'I first met Bogey when I was nineteen. My God, I can't be expected to ignore those years. Bogey had so much to do with the kind of person I am today: Jason has to recognize *that* as a plus. I'm afraid the Bogey interest is always going to be there. I would say the staying power of that man is extraordinary.'

Resolving her conflict over the two husbands, she stated in *This Week* magazine, 'I received many angry letters about my marriage to Jason. But anyone with any sanity realizes that four years were long enough to wait. Bogey would have insisted I remarry. He would see it as proof that our marriage had been good.

'I am back living my old life again,' she said, finally seeming to have decided in favour of Bogart over Robards. It seemed that the greater celebrity had won, again proving Romanoff's theory about fame being her spur. 'I look at Bogey and it revives my life—the best years of it. I guess that's got to be hard on another man. Jason never said anything. He tries to understand. But I know I'd resent it terribly if the shoe were on the other foot.

'Only one thing I didn't like about Bogey: he was always right—that infuriated me.

'We were such an integrated pair that when he died I felt I had lost half myself and I was inadequate to hold my friends. It was Bogey and not me, I felt, who had been the attraction. Bogey who was the star. I felt people had just been thinking of me as Bogey's wife. So I became bitter. I walked out on my friends before they could walk out on me. But time proved me wrong. With the success of my play, all those old friends I had doubted were genuinely pleased. Those big lines in front of the theater are marvelous for my ego. This is the first time in my life I have earned the right to be called a full-fledged star. It's beginning for me again. I have to get along with my life.

'I'm not one who feels that everything happens for the best. Men

die in the full bloom of their power. When people talk about justice, I don't get it. The good still die young. Eternal youth—that's
what you need. Nothing improves with age.

'Oh, let's face it. Bogey has taken over my life all over again.
My brain is full of him—more acutely than when he died. Nine
years have gone by, but I'll never get away from him—and I don't
think that's bad.'

After a brief separation, Betty charged Robards with incompati-
bility and went for a divorce to Juarez, Mexico, the country where
they had been wed eight years earlier. The decree was issued on
September 11, 1969, five days before she became forty-five—the
same age as Bogey when they were married.

Robards did not contest the action, but commented, 'I am tired
of being Mrs Bogart's Second Husband.'

Applause

A Star is Born ends as the left-over wife faces an adoring crowd with the reminder of her indebtedness to the deceased husband. Vicki Lester corrects the introduction that used her professional name, and announces, 'This is Mrs Norman Main.'

Betty had always preferred men who shone brighter than herself—the superior father she never had. Testing their strength, she would compete, and when she overtook her last husband, they had to part. And she returned to the one who was still greater than her. To rid herself of this unreal attachment, she had to believe in her own worth without the need of constant striving. That acceptance of herself would have to come from the overwhelming approval of others, just as this need probably originated from her rejection by someone else—her father. To be at peace with herself, her total triumph would have to come from a declaration of her own identity, unlike Mrs Norman Main's merging of her own personality in that of her husband.

Though Betty was on high ground after *Cactus Flower*, the overflow from the Bogey flood still threatened to drown her. The only safety for her was in reaching a summit where she could glory in having arrived there by herself.

An unexpected chance for that self-recognition came when she was offered *Applause*. In *Cactus Flower*, which closed on November 23, 1968, she played her part well enough to be considered a talented stage actress, but almost any capable performer could have done the same. Her only personal contribution was in starting a fashion trend with her climactic costume, a Norman Norrell sequined ballgown. Otherwise, it was just another job for an actress and she kept it beyond any advantage to her. 'I tend to do that, and it's too long,' she explained to Eugenia Sheppard of *The New York Post*. 'People think that the longer you play a part, the easier it must get to say the lines, but they're wrong. It gets harder.' The comedy was not a star vehicle on which she could put an indelible imprint. This was proven when the picture was made and Bogey's partner in *Casablanca*, Ingrid Bergman, played the role, however awkwardly. Betty's reaction? 'I was very angry, but it's all over and to hell with it.'

By any standards, *Applause* would not have seemed a likely prospect in which to make an enduring impression. The book, music and lyrics were adequate enough reminders of the greatness of the source, *All About Eve*. And for Betty in her late forties to gain acceptance as a singer and dancer in her first musical was too much to expect. Even if the production and performance worked, the almost insurmountable obstacle would be to overcome the complete association in the public's mind of the Margo Channing role with Bette Davis. To do that would require a miracle and Betty would be truly a goddess. In accepting the challenge, Betty expressed the attitude: 'I've made an ass of myself before.'

Originally the part had been written by Joseph L. Mankiewicz for Claudette Colbert, but when she became ill Bette took over and made the role of Margo all hers. Similarly, the first choice for the musical was Anne Bancroft who had tried unsuccessfully to repeat on-stage the Davis part in *The Little Foxes*. Bancroft anticipated getting sick of playing Margo for more than six months and refused to sign for a year as the producers insisted. And so Betty got a run-of-the-play contract for ten thousand dollars a week. This made her declare, 'You back into the best things in life.'

Margo Channing was the kind of dynamic character that Betty always tried to be. Also, the fictional actress had problems with which the real one could identify. As an ageing star, Margo was forced to face the realisation that Betty had voiced a long time before: 'A woman doesn't know any fulfilment alone.'

The reverse of that premise was being promulgated ineffectively by Betty's close friend, Katharine Hepburn, at the same time in *Coco*. She, too, was making her Broadway musical debut. Like Betty, she had just lost the most meaningful man in her life, Spencer Tracy. So Hepburn also turned to a new venture for distraction. Her show concerned itself with Coco Chanel's self-reliance. Much too indirectly, the musical posed the question: Can an independent woman find complete love? The on-stage answer was negative and this was also true of Hepburn's personal life. Not only was she willing to accept Tracy's being married to another woman, but also, because of her powerful, father-influenced nature and her success, Hepburn did not need total commitment from a man.

The difference between the outlooks of Betty and Hepburn regarding male–female involvement did not prevent the feminist critic Molly Hakell from citing Betty and Bogey in *To Have and Have Not*, and Hepburn and Tracy in *Adam's Rib* as 'classical couples'. In her book *From Reverence to Rape*, Ms Hakell extols these two pairs for bringing to the screen 'the kind of morally and socially beneficial "pedagogic" relationship that Lionel Trilling finds in Jane Austen's characters, the "intelligent love" in which the two partners instruct, inform, educate and influence one another in the continuous college of love. In the confidence of mutuality, individuals grow, expand, exchange sexual characteristics.'

Now both friends were competing to express what Ms Hakell described as a woman's 'interior life: a continuum which precedes her relationship with men and by which she, too, defeats time temporarily and transcends her biological fate'. Hepburn had already achieved this as an actress and as a woman. Betty had once given that impression on the screen and had tried to transfer it to her real life, but could not maintain equality with her partner. But then, perhaps, for all her show of strength she might have preferred the more romantic notion of being protected without feeling guilty that it was a compensation for her lack of self-esteem. She often said as much, but no one believed she needed that kind of tenderness because she had learned to hide her vulnerability. The realisation she sought could come from *Applause*—a title that suited her needs because of the hope it promised.

The characteristics that Hepburn saw in Betty were expressed for *McCall's* in such poetic terms as: 'Soft and sleek—and looking—

looking ... best—and long—and deep ... No sound—only rhyth-
mic beat—Honey dripping from her temples—Eyes unblinking—
glinting green—challenging—Her texture bread-dough soft—and
smooth and tawny—rising alive—He has penned a lioness—No
claws for those she loves ... You are subdued by her lavish enthusiasm—lulled by the repetition of your own extraordinary virtues—
You are a king among mice—secure ... You belong to the
kingdom of her children—she will protect you—But if you do not
belong—: look out—No zulac from the bazaar has a sharper
knife—can use it without pause—direct—piercing—Love or
Hate—Victorian clarity—Soft—sun serene surface ... and under
it—Woman.'

That August, Betty had prepared herself for the change in her
future the show might initiate by getting ready to free herself of
Robards. Unexpectedly, she suffered another emotional loss. Her
mother died. 'Life is rotten ... there's no justice. There really isn't,'
a distraught Betty exclaimed. 'I guess that's the worst experience
I've ever had. There's nothing quite as final as losing your mother.
Suddenly you're nobody's child.' With her mother, the personification of her driving force, no longer there as Betty was approaching her goal, the accomplishment would have to be done by and
for herself.

Betty's supply of energy during rehearsals seemed endless. In
addition to the preparations for the show itself, she had to be trained
for the musical sequences. So that she could seem like she was a
singer without straining her voice during eight performances a
week Betty took vocal coaching from Peter Howard. Also, she
had to take special dance lessons. Even though a childhood ballet
teacher had once told her she had 'the wrong feet' for it, Betty
was going to kick up her heels on Broadway. The run-through
for people in the theatre, prior to the two-month Baltimore and
Detroit try-out, went so well that everyone became nervous. The
word-of-mouth would build too great an expectation before the
Palace Theater première on Broadway, March 30, 1970.

The amazement at Betty's accomplishments made her a triumph
for the critics as well as the audience. Everyone had anticipated liking her as an actress, but the surprise came from the agility and
downright sense of fun she showed as she threw herself into the
musical numbers. Her singing and dancing abilities may have been

limited by her lack of being truly talented, but her contagious exuberance more than compensated.

But Alive was her first song, and its title keynoted her explosive vitality. Obviously, she was out to win, and that determination created an empathy to which all responded as never before. Released was the drive that had always been intrinsically hers, but that had been manipulated by the domination of her mother, the direction of Hawks, the love of Bogey, the seduction of Sinatra and the competitiveness of Robards. And because this propulsion was true to her very being she was able to give of herself 'one-hundred-and-fifty per cent', as she rightly estimated.

Not even tearing two cartilages in her left leg could stop her. The accident happened one night early in the run while she was doing a high kick during her first dance in the gay discotheque number, a scene which shocked some of the prudish. Fortunately, she was caught before she fell by members of the chorus, but after that she had to wear a bandage for a long while and be careful how she danced, otherwise she could cripple herself for life. However, she never missed a performance. Besides the two months of pre-opening performances, Betty was in the show fourteen months on Broadway, five months in the cross-country tour and eleven months in London. While on in the West End, she filmed the television production that proved to be almost overwhelming—for her and for the audience.

The entire time, those on both sides of the footlights wondered how Betty could keep up the pace since she had not had long training to perform such pyrotechnics. A programme note gave some hint of the answer: 'She's having the time of her life.' But Betty revealed that the source of her fire was in rejecting her role as keeper of Bogey's flame. 'Being a widow is not a profession,' she said. 'It's not a lack of appreciation for what I had. It's just that you want to contribute something that is yours.'

That is why she could not be upset by Bette Davis's opening-night telegram that read, 'The years have gone and now you are me.' A quarter of a century earlier, Betty had anticipated this moment when she had expressed the hope, 'I don't want to be another Bette Davis ... I'm not "another" anybody.' Betty was now a somebody in her own right who had a longer run on Broadway than Davis was ever able to attain.

Signalling this new phase of self-possession, Betty told *The New York Post*'s Ralph Blumenfeld, 'I really don't anticipate ever getting married again. I'm anti-being-without-men. I think the Women's Liberation movement is a disaster. I'm totally against it. I think it's ridiculous. I mean, to be so against men to think you can function in a world without them. I'm not saying let 'em drive you up the wall but, good God, I need, I know emotionally I need a man. I don't want to live without one. I just can't. I mean I've done it and I'm doing it. But I don't like it ... I don't want to get married now because I think for the first time I would like to do what I would like to do. And if I meet a man that I would like to be with, I would love to be with him and to have him be with me because we would like to be together and not because someone says you gotta take that piece of paper out and sign it and lock up for life. 'Cause it's not for life anyway.' Betty was discovering what Hepburn knew: independence sometimes means being left alone.

More than ever, she was annoyed that 'even when I'm out with a man people talk about Bogey'. Although Robards had been gone for some time, she still kept no pictures of her first husband on display in her flat. 'He's been dead thirteen years. I'm still alive,' she declared, almost repeating the content of her opening number in the show. 'I think I've damned well earned the right to be judged on my own, as a person, as me. Christ, what have I lived for if I can't have something that's mine.'

That *something* that was completely her own came to her through working on the stage rather than in films. 'Perhaps because the theater is live, more real,' was the reason Betty gave for the fulfilment that came to her after being frustrated half her lifetime by the world of projected illusion.

As a tribute for having single-handedly conquered Broadway, Betty received the Antoinette Perry Award for being the Best Actress in a Musical for 1970. The gold medal that was the equivalent of Hollywood's Oscar glistened even brighter because her major competition was the glorious Hepburn. A winner of so many other accolades, Hepburn also proved to be a good loser on this occasion. 'Isn't it simply *great* about Betty,' Hepburn telephoned a friend to say. 'She tells me she's never won a prize for anything—think of it—so you can imagine how much this one means to her—and after all she's been through lately—it's sort of balm. Freddie Brisson and Alan Jay Lerner are furious—I can't imagine what's got into them.'

The significance of getting the theatre's highest honour was augmented for Betty by the awareness that Bogey never achieved this recognition, and was not in any way responsible for her accomplishment except that his after-life had goaded her on to avoid being obliterated. And so, after being presented with the Tony, Betty announced, 'It means a great deal to me at this particular juncture of my life. It seems to me for the first time I've really felt I've earned something on my own, that I've done something that has to do with my ability.'

The conclusion of *A Star is Born* had the actress paying homage to the memory of her husband. Betty, however, did Bogey a similar service by laying his ghost to rest. What she seemed to be saying so emphatically that her meaning came across in capital letters was: 'THIS IS BETTY BACALL!'

Encore: As Time Goes By

The themes continue for those who are *But Alive*.

Stephen is in his mid-twenties and married to Daletrend Gemelle of Torrington, Connecticut. They have a son named James Stephen Humphrey Bogart, but Betty insists, 'That doesn't make me a grandmother. I refuse to be a grandmother. "You rat fink," I said to him when it happened. "How dare you do this to me when I'm trying to look younger?' An inquiry about Stephen's ambition brings an exasperated reply from Betty: 'Don't ask me what he's doing. I think being Bogey's son has been quite a problem for him. Perhaps he'll act but he'll have to find the right thing. He's a late developer, I suppose, but so was his father.'

Leslie has grown into a blonde beauty like her mother, but with a will of her own. As a youngster, she wanted to be an artist. Then she thought she might be an actress, but was 'scared to death' in her stage debut at a summer camp. Now nursing is her occupational interest. This causes Betty to say, 'She likes it. She's lovely looking. She could be a model and make lots of money. She wants to have an identity of her own.' To be like her mother, the girl must realise, she must be unlike her mother.

Sam Robards provokes this reaction from Betty: 'I'm bringing up my third child without a man around to help. That's not fair either

213

on the kids or on me.' She keeps him with her wherever she goes because, 'although I've always had to work where the work was, I recognize, as a mother, that you can't take a kid out of school every three months and you have an obligation to be with him.' Yet she complains that Sam has 'teenage problems'.

Sinatra never changes, only grows older. After Betty, he went to another Hawks girl, Angie Dickinson, but wound up in a parody of the Betty–Bogey, May–December marriage by being briefly wed when he was fifty to the twenty-one-year-old Mia Farrow. The bride's waifishness supposedly prompted a remark that became an apocryphal underground joke: 'I knew someday Frank would marry a boy.'

Robards is still being bugged by Bogart. In 1970, he married Lois O'Conner, his fourth wife—like Betty to Bogey. He now blames his rift with Betty on her 'socialising', while she maintains that his career, his in films and hers on-stage, kept them apart—as was true of Bogey and Mary Philips. Robards had completed his image by bearing the mark of Bogart. When Robards did not get his Hickey part in the film version of *The Iceman Cometh*, he was so despondent that he went on a binge and wound up in a devastating automobile accident. His face had to be completely reconstructed. The only part that did not heal is his upper lip which now bears the scar of Bogey.

Bogey is everywhere. ... In 1971, Betty forced Pan American Airlines to desist from using a shot of Bogey in a scene from *Casablanca* to promote flights to Morocco, 'Listen, kid, Bogey didn't do that sort of advertising when he was alive,' Betty claimed, 'so why should they be able to do it when he is dead? How dare they?' She might have lost her suit had the case come to court because the airline could have shown an ad in *The New York Times* of October 11, 1955. Posed in a full-page picture are Betty and Bogey ready to board a plane. The headline reads 'The Bogarts Fly Home From Broadway', and the advertisement was for American Airlines. The latest word that Betty has said about Bogey is, 'He has lasted so long and will last forever.'

A Star is Born is making movie news again because another girl with 'chutzpah' is talking about doing a remake and her hairdresser is announced to be the producer. Her usual boss, Ray Stark, lives in the Holmby Hills house that once belonged to the Bogarts.

Betty has settled once again in her Dakota apartment with Sam and Blenheim, a cocker spaniel like the one she had when she was a young girl. When *Applause* closed in London, she stayed on for a couple of years. Before returning to New York, she was interviewed by Julie Kavanagh for *Women's Wear Daily* and said, 'I like many aspects of my life alone. I've become more selfish and I feel I could live anywhere so long as there was a reason. I never felt that way before, even though I've been alone for a long, long time.' Lately she has been attracting younger men because they are 'less intimidated' by her. 'Not that there's an army of young guys knocking down doors to get me,' she added. 'Besides, I don't want to settle for just anything.' Her publicised romance with her leading man in the London production of *Applause*, Basil Hoskins, ended soon after the show closed and he announced, 'She's a great girl. Of course I will miss her, but we both have our own lives to lead.' Though she won her Broadway battle with Hepburn, she was losing the war between the sexes to the 'Coco' theory that independence is an obstacle to love.

One of her last interviews abroad was for the London *Times*, and she ended on a hopeful note: 'I'm Virgo. The influences have been disastrous for the last fifteen years. Saturn, or one of those damned things has been trouble making and upsetting my sign. I don't live by such things, but there is an element of truth in it. I don't mean that I've been living in a state of total lunacy; I've had some good moments. But they were nothings taking me nowhere. That's all over now and things must get better.'

As soon as she came back, Betty began plugging the all-star movie she made in England, *Murder on the Orient Express*. 'My first film in eight years,' she reminds everyone when she appears on television shows and the first ever with Bogey's co-star Ingrid Bergman.

Negotiations have been completed for her to be with Jason Robards in *All the President's Men*, but they will not have any scenes together. In discussing recent events with interviewers, she reveals 'loving is giving' and she has given but has been disappointed. Yet

215

she does not want a duplicate Bogey. Even now, Betty says to Sally Quinn of the *Washington Post*: 'I guess it was when I was in *Applause* on Broadway that I finally was free of Bogey and of being his widow. At that moment I earned my own spot on my own nickel.'

The themes go on and new forms are created, otherwise there is no art in living. What happens on the cessation of growth is described by Bogey in the concluding speech of *The Barefoot Contessa*, a fictional actress's biography:

'Life every now and then behaves as if it has seen too many bad movies, when it winds up in a pattern that's too pat, too neat. As it was in the beginning ... you fade out where you fade in.'